IN OTHER WORDS

IN OTHER WORDS

Incarnational Translation for Preaching

Charles H. Cosgrove *&* W. Dow Edgerton

WILLIAM B. EERDMANS PUBLISHING COMPANY
GRAND RAPIDS, MICHIGAN / CAMBRIDGE, U.K.

Published 2007 by

Wm. B. Eerdmans Publishing Co.

2140 Oak Industrial Drive N.E., Grand Rapids, Michigan 49505 /

P.O. Box 163, Cambridge CB3 9PU U.K.

Printed in the United States of America

12 11 10 09 08 07   7 6 5 4 3 2 1

Library of Congress Cataloging-in-Publication Data

Cosgrove, Charles H.

In other words: incarnational translation for preaching / Charles H. Cosgrove & W. Dow
Edgerton.

p.   cm.

Includes bibliographical references (p.   ).

ISBN 978-0-8028-4037-0 (pbk.: alk. paper)

1. Bible — Homiletical use.   2. Bible — Translating — Miscellanea.

3. Contemporary, The — Religious aspects — Christianity.

I. Edgerton, W. Dow, 1948-   II. Title.

BS534.5.C67 2007

251 — dc22

2007003163

www.eerdmans.com

For our students in the Association of Chicago Theological Schools
Doctor of Ministry in Preaching Program

Contents

Foreword

I had the best seat in the house. In the 1990s, as director of the Association of Chicago Theological Schools' Doctor of Ministry Program in Preaching, I saw Charles Cosgrove and Dow Edgerton putting the meaning of this book into classroom practice long before they got it into writing. Theirs is the first required course in the program, "Preaching as an Interpretive Act." They have been co-teaching the course for a decade now.

The average participant in the A.C.T.S. D.Min. in Preaching Program has been away from formal theological education for one to two decades. Many of these pastors have not been previously exposed to the kinds of insights about *homiletical* biblical interpretation that Cosgrove and Edgerton bring to the classroom. But once into this course, the participants have consistently shown a newborn facility not only for allowing the biblical passage to sing its song, but also for transposing that melody into a new key. Working with these same students in the second-year required course, I have seen how Cosgrove and Edgerton have led these participants to think beyond traditional homiletical hermeneutics. They have enabled the students not just to explain a biblical passage, but to make meaning with it, to free it to say and do with us *analogously* what it said and did with its ancient hearers. And the key pedagogical instrument for this classroom breakthrough? The incarnational translation.

Incarnational translations combine both commentary and recital, the kind of retelling of a biblical passage that holds the sense of the passage while reclothing it in contemporary dress. Too many sermons fail to keep this balance, either worrying a passage into irrelevance or reaching for modernity at the expense of the sense of the passage. Cosgrove and Edgerton show us how to live in a creative tension between the Then and the Now. Such a translation seeks functional rather than formal linguistic equivalents, thus enabling the preacher to retell the text as an analogy ringing with contemporaneity. Exegesis, once akin to working with a passage like an algebraic equation, can become, with Cosgrove and Edgerton, the pleasure of freeing a passage to do its dance, and to do it on our stage.

Yes, I had the best seat in the house. As I worked with the second-year students in the required preaching course, I saw proof of the value of incarnational translations in how the participants formed and preached their sermons. I was struck with how *the fact of* making a contemporary rendering of a biblical text, with well-chosen imagery and thought-forms, gave energy and zeal to the preacher. As if the incarnational translation so synthesizes the Then and the Now as to become a Presence that ignites the preacher with a self-possession that, strangely, transcends self. As if the act of converting past echoes into a present voice kindles in the preacher's heart the conviction that this gospel is, *de facto,* a present reality. Watch, then, what this spiritual awareness does to the "accidents" of preaching, to the body language, to the voice use, to the eye contact. Or, more deeply, look at what this new-found sensibility does to the preacher's sense of being there, mainly because of the sense of Being, *here.*

Charles and Dow, look at what you have turned loose with your incarnational translations. You have turned *us* loose.

DON M. WARDLAW

Preface

This book was inspired by many richly rewarding years of team-teaching in the Association of Theological Schools Doctor of Ministry in Preaching Program in Chicago. Founded by Chicago-area homileticians led by Don Wardlaw some twenty years ago, this program has been an important force in narrative preaching and the significance of biblical genres for preaching. We have been honored to be a part of this work and to have made some modest contribution to it.

This is not a book about preaching in general or even about a certain kind of preaching or approach to preaching. Instead, it focuses on a way of engaging the biblical text for preaching. We call it a kind of dynamic, or "incarnational," translation that renders the form and content of the text in functionally equivalent contemporary terms. As an interpretive process (a way of understanding the text) and as a product (a contemporary "version" of the ancient biblical text), incarnational translation can serve any number of approaches to preaching.

An incarnational translation is a kind of illustration, an illustration that imitates the form and content of the text. That imitation aims to be an accessible contemporary rendering of the text — story for story, psalm for psalm, proverb for proverb, oracle for oracle. The process that leads to this rendering is a sophisticated hermeneutical engagement with the text. The sermon illustration has always been an act of interpretation. We press for rigor and self-awareness in an approach to the sermon illustration that draws on recent attention to genre in contemporary biblical studies and hermeneutical theory.

The first chapter describes tendencies in the field of homiletics today as a way of situating the interests and approach of incarnational translation. Chapter Two introduces incarnational translation, and three more chapters introduce incarnational translation for a variety of biblical genres. A closing chapter deals with hermeneutical questions that are raised by this method. In this final chapter, the work of Paul Ricoeur figures importantly in helping us frame our conception of the hermeneutical circle (or "spiral") of preaching as an interpretive act.

We write as Westerners and "Americans" whose social location is the United States and the middle class. When we say "we" in a general sense in this book, it tends to mean the "we" of the Western church or, more specifically, the church as we know it in the United States. The same goes for the examples of incarnational translation in the book. Admittedly, this orientation in our discussions and examples is parochial. But we do not presume to speak for and about contexts we do not know well or at all.

We have had extraordinary experiences with students through the long process of developing this book. We owe them all a great debt — for their enthusiasm and encouragement, their acute questions and annoying discoveries of holes in our thinking, their wonderful imaginations and adventurous spirits, their honesty and transparency, and, above all, for their devotion to ministry and to the grave and wondrous task of preaching. To all of them we are proud to dedicate this book.

CHAPTER ONE

Preaching and Interpretation in Transition

Open the pages of a few books on interpretation and preaching, and it soon becomes evident that you have walked into a room full of people engaged in a long conversation already in progress. In one corner of the room is an animated theoretical argument with sharp disagreement. In another corner they are telling stories. In another, someone has set up a chalkboard and filled it with diagrams of different kinds. In yet another, they are pointing at the pages of a Bible, while others point to the pages of a book of worship. Another group has gathered itself into a circle for prayer. Listen in and you will hear talk of subjects such as theology, faith, hermeneutics, modernism, postmodernism, premodernism, history, creeds, ecclesiology, liturgy, communication theory, performance, ritual studies, psychology, poetics, narratology, context, culture, race, gender, ministry, rhetoric, and what makes people tick.

Some parts of the conversation may sound so highly specialized and abstract that you begin to wonder how on earth they could yield anything an actual preacher could use on any ordinary Sunday. Some parts may sound so much like sharing recipes that you may wonder whether that's really all there is to it. Some parts may sound so urgent that you fall silent at the thought of what is at stake in all this — and for whom. All around the room, different forces converge into a practice and reflection for a time, then they diverge once again, rearrange the partners, and converge once again into a new practice and reflection.

The last few decades have seen a dramatic flowering of homiletical and hermeneutical reflection, arguably the most complex and interdisciplinary approaches the practices of interpretation and preaching have ever known.

1

The conversation partners we have named above make up only a brief and incomplete list. With so many new questions and possibilities to consider, how could interpretation and preaching *not* be in transition?

For some, the transitions may be tough news because they grow from critiques of cherished practices and assumptions. It is a sickening feeling to suddenly suppose that what we have been doing with the best of intentions and the highest of ideals may have offered much less than we had hoped for — perhaps even the opposite of what we had hoped for. For others, the transitions may be good news because they open up paths away from practices that never seemed quite right in the first place. Like David shrugging off Saul's armor in favor of five smooth stones and a leather sling, some preachers find that new approaches to interpretation and preaching offer them ways to grasp and appreciate much more deeply the possibilities that have been there all along, possibilities they never really had the framework to understand or the permission to embrace. For still others, the transitions are no transition at all but a long-delayed recognition of homiletical approaches and understandings they have already made their own on the margins of accepted practice. Perhaps, for many preachers, the situation is a mix of all three: tough news, good news, and recognition.

Some Shifts

By way of a broad summary, we shall present a number of shifts that have been taking place over these last decades. All of these shifts are concerned with the intersection of biblical interpretation, theology, and preaching, which means that they all have multiple complex histories behind them, including whatever inter- and intradisciplinary conflicts may exist at any given moment. The story of these disciplines and their interaction involves theory and practice at every turn, and since what people say they are doing and what they actually do are not necessarily the same, the issues are complex indeed.

The relationships among the fields have been configured in sharply different ways during the last two millennia, and since at least the third century CE there has been an active combination of Scripture, tradition, philosophy, and practical reason in all of them.[1] Certainly, one of the

1. For Bible and theology, see Robert M. Grant and David Tracy, *A Short History of Interpretation of the Bible*, 2nd ed. (Minneapolis: Fortress Press, 1984).

strong concerns of the Reformation was the nature of this combination, particularly the criticism by the Reformers that theology and philosophy were determining the meaning of the Bible, rather than the other way around. Wesley Kort describes Calvin's view on this issue as follows:

> The idea that one reads Scripture in order to develop a theology that one then substitutes for or imposes on the reading of Scripture is antithetical to Calvin's doctrine. Theology does not determine the reading of Scripture and reading Scripture does not harden into a doctrine of the text or of the reading of it. Theology, doctrine, and even dogma are always vulnerable to correction by reading Scripture.[2]

To what extent Calvin and other reformers were able to follow through on this conviction is a matter for debate, but as a principle it had great motive force. One did, nevertheless, read Scripture in order to draw doctrine from it, and preaching had the responsibility of presenting this doctrine and its implications for life to the community.

Following the Enlightenment, the rise of biblical studies as a historical field (operating within the terms of historical study in general) and as a literary field (operating within the terms of literary studies) created a degree of independence from the needs and demands of dogmatic theology, with inevitable effects of conflict or alienation. By the same token, where confessional forces made aspects of historical-critical exegesis problematical, this also had significant effects of conflict or alienation between the fields. Where theology entered into closer dialogue with other disciplines — philosophy, psychology, history of religions, critical theory, and so forth — its relationship to biblical studies also changed. The question of correlation between confessional and cultural sources required both theoretical and practical attention. Preaching has always had to confront the question of its relationship to the interplay of Bible, theology, and culture, with the added dynamic of ordinary Christian life.

The last thirty years or so have witnessed a tremendous "complexification" of all these relationships as the dynamics of late modernism and postmodernism have successively shaken the authority of Scripture, tradition, reason, and experience, to say nothing of the authority of the "authorizing" religious institutions. Far beyond the sphere of the church, these de-

---

2. Wesley A. Kort, *"Take, Read": Scripture, Textuality, and Cultural Practice* (University Park, PA: Pennsylvania State University Press, 1996), p. 34.

cades have seen the shaking of the foundations of language, knowledge, culture, cultural and political institutions, and personal and communal identities. But the shaking of the foundations is only part of the story. Another part of the story is the recovery of previously marginalized, subjugated, or simply ignored countertestimonies, and with them the introduction of new possibilities. Preaching, of course, has been affected by all of this.

In a recent volume, ten leading North American homileticians were invited to address the question of the purpose of preaching.[3] Their responses give some indication of the range of perspectives currently in play: preaching as "mutual critical correlation through conversation" (Ronald Allen); preaching as "exorcism of the powers of death" (Charles Campbell); preaching as "incarnational act" (Jana Childers); preaching as "hospitality, de-centering, re-membering, and right relation" (Christine Smith); preaching as illumination of the "essential paradox of human experience of being simultaneously in and out of touch with God" (Tom Troeger); preaching as "living between the Alpha and the Omega" (Lucy Lind Hogan); preaching as a "disruption of a ruptured world" (Mary Donovan Turner); preaching as "redeeming language through a language of resistance and 'signing' of love" (John McClure); preaching as "communication of the means of faith development" (Teresa Fry Brown); and preaching as "communication of faith" (Paul Scott Wilson). Each of these responses leads back into a rich and varied range of resources, locations, and analyses. Each is concerned with some aspect of the challenge of preaching that seems particularly acute in this time. Each articulates (explicitly or implicitly) a strong interpretive relationship with the Bible. And if ten more homileticians were invited to address the question, there would be ten more responses with equally vigorous claims for our attention.

The full breadth and complexity of the hermeneutical and homiletical discussion exceed our scope here, but certain dimensions have special importance for our purposes.[4] We shall lay them out as a series of movements

---

3. Jana Childers, ed., *Purposes of Preaching* (St. Louis: Chalice Press, 2004).

4. An account of the last century's homiletical development that is especially insightful regarding theory can be found in John S. McClure, *Other-wise Preaching: A Postmodern Ethic for Homiletics* (St. Louis: Chalice Press, 2001). For a helpful descriptive overview of the last forty years in homiletics, see the following three books by Richard L. Eslinger: *A New Hearing: Living Options in Homiletic Methods* (Nashville: Abingdon Press, 1987); *Narrative and Imagination: Preaching the Worlds That Shape Us* (Minneapolis: Fortress Press, 1995); *The Web of Preaching: New Options in Homiletical Method* (Nashville: Abingdon Press,

from prior dominant understandings to recent developments. Although we will accentuate the contrasts in these shifts, they are best imagined not as mutually exclusive alternatives but as dynamic movements or tensions along a continuum from a set of dominant understandings toward a different set of possibilities. As we unfold these movements, the reader will begin to notice a certain resemblance among the understandings on the *from* side, and a different resemblance among those on the *toward* side. Resemblance is not identity, however; nor does it necessarily mean family. The perspectives on each side have significant points of disagreement among them, and preachers who might share a perspective on one issue may have major differences on another. The purpose here is not to create a taxonomy but rather to orient readers to important tensions and alternatives that are present in the homiletical world.

Broadly speaking, the *from* side represents perspectives that are strongly founded in the world of modernity (and, in some cases, in premodernity), and the *toward* side represents perspectives shaped by late modernity and postmodernity. We might think of the *from* side as a dominant homiletical paradigm and the *toward* side as a set of critiques of that paradigm. The critiques suggest a new homiletics, a certain coalescence of perspectives in a field that is, nonetheless, very much in flux and marked by variety and diversity of opinion and practice. Likewise, there is more variety and diversity on the *from* side than our characterizations may suggest. Categorization and periodization are risky business if one supposes that the history of ideas and their effects lines up neatly, with tidy and well-marked beginnings, middles, and endings. Reduction and distortion inevitably occur when complex ideas are subsumed under common denominators, which leads to the loss of real — and sometimes crucial — differences. What appears to be quite new may have important anticipations, and what is chronologically old may be more contemporary than something written last week. This is, indeed, one of the characteristics of a postmodern situation. As individuals and as a culture, we find a plurality of often competing paradigms not only available to us as options but already at work within us and among us.

2002). For a helpful descriptive summary of major themes in interpretation of Scripture, see John Goldingay, *Models for Interpretation of Scripture* (Grand Rapids: Eerdmans, 1995). For particular attention to postmodern biblical interpretation, see George Aichele et al., *The Postmodern Bible* (New Haven: Yale University Press, 1995), and Fernando Segovia and Mary Ann Tolbert, eds., *Reading from This Place: Social Location and Biblical Interpretation*, 2 vols. (Minneapolis: Fortress Press, 1995).

Plurality of competing paradigms has long been true in the heritage of the Jewish-Christian tradition. Our texts and practices have their origins in vastly different places and times, are formed within and among very different peoples and paradigms, have been handed along through very different intermediaries with very different understandings, and are received in a staggeringly wide range of contexts. Because texts of tradition function with a certain authority, varying in kind and degree according to time and place, they are repeatedly being retrieved, reconsidered, reinterpreted, and re-presented. This is certainly the case in preaching: sermons are webs of intertextuality. A single sermon may include materials stretching over thousands of years (in influence, if not quotation). The influence and even the words of a fourth-century BCE Hebrew prophet, a fifth-century CE African bishop, a fourteenth-century German mystic, a sixteenth-century Protestant Reformer, a nineteenth-century American hymn, a twentieth-century Latin American theologian, and a twenty-first-century novelist can all cohabit the same address. This is to say nothing of the presence of advertising slogans, current political rhetoric, or a line from a sitcom. Even when they know that all these sources may be drawn from very different worlds and have very different (even contradictory) claims, listeners can and do make meaning out of these intertexts without accepting as normative any of the paradigms from which they have come.

It is one thing, of course, to make meaning of intertexts when one is unaware of the differences between the sources that inevitably appear in our discourse or feels that the differences do not matter. It is another thing to make meaning of them when one is aware of the sources, taking responsibility for the retrieval, reconsideration, reinterpretation, and re-presentation of the traditions that shape us. This is where the interpretive process finds (or misses) its integrity: at the point where we do discover and name the choices we make, why we make them, and in the service of what interests or claims.

From the Priority of Reasoned Argument
Toward the Priority of Constructive Imagination

To one degree or other, all of the shifts reflect something of the first, particularly momentous shift, so we will present that in somewhat greater elaboration.

"Homiletics is exiting the house of reason constituted by representational epistemology and propositional-deductive homiletics," says John McClure.[5] The term "exiting" is especially apt because it points to something that is still underway. A change has begun in the way preachers understand how we know things and how that affects what happens in preaching. Of course, those who are exiting the house do not necessarily do so for the same reasons, nor go out by the same door. For many preachers, however, the door of choice is that of imagination.

A commonly acknowledged point of reference for this shift in homiletics was the publication of the first edition of Fred Craddock's book *As One Without Authority* in 1971.[6] His work resonated deeply and widely among homileticians because it brought together concerns that were already widely shared. Drawing on a broad range of biblical studies, hermeneutics, contemporary theology, communication theory, and homiletics, Craddock presented both an assessment of what was wrong with the dominant preaching paradigm and proposals for change. Among a number of telling analyses, Craddock crystallized a critique of the dominant paradigm of Western preaching as *deductive*. By that he meant a process by which the preacher interprets a Scripture text so as to produce a thesis, which is then broken down and presented in a series of "points," or subtheses (with various illustrations), and finally applied to some situation.[7] This approach grew out of the tradition of Greco-Roman rhetoric; it was transmitted and developed (along with Aristotelian logic) down through the Middle Ages; and it was reshaped by the Reformation and again under the conditions of the Enlightenment and the modern era. In the words of Don Wardlaw, "Preaching, per se, has meant marshaling an argument in logical sequence, coordinating and subordinating points by the canons of logic, all in a careful appeal to the reasonable hearer."[8] In the deductive mode, the sermon was essentially an "oral essay," and the

---

5. McClure, *Other-wise Preaching*, p. 131.

6. Fred B. Craddock, *As One without Authority*, 3rd ed. (Nashville: Abingdon Press, 1979). On the significance of this book, see, for example, Eugene L. Lowry, *The Sermon: Dancing on the Edge of Mystery* (Nashville: Abingdon, 1997), p. 11. McClure points back further to H. Grady Davis, *Design in Preaching* (Philadelphia: Muhlenburg Press, 1958). See also Eslinger, *The Web of Preaching*, pp. 16-17.

7. *As One without Authority*, p. 54.

8. See Don M. Wardlaw, ed., *Preaching Biblically: Creating Sermons in the Shape of Scripture* (Philadelphia: Westminster Press, 1983), p. 12.

preacher used whatever other imaginative forms it contained — stories, poetry, metaphor — in the service of persuading listeners of the main point.[9]

Propositional-deductive logic, according to the critique that developed in the wake of Craddock's book, is too small for the subject matter (whether Christian faith in general or Scripture in particular) and too constrained for the task of communication. Although Scripture does indeed contain significant material in the form of argument, it contains many other forms or genres that function in ways quite different from that of argument and the appeal to the unfolding of a deductive logic. The diversity of communicative forms in Scripture calls for preaching that goes beyond elucidating and applying principles and speaks to the larger imagination.

Now the appeal to imagination has been well established since ancient times, and it certainly was part of the homiletical practice in the nineteenth and twentieth centuries, so that constituted nothing new. In the prior practice, however, imagination was part of the means of persuasion, that is, it was in the service of logical argument. This produced an often uneasy relationship between logic and imagination in modern homiletics. Richard Eslinger speaks of "a methodological schizophrenia" in sermons that present "rationalistic points, propositions, and sub-themes illustrated by emotive, pathos-laden anecdotes."[10] In this kind of preaching, "imagination's role becomes that of providing the illustrations whereby the truths of the sermon will be driven home and the sermon's themes kept interesting to the audience."[11] The epistemological status of "illustration" was left unexplored (at least in preaching textbooks), and the priority of deductive logic was assumed. Ironically, what listeners tended to remember were the illustrations, not the logical chains of persuasion!

The shift heralded by Craddock brought the role of imagination to the foreground as a *way of knowing* that has its own validity and makes its own kind of claim to truth. For homiletics this meant that imaginative forms such as symbol, image, metaphor, and story could be regarded as both the content and the means of preaching. They were not inferior or naïve forms to be translated into propositions; they were indispensable as themselves and offered models for preaching.

9. Wardlaw, p. 13.
10. Eslinger, *The Web of Preaching*, p. 258.
11. *The Web of Preaching*, p. 258.

The understandings of what is meant by imagination make a fascinating history in the West. Imagination has been praised and pilloried, lauded and lambasted. Plato excluded the poets from his ideal republic because they contributed nothing to the determination of the truth. On the other hand, the Romantics believed that imagination was the unique faculty of human genius and the contact point with the divine. Some philosophers and theologians have seen it as the antithesis to truth, and others have seen it as the means to truth. For some, imagination has meant the realm of the imaginary, the unreal; for others, it has meant the realm of the imaginative, the possible.

Since Kant, it has been fairly common to distinguish between imagination as a "reproductive (or receptive)" faculty and imagination as a "productive (or constructive)" faculty. Kant's influential insight is that we do not perceive "things in themselves"; we perceive them as they appear to us mediated by our senses and the structures of our minds. As a reproductive faculty, imagination is the means of perception by which phenomena appear to us: the disparate sensory impressions of perception are combined by imagination to make a "tree," let's say, or a "person." I grasp this bundle of perceptions "as" something. The productive imagination builds these perceptions into larger and larger wholes, into a constructed world. However, the productive (or "constructive," in our usage) imagination also turns back on the reproductive, and it supplies the categories and paradigms through which it perceives. There is an inherent circularity in all of this — or at least a dynamic of "looping back": we see what we have categories to see.

The constructive imagination is both personal and social. An individual construes and configures a world out of his or her distinct experiences and perceptions, but the individual's world is also powerfully shaped by the surrounding world, particularly as it is represented and socially constructed in language. The images, metaphors, symbols, and stories available to us create a prior understanding of what we experience, and they strongly influence us to see what we see through that understanding. Some take the position that this influence is so strong that there really are no individual perceptions, only repetitions and recombinations of the "texts" of the previously imagined world. Others allow for more novelty or originality, whether on empirical, philosophical, or theological grounds. In any case, the power of the socially imagined world is difficult to deny and, more importantly, dangerous to ignore. This is, in fact, one of the most important services that critical reason offers us: to give us some distance on the worlds we inhabit unreflectively.

One of our theology teachers liked to illustrate the role of the imagination by placing it in a three-story house.[12] In the basement he would put the word "Experience," on the first floor the word "Imagination" and on the third floor the word "Reflection." He would then ask the class, "If you are on the third floor, how do you get to the basement?" Thinking there was probably some trick involved, the more theoretically inclined class members would scratch around for something theoretically profound to say. But one day a more concrete-minded student took the question at face value and said, "Well, you *could* jump out the window and hope you don't break your leg, then see if there is some cellar door you can get in and hope it's not locked. Or," he concluded, "you could go down the stairs to the first floor, and from the first floor go to the basement." In good Socratic style, the teacher asked, "And how would you say that using the terms of the diagram?" The student answered, "If you want to get from Reflection to Experience, you have to go through Imagination." "Exactly so," said the teacher.

Reflection has access to experience only by means of the imagination. Lived experience is available to us insofar as it is transformed into the symbolic forms of the imagination, especially language. These first-order transformations both preserve experience and construct it according to the imaginative world, forms, and dynamics available to us. If I want to reflect on my experience, I must reflect on it as it resides (preserved and constructed) in my imagination.

Explanatory or analytical processes take place as a second-order reflection on these "originary expressions" (Ricoeur).[13] Quite properly, such reflection seeks to generalize, organize, and theorize, that is, to make critical sense of the world that confronts us or to deconstruct aspects of the presumed world of our imagination and/or reflection. In theology this is the (re)constructive, systematic, or dogmatic task. Poetic or artistic processes, we could say, also work constructively and deconstructively with the symbolic forms of imagination, but through different means. Through such approaches as narrative, metaphor, poetry, music, visual representa-

---

12. For a more extended discussion, see Theodore W. Jennings, *Introduction to Theology: An Invitation to Reflection Upon the Christian Mythos* (Philadelphia: Fortress Press, 1976), esp. chs. 2-4.

13. Paul Ricoeur, *Essays on Biblical Interpretation*, Lewis S. Mudge, ed. (Minneapolis: Fortress Press, 1980), p. 73.

tion, material representation (e.g., sculpture or clothing), transformations of form or genre, enactment or ritualization (e.g., drama, dance, or liturgy) the imagination is addressed and configured more directly. One is not thinking *about* the imagination (as in philosophy or dogmatic reflection), but thinking *with* and *by means of* the imagination.

As the twentieth century unfolded, particularly in its later decades, it became increasingly difficult to maintain a sharp dividing line between reason and imagination, even in the world of science. There is now a recognition that what has been considered reason or rationality is not necessarily, in fact, objective and impartial, especially when we move beyond strict empiricism. Reasoning is built on many layers of assumption, framing, "seeing as" — all of which are open to question. It may participate in a fiction of objectivity, which serves to obscure the ways in which reason is based on something that is "unreasonable," or produced by the imagination. There is also a recognition that the processes of imagination themselves operate through various kinds of implicit rationality. Reason imagines, and imagination reasons. Reason critically examines imagination; imagination proposes critical alternatives to reason. Except for the most hardcore empiricists or the staunchest "imaginationists," there seems to be significant recognition that a great deal of imagination is at work in what we call rationality, and a great deal of rationality operates in what we call imagination. Both imagination and rationality take many forms, and sometimes what we call one may be better understood as the other.

The three floors of the house, it must be remembered, are of one house, not three different houses. This implies that they all stand in relationship to one another, influencing each other, and in need of one another. Experience needs imagination in order to come to expression and make a world. Imagination needs reflection in order to critically test the worlds it constructs. Reflection needs imagination to be connected to the worlds of experience and of possibility.

It may be tempting to "abandon" the *from* side of rationality in favor of imagination, and there are surely those who leap at the opportunity to do so. But the broad concern among homileticians has been to address a distortion in preaching created by the dominance of one kind of understanding — not to abandon rationality or conceptual forms of thought. The distortion occurs when a dominance of explanatory rationality in interpretation and preaching functions to reduce meaning rather than enlarge it. By turning toward the larger world of meaning through rationality and imagination, we discover how these two complement and challenge each other by their difference rather than simply going their different ways with little regard for each other. Much of the homiletical discussion of the last few decades has been centered on the question of just how that can actually be done.

For preaching, the question now is what *kinds* of imagination and rationality are at work, how they are at work, and why. For preaching to shift from reasoned argument as its primary mode toward the constructive imagination signals a larger — and in some instances more fragmented and diffuse — vision of how the world is configured in our minds, and how that configuration is best addressed. When the priority shifts toward the constructive imagination, reasoned argument takes up a critical role, but not that of sole author and adjudicator of the truth.

From Meaning as Grasping a Proposition *Toward* an Experience of Meaning-Making

A related movement over the last decades has been a change in what is meant by "meaning." In the dominant prior understanding, as we have discussed, meaning referred to content: to grasp meaning meant to grasp an idea, proposition, or truth located within or behind the text.[14] Meaning was understood as cognitive and ideal (or abstract), and the ultimate task of interpretation was to discover the ideas residing in or implied by a passage. Frequently guided by some prior confessional perspective, interpretive tradition, ethics, philosophy, or piety, the interpreter aimed to discover the cognitive content of the text and bring it into correspondence with some larger pattern of meaning. Thus the task of preaching was to communicate that meaning to the listener.

In cognitive terms, the "meaning" of the story of the binding of Isaac, for example, is that one must be obedient to God no matter the cost. The "meaning" of the parable of the Prodigal Son is that God welcomes penitent sinners. The "meaning" of Romans 8 is that God's providential love

14. See George A. Lindbeck, *The Nature of Doctrine: Religion and Theology in a Postliberal Age* (Philadelphia: Westminster Press, 1984). Lindbeck uses the categories cognitive-propositional, experiential-expressive, and cultural-linguistic as ways of categorizing approaches to theological understanding.

can never be defeated. All of these statements may, indeed, be true (and also open to debate on the basis of other texts and those texts themselves); but all of them are also both reductions and generalizations. They *render* the passage, a term we use in cooking to indicate extracting the essence of something by boiling it down. They stand as conclusions, as explanations of a passage's meaning. When we have grasped the explanation, we have grasped the meaning — that is, the reduction — and the work of the text is done. The explanatory summary also functions to make texts less specific and more general. They are subsumed under larger theological categories for which they serve as supports, when the texts are pointed to as evidence for the validity of the generalization, but also as the interpretative framework for the texts that support them.

The problem is not that such an approach is invalid or has no place. The problem is that it became so *normative* in interpretation and preaching that it functioned to silence other strategies of understanding and communicating Scripture that had special value themselves. One could argue that in the cognitive-propositional approach the texts meant less rather than more, because the vision of what constituted meaning was restricted.

If this is the case, what other understandings of meaning might there be? It is helpful to distinguish two different aspects of the question: the hermeneutical and the homiletical. The hermeneutical question asks what is involved in understanding; the homiletical question asks how such understanding may take place in the event of preaching. In his seminal book Craddock observes that a cognitive-propositional mode of understanding leads to deductive homiletical methods. When the mode of understanding shifts, the homiletical method needs to shift as well. Craddock also suspected that, in the older model, the interpreter actually goes through an inductive process in coming to meaning but then turns it into a deductive sermon. Why not engage the listener in an inductive process of meaning-making as well? In that way the listeners could also participate in the making of meaning, and in a way that is potentially much more powerful because it is their own.[15]

The issue, however, goes beyond the question of inductive-versus-deductive thinking. One can engage in an inductive process in the cognitive-propositional mode, then serve as a guide for others in a similar process. It is another step to identify a process of coming to meaning in

---

15. Craddock, *As One without Authority*, p. 57.

which the experience of the listener is not only engaged and necessary but, even more importantly, is actually constitutive of meaning. We have all probably had the experience of being given an explanation that we grasped in its entirety but that then proved meaningless to us. This is the hermeneutical contrast (or tension) between explanation and understanding.[16] The explanation may make sense and yet may still not be meaningful. Meaning extends beyond grasping an idea or the "sense" of a text and encompasses an *experience* that is meaningful, an experience of meaning. When people say that something is meaningful, what do they mean? Whatever technical or philosophical account one may give, ordinary usage points to an experience of connection and relationship; it points to an experience of recognition of place, time, and pattern. In particular, it points to a taking-to-oneself, a coming to awareness of the situation and how one stands in it.[17]

Such an understanding of meaning may properly be called existential, in that it brings the question of one's actual life into the foreground. Tillich's famous sermon "The Depth of Existence" is an evocative depiction of the tension between these two understandings of meaning.

> Look at the student who knows the content of the hundred most important books of world history, and yet whose spiritual life remains as shallow as it ever was, or perhaps becomes even more superficial. And then look at an uneducated worker who performs a mechanical task day by day, but who suddenly asks. . . "What does it *mean*, that I do this work? What does it mean for my life? What *is* the meaning of my life?" Because he[18] asks these questions, that man is on the way into depth, whereas the other, the student of history, dwells on the surface among petrified bodies, brought out of

16. A classic description of the tension between explanation and understanding can be found in Ricoeur, *Interpretation Theory: Discourse and Surplus of Meaning* (Fort Worth, TX: The Texas Christian University Press, 1976); Ricoeur, "Explanation and Understanding," *in The Philosophy of Paul Ricoeur: An Anthology of His Work,* Charles E. Reagan and David Stewart, eds. (Boston: Beacon Press, 1978), pp. 149-166. E. D. Hirsch approaches the question through the distinction between "meaning" and "significance"; see Hirsch, *Validity in Interpretation* (New Haven: Yale University Press, 1967).

17. This is what Ricoeur means by "appropriation." For a fuller discussion, see ch. 6 below.

18. Tillich, a child of his era, did not use gender-inclusive language. What he describes applies, of course, equally to women as to men.

the depth by some spiritual earthquake of the past. The simple worker may grasp truth, even though he is unable to answer the questions; the learned scholar may possess no truth, even though he knows all the truths of the past.[19]

Here the question of meaning has the sense of connection, relationship, coming to awareness of self, place, and time. As a hermeneutical dynamic, then, the question of meaning does not require an opposition between explanation and understanding (although there are positions that push in that direction), but it recognizes the difficulty — perhaps even the danger — of contradiction. I may insist on explanation at the expense of understanding, and may substitute an explanation for a living understanding. I may even use the explanation to avoid understanding.

"Understanding envelops explanation," as Ricoeur has said.[20] That is, the process of understanding, the work of meaning-making, is larger than the task of explanation. Explanation, cognition, proposition constitute a particular critical and formal moment in understanding a text, but they are neither the starting point nor the goal.

On the *toward* side of the shift from meaning as grasping a proposition toward an experience of meaning-making, proclamation is concerned with the experience of meaning — not simply the re-presentation of meaning. The role of the preacher, beyond presenting an interpretation, becomes one of leading or guiding a process of interpretation by which the listeners become co-interpreters. The interpretive methods of the study become linked in a different way to the homiletical methods of the proclamation.[21] If the dominant patterns of cognitive-propositional thinking led to a deductive homiletical practice, the newer trend is toward an inductive practice by which the listener takes up an active and necessary role in meaning-making. Thus the listener is not just the receiver of meaning but a maker of meaning. This hermeneutical dynamic clearly has implications for both what and how preaching goes forward, as may be seen in the shifts that follow.

---

19. Paul Tillich, *The Shaking of the Foundations* (New York: Scribner's, 1948), p. 55.

20. "Explanation and Understanding," p. 165.

21. This is a significant aspect of Craddock's work, in which he has linked the inductive method of preaching to the process of interpretation and the experience of the formation of meaning.

From Preaching as Interpretation of a Text
Toward the Text as an Interpretation of Life

When preaching is rooted in the *from* side, the side of explanation and commentary, it inevitably takes the shape of propositions, illustrations, and application. This shapes the relationship of the interpreter to the text, of the interpreter to the hearer, and of the hearer to the text. Although one may use the metaphor of "listening" to the text and honestly claim that one is seeking only to hear "the voice of the text itself," this nonetheless sets up the text as a problem to be solved. If there is need for interpretation, then it is because the meaning of the text doesn't give itself but requires special strategies and approaches that ultimately allow the interpreter to set the text aside in favor of its "meaning (explanation and application)." This is objectifying the text, that is, treating it as a problematic object to be interrogated and determined. And the interpreter's relationship to the text is configured accordingly.

This also affects the relationship of the interpreter/preacher to the hearer, which becomes one of expert and surrogate: my reading takes the place of the listener's reading; my commentary takes the place of the text; my application takes the place of the listener's appropriation. The interpreter becomes the authority who has the responsibility to bring an authoritative interpretation. Indeed, the listener is not even strictly necessary for the interpretation. Now this description may be a bit overdrawn, but the tendency and dynamic are very much at work in varying degrees.

On the *toward* side, the concern is to refocus the nature of the problem. To put it in rather bald terms, the text doesn't need interpretation. It doesn't need anything: it is a text, not a person. As a text it may be read or not, interpreted or not, and it still remains itself. The text does not need interpretation; life does. Therefore, the question is not "how can we understand this text?" but "how can we understand our life?" The purpose of interpretation is to seek, with the help of the text, to understand ourselves and our situation. This orientation places a primary emphasis on the place of understanding: where, when, and by whom does this text need to be heard? Where in the midst of life will we stand and seek to understand — with the help of the text?

Ernst Fuchs, one of the leaders of the New Hermeneutic, likened this interpretive approach to putting a cat in front of a mouse.[22] If you want

22. See *The New Hermeneutic*, James M. Robinson and John B. Cobb, Jr., eds. (New York: Harper & Row, 1964), p. 54.

to know something about a cat, after all, there are different ways to go about it. You can buy a book about cats that has thorough descriptions, explanations, and illustrations, perhaps a lovely coffee-table sort of book with acetate overlays showing all the successive layers of the cat's physiology (perhaps even with different kinds of fur to try out!) and delicious histories, categories, species, and so forth. This is the kind of children's book Dylan Thomas wrote about, saying it told him "everything about the wasp, except why."[23] One could learn a great deal from such a book — in a certain way.

However, instead of a discussion about cats in a book, one could follow Fuchs's lead: one could take an actual cat and place it in front of an actual mouse, and the cat itself would show what it is and what it does. In this orientation the interpretive process does not ask, Where will the meaning I have grasped be put to work? Rather, it asks, Where in the midst of actual life shall we bring this text—so that it will show us itself what it is? Where in the life of an individual? Of a family? Of a community, a nation? Where in the life of the world? "Come, go down to the potter's house, and there I will let you hear my words," God says to Jeremiah (Jer. 18:2). There are some things we cannot begin to understand from where we are standing, and every place we stand may offer yet another possibility to hear.[24]

This recognition of the hermeneutical importance of the *situation*, as contemporary as it is, also has ancient roots in rabbinic midrash, a process that has been described by Gerald Bruns as "exemplary of all interpretation that is open to the historicality of human life."[25] Scripture is overflowing with meaning, and the meaning requires the history and experience of the community to bring it to light. Thus there are both a written and an oral Torah. Both are given by God at Sinai; both are divine. Interpretation unlocks the richness of the book, which is the Torah in time and place. The two Torahs are given together, but the Torah as writing must unfold and be

---

23. Dylan Thomas, *A Child's Christmas in Wales* (New York: New Directions, 1995), p. 29.

24. We elaborate on this theme in our discussion of decontextualization and recontextualization in ch. 6.

25. Gerald Bruns, "Midrash and Allegory," in Robert Alter and Frank Kermode, eds., *The Literary Guide to the Bible* (Cambridge, MA: Harvard University Press, 1987), p. 636. See also Michael Fishbane, *The Exegetical Imagination: On Jewish Thought and Theology* (Cambridge, MA: Harvard University Press, 1998).

read in sequence. Therefore, interpretation unfolds through time and community.[26]

The question of the situation inevitably directs the issue of meaning from the abstract to the particular. It inevitably brings to the foreground the identity of the interpreter, the community, and the time in which they must understand and act. By shifting the nature of the problem from that of understanding a text to that of understanding our life, we bring about a strong reorientation toward meaning as embodiment or reflective practice (or *praxis*). This can be seen in the enhanced importance of social location in the interpretive process.[27] The location of the interpreter shifts from that of the "omniscient reader" to that of a particular reader in a particular time and place, a reader confronted with a need to understand and act. The direction of interpretation shifts from universalization to particularization. Indeed, the context of interpretation discloses features and dynamics of the text (and the interpretive tradition attached to it) that had been hitherto unmarked, and it "talks back." Precisely because texts do interpret life, life must talk back and thereby deepen the encounter with what is at stake in interpretation.

From Preaching as Instruction/Cognition
Toward Preaching That Seeks to Address the Imagination

As preaching has sought to address the imagination, the roles of image and narrative have come to the fore. If it is true that we live first of all within an imaginatively constructed world, and if preaching seeks to offer an alternative world in which to live, then preaching must address the imagination in its own forms and dynamics. The extensive arguments swirling around theories of image and narrative would take us far beyond the scope of our discussion; indeed, different homileticians will use the terms in very different ways. But the concern for image and narrative is a strongly recurring hermeneutical and homiletical theme.

For our purposes, we mean "image" in the common sense of metaphorical or figurative language. Metaphorical language, far from being

26. See W. Dow Edgerton, *The Passion of Interpretation* (Louisville: Westminster/John Knox Press, 1992), pp. 46-48.

27. See Segovia and Tolbert, *Reading from This Place.*

merely decorative, grants us access to dimensions of ourselves and our world beyond that of discursive reason. The poet Percy Shelley once observed, "Metaphorical language marks the before unapprehended relation of things." Owen Barfield modified this to say that metaphorical language marks the forgotten relationships of things.[28] Image has the power to restore the memory of connections, to return to the center what has been left out or exiled to the margins. Image can integrate experiences, times, and places that memory has displaced and separated. Hence, image can join horizons that we cannot bring together in any other way. "The image has touched the depths before it stirs the surface," says Bachelard.[29] He means that the image circumvents the surface structures of concepts and explanations and sets the web of imagination reverberating. The image troubles the waters, we might say, reordering and recombining elements of the imaginative world — perhaps in surprising or even explosive ways. In time we may come to reflect on how and why an image has the effect it does; we may investigate the image through more discursive language, the surface to which Bachelard refers. But the image does its most powerful work in the imagination itself.

"Real metaphors are not translatable," Ricoeur observes.[30] By that he means that they cannot be converted into literal speech. Metaphor, properly understood, goes beyond merely clothing an idea in an image; it creates a "semantic impertinence," a contradiction, or an absurdity.[31] This draws us beyond the literal (or denotative) meaning of the words to figurative (or connotative) meaning, a movement that is provoked by the contradiction of the surface. Let's take, for example, "I am the bread of life "(John 6:35). At the literal level this statement is absurd: bread is made of flour and water, not flesh and blood. Not only is it absurd, it is offensive and alarming; in the story itself, the metaphorical usage is scandalous, provoking interpretation and counterinterpretation. It leads out into a whole series of other statements (themselves narrative and metaphorical) and finally ends with even the disciples unable to "translate" Jesus' words into something they can comprehend. Resistance or refusal of translation means that the metaphor is not simply a code to be deciphered into something we already know, but

28. See Robert Bly, "What the Image Can Do," in Donald Hall, ed., *Claims for Poetry* (Ann Arbor: The University of Michigan Press, 1982), p. 42.

29. Gaston Bachelard, *The Poetics of Space* (New York: Orion, 1964), p. xix.

30. Ricouer, *Interpretation Theory*, p. 52.

31. *Interpretation Theory*, p. 50.

"tells us something new about reality."[32] It breaks open the possibilities of the world through a disruption of the settled pattern of language.

However, a metaphor can become dead, so much a commonplace and so accepted into the language landscape that it no longer reads as a disruption, no longer draws us past the surface. It has the form of a metaphor but the function of an identity, substitution, or decoration. On another hand, it can also become a "root metaphor."[33] That is, a metaphor can gather together a range of other submetaphors and configure them so strongly that they form a whole metaphorical architecture or complex, held together at the root. This gathering together of metaphors also serves to "scatter" concepts by leading to a profusion of possible interpretations at the conceptual level.[34] Hence root metaphors (such as "I am the bread of life") both bind and loose: they bind together a complex of other metaphors and set loose conceptual reflection by their irreducibility.

The more that meaning is conceived to be larger than explanation, and the more that the function of metaphorical language is understood as opening up and (re)constituting a world and not just decorating it, the more important the task of addressing the imagination becomes. In recent years the role of narrative in constituting our imaginative worlds has been, if anything, even more emphasized than that of image. Narrative theology and narrative homiletics began blossoming in the 1970s and would seem to have continued unabated.[35] Stephen Crites's provocative and hugely influential article "The Narrative Quality of Experience"[36] set off a discussion that is still unfolding. "There is no point so deep in the life of a culture," Crites argued, "that it is free from the narrative form, nothing prior to narrative upon which narratives depend."[37] This is to say that we live and move and have our being in narrative. Narrative is, in effect, the very lens through which we perceive the world, a fundamental structure of human imagination — hardwiring.

We live in story-shaped worlds, perceiving and ordering experience in

---

32. *Interpretation Theory,* p. 53.

33. *Interpretation Theory,* p. 64.

34. *Interpretation Theory,* p. 64.

35. See the previously cited works of Eslinger and McClure on this, especially Eslinger's *Narrative and Imagination.*

36. Stephen Crites, "The Narrative Quality of Experience," *Journal of the American Academy of Religion* 39 (1971): 291-311.

37. Crites, p. 308.

narrative form. How consolidated or fragmented the story worlds may be is a matter of considerable discussion. The movement from premodern to modern to late modern and postmodern situations can be described as a movement from an overarching real (or realistic) metanarrative to a constantly shifting kaleidoscope of narrative fragments. Even the possibility of a coherent personal narrative (or subjectivity or identity) has come under scrutiny and cannot be taken for granted.[38]

An emphasis on the role of narrativity as a feature of human consciousness, however, does not speak to the particular role of narrative in Jewish-Christian usage. H. Richard Niebuhr argued that what moves a narrative into the field of revelation is its power to found a pattern or paradigm.[39] If it does, then perceiving the pattern in relationship to a new context transforms both the context and the paradigm narrative. The context is seen as it stands in light of the narrative, disclosing possibilities, limitations, contradictions. Similarly, the narrative is seen as *it* stands in light of the context. The relationship is metaphorical—or, to use a narrative term, parabolic.[40]

One does not have to agree with the strongest formulations of the importance of narrative to recognize the power of narrative to shape our understandings of ourselves and the world. By the same token, we do not have to see narrative as a fundamental structure of the human imagination to recognize that it is nevertheless a fundamental structure of the Jewish-Christian world. Whatever else it means to understand ourselves as Jewish or Christian, it means that we take our bearings within an overarching story of creation and redemption as it is configured within the Bible. *How* we name the plot and characters of the story, of course, is a matter of serious difference and debate, whether in the exegetical or dogmatic sense. The same is true for how the implications of this narrative frame play out in the actual work of preaching (from preaching as storytelling, let's say, to preaching as story-like telling, to preaching as telling The Story). But the importance of the role of narrative in shaping us — and therefore the way

---

38. For a consideration of the implications of this for homiletics, see McClure, "Exiting the House of Experience: Preaching and Fragmented Subjectivities," in *Other-wise Preaching* pp. 47-66.

39. H. Richard Niebuhr, *The Meaning of Revelation* (New York: Macmillan, 1941), p. 69. See the discussion of this in Paul Ricoeur, "The Bible and the Imagination," in *Figuring the Sacred: Religion, Narrative, and Imagination* (Minneapolis: Fortress Press, 1995), pp. 144-166.

40. See Paul Ricoeur, "Interpretive Narrative" and "Toward a Narrative Theology: Its Necessity, Its Resources, Its Difficulties," in *Figuring the Sacred*, pp. 181-199, 236, 248.

in which preaching responds to the role of narrative imagination — has been central to the hermeneutical and homiletical discussion.

From Preaching That Seeks to Comment on (or Repeat) What the Text Says *Toward* Preaching That Seeks to Do What the Text Does

Preachers have long sought to grasp the relationship between the eventful nature of the Word of God and the actual event of preaching. "Whatever precise theological definition may be given to the *concept of the word of God,* at all events it points us to something that happens, *viz.,* to the movement which leads from the text of Holy Scripture to the sermon ('sermon' of course taken in the pregnant sense of proclamation in general)."[41] To speak of the Word of God is to refer to the speech encounter (speaking and hearing), in which what the text is about confronts us and interprets us. "Word event is the event of interpretation taking place through the word."[42] The Word of God is not communication *about* God, but rather something that happens. The criticism of an older orthodox Protestant view was that it simply identified the Word of God with the words of Scripture, thereby losing the crucial element of eventful address, speech, proclamation, and understanding.

Speech does not only say something — it does something. The work of J. L. Austin focused attention on the different ways in which ordinary speech functions.[43] Two distinctions are especially important in speech functions: the locutionary and the illocutionary. The locutionary function of language refers to the content of what is said; the illocutionary refers to the action that the saying performs. We could describe the locutionary meaning of the statement "I forgive you" by discussing the meaning of sin and forgiveness; but the illocutionary meaning — the action when one person says this to another — is an act of forgiveness. Talking about forgiveness and forgiving are two different things.

Hermeneutically, this involves the dialectic of speech as event and

41. Gerhard Ebeling, "Word of God and Hermeneutic," in Robinson and Cobb, *The New Hermeneutic,* p. 85.

42. Ebeling, p. 68.

43. J. L. Austin, *How to Do Things with Words* (Cambridge, MA: Harvard University Press, 1962).

speech as meaning.[44] As an event, speech is an action that begins and ends. When the event comes to an end, what becomes of it? It persists as meaning (whether orally — in memory — or in writing). Speech comes to an end, and what is preserved is meaning, not speech. Yet preaching is concerned with a speech event also, and it will take place as a speech event. For homiletics the question is that of the relationship between the locutionary meaning and illocutionary action of the text and the locutionary meaning and illocutionary act of preaching. What is the relationship between what the text says and does and what I am saying and doing?

This opens up all those dimensions of preaching that go beyond the sense of the words. Communication theory suggests that, in a face-to-face setting, listeners are affected more by body language than by vocal inflection, and more by vocal inflection than by the particular words that are said.[45] This can be an appalling thought to those of us who agonize over the crafting of each sentence and take great care to say things just so. Speech has sense, but it also has feeling, tone, intention, and action — all coming to expression (or failing to) through voice and gesture. We are always enacting *something* when we preach; we have no choice. If I try to empty my voice of all inflection and hold my body as perfectly still as I can (and still move my lips), then I am enacting someone who is frozen and empty of inflection. The question is not whether or not I will perform some action, only what that action will be. Performance is not just decoration or staging; it helps make the meaning.

Performance is hermeneutical. Interpretation is "an act and an art of performance not apart from but including cognitive study and analysis [as well as] commitment to the whole physical process of interpretation."[46] Alla Bozarth-Campbell synthesizes understandings from hermeneutics, literary criticism, performance studies, and theology, and she provides a highly nuanced theoretical framework for homileticians thinking about performative hermeneutics.[47] Every interpretation, she argues, whether pri-

---

44. Ricoeur, *Interpretation Theory,* pp. 8-23.

45. Jana Childers, *Performing the Word: Preaching as Theater* (Nashville: Abingdon Press, 1998), p. 57.

46. Wallace A. Bacon, as quoted in Alla Bozarth-Campbell, *The Word's Body: An Incarnational Aesthetic of Interpretation* (Tuscaloosa, AL: University of Alabama Press, 1979), p. 7.

47. Bozarth-Campbell, *The Word's Body.* See, for example, the use of her work by Jana Childers, *Performing the Word,* and Richard Ward, *Speaking from the Heart: Preaching with Passion* (Nashville: Abingdon, 1992).

vate or public, involves performance. Even the person reading alone is engaged in a performance of the text, an "incarnation," in her terms, "that results in the speaking and hearing and final embodiment of the word within human flesh, blood, and psyche."[48] The process of preparing to preach and preaching is a whole series of performances, each leading to the next, and finally to the preaching event itself. Interpretation is eventful and embodied: the preacher performs the interpretation, and those present interpret the whole performance. The listeners, in turn, will perform their understanding in speech and action. How can the preacher be a *doer of the word?*

For philosophical, theological, and hermeneutical reasons, therefore, homileticians began exploring what it might mean for texts not simply to be explained (however clearly), commented upon (however astutely), or mined for sermonic ideas (however creatively), but *performed.*

From Preaching as an Independent Rhetorical Genre *Toward* Preaching That Is Shaped by the Forms of the Texts

In biblical studies there has been another influential line of development, focused on the literary forms or genre, that has had a great impact on homiletics. In this shift, the *from* side represents hermeneutical and homiletical approaches in which the content of texts could be separated from the form and made the subject of some other form of communication. The *toward* side represents those approaches that seek to hold together form and content in both interpretation and preaching.[49]

In the hermeneutical and homiletical fields, the work of theoreticians such as Ernst Cassirer, Martin Heidegger, Philip Wheelwright, Susan Langer, and Paul Ricoeur was energetically appropriated in the latter half of the twentieth century. In addition to this, new perspectives and approaches of literary criticism came into play, particularly in narrative and parable studies. Biblical scholars increasingly focused on both the *what* and the *how* of biblical texts, and homileticians increasingly focused on the ways in which the *how* really shaped the *what* of preaching. Ron Allen offers a succinct summary:

48. Bozarth-Campbell, *The Word's Body,* p. 1.

49. For an excellent discussion of the development of the use of formalist literary criticism in biblical hermeneutics, see Lynn M. Poland, *Literary Criticism and Biblical Hermeneutics: A Critique of Formalist Approaches* (Chico, CA: Scholars Press, 1985).

In this view, the form of the text — its particular configuration of words, images, thoughts — cannot be separated from the meaning of the text, because it is precisely through the form that the fullness of the text's meaning is imparted. In this context, "meaning" includes that which is rational, cognitive, and discursive as well as that which is intuitive and emerging from the life of feeling. The form itself is an embodiment, an incarnation of meaning.[50]

If genre is, indeed, an essential aspect of meaning, then the preacher must ask how that essential dynamic can be present in the preaching. The preacher must ask if and how preaching can somehow realize the meaning created by form and content together. As Craddock puts it, "Let doxologies be shared doxologically, narratives narratively, polemics polemically, poems poetically, and parables parabolically. In other words, biblical preaching ought to be biblical."[51]

Samuel Terrien links the question of literary genre in the Bible to shifting, differing, and sometimes competing testimonies in the life of Israel to God's presence and absence, bringing the question of genre together with the question of revelation.[52] Paul Ricoeur explores this in a different way in his essay "Toward a Hermeneutic of the Idea of Revelation."[53] Ricoeur argues that the classic doctrine of revelation depended on the speech-model of the prophetic oracle: in the oracle a voice speaks behind and through another voice. The voice of God speaks behind and through the voice of the prophet. The affirmation of Scripture as the Word of God carried this dynamic of double speaking implicitly or explicitly. Yet Scripture itself contains a number of different genres; indeed, prophecy may not be the dominant one. Ricoeur asks why the dynamic of one speech model should displace the others, which operate in quite different ways. He then explores how various biblical genres present different possibilities for understanding what is meant by "revelation."

Seen in this light, the question of genre becomes the question of ways of knowing. The different genres testify that we know differently when we

---

50. Ronald J. Allen, "Shaping Sermons by the Language of the Text," in Don M. Wardlaw, ed., *Preaching Biblically*, p. 32.

51. Craddock, *As One without Authority*, p. 163.

52. Samuel Terrien, *The Elusive Presence: Toward a New Biblical Theology* (San Francisco: Harper & Row, 1978).

53. In *Essays on Biblical Interpretation*, pp. 73-117.

prophesy, narrate, prescribe, compose a parable, voice a hymn, and so on. Different forms make different claims to authority. Different forms locate speaker, listener, and meaning in different configurations and relationships, and these configurations are essential to what and how we know. Different forms invite different ways of participation and validation. In subsequent chapters we shall take up these dynamics as they relate to various biblical genres and to a practice of interpretation for preaching.

From Preaching as Discourse about the Text *Toward* the "Displaying of the Icons"

In the shift from preaching as interpretation of a text toward the text as interpretation of life, we discussed the question of where in life a text would be placed in order for it to give what it has to give. The shift toward "displaying the icons" has a similar direction of movement but with a special dynamic related to the sacred status of Scripture. Here the dimension of meaning flows less from what or how the text says what it says and more from the very fact of the presence of the text itself.

People use the term "holy" in quite different ways, but it usually indicates something of great (perhaps even ultimate) power and value, whether because of where it comes from, what it is (or says), how it affects us, or what it does in the world.[54] As with the discussion of revelation and genre, in which the possibility of a broader and more pluralistic understanding of revelation grows from recognition of dynamics of different literary forms, Scripture itself may be seen to model a pluralistic approach to what it means to have a sacred text. Multiple dynamics of form invite recognition and response to multiple dimensions of holiness.

---

54. Like the question of revelation, the discussion of what it means to call Scripture "holy" is long and complex, far beyond our scope here. For the sake of rough approximation, however, we could group the approaches to the concept of Scripture as holy under four categories, which indicate the loci of the sacredness of Scripture: origin, content, effect on the reader/hearer, and function. See M. H. Abrams' classic schematic of literary-critical theory *The Mirror and the Lamp: Romantic Theory and the Critical Tradition* (London: Oxford University Press, 1953). See also the more recent poststructuralist perspective in, for example, Wesley A. Kort, *Story, Text, and Scripture: Literary Interests in Biblical Narrative* (University Park, PA: The Pennsylvania State University Press, 1988). See further W. Dow Edgerton, *Speak to Me That I May Speak: A Spirituality of Preaching* (Cleveland: Pilgrim Press, 2006), ch. 4.

Quite apart from theories of sacredness, however, we have witnessed repeatedly the way in which the sacred status of Scripture creates an experience of meaning that is not confined to the particular sense of the words and their interpretation. Scripture not only contains symbols but *is* a symbol, and particular texts come to have particular symbolic value. A family gathers in a hospital room at the time of death. Someone asks the pastor to recite Psalm 23. Surely this is the time for recitation, not explication. Why? Because the text itself is more than what it says; it is an "icon." The function of an icon is translucency: one's gaze is drawn through the surface of the icon toward the divine. It is not a representation or "likeness" of the divine but a means through which one contemplates the divine. To follow Baudrillard, an idol stops and captures the gaze; an icon directs and guides the gaze through and beyond itself.[55]

To be sure, there can be an idolatrous use or function of Scripture as well as of an icon. Certain kinds of literalism or fundamentalism work in that way, which has been recognized since ancient times. One could argue that the history of hermeneutics is an extended discussion of just that issue. But certain scriptural and liturgical texts function not idolatrously but iconically for many people. They are overcharged with memory, association, special significance, and meaning. We ask not to have them explained to us, or commented upon, or applied to our situation; rather, we ask to be allowed to spend time in the range of their power. We ask to "tarry with them" a little longer because they hold together dimensions of experience, imagination, and meaning in ways that other texts do not. And in some cases one may *experience* that meaning only through the very recitation. How will we find ways to dwell within the words of this text? How will we find ways to allow ourselves to embrace and be embraced by it? How will we structure the time of speaking and hearing so that the reverberation of this text will have time enough to do what it (alone) can do?

As fewer and fewer listeners come with a strong prior relationship with Scripture, however, we also find that what may have functioned as an icon at one time may now be heard as little more than vaguely familiar religious language. The texts may be recognized as Scripture but have (at best) only a formal authority, an authority in principle but not in the

---

55. For Baudrillard's discussion of the transformation of an image from a representation of reality to a "simulacrum" representing itself, see Jean Baudrillard, *Simulations*, trans. Paul Foss, Paul Patton, and Philip Beitchman (New York: Semiotext(e), 1983).

hearer's life. Over the last few decades one has heard preachers asking more and more how to preach for people who have virtually no knowledge of the Bible. The biblical texts, so "fraught with background" (to recall Eric Auerbach's phrase) to the experienced reader of the Bible, so resonant with other texts and overcharged with connections for the preacher, may have no such echoes and resonances for the contemporary listener. This is, at least in part, a source of the urgency in "postliberal" approaches to preaching and their emphasis on the creation and nurture of the cultural-linguistic community of faith. Perhaps Scripture can become an icon once again through the act of preaching itself.

If that is so, then it certainly affects the hermeneutical and homiletical approach. At the level of reading and explanation, there may be no special "sacred hermeneutic" (a foundation of historical-critical method and any critical methodology), but at the level of proclamation the question of holiness is still very much in play. What do we mean when we call the Bible "holy"? What does it mean that the texts we handle are Scripture? What is required for the words of the Bible to be known as holy?

Such questions naturally lead to the liturgical function of preaching and the preaching function of liturgy.

From Preaching That Is Considered in Isolation from Liturgy *Toward* Preaching That Is Liturgically Integrated

Although the liturgical context of preaching has long been presumed, attention to the significance of that context for the practice of preaching has been highly uneven. It has been quite possible to consider preaching as an effectively isolated rhetorical act; indeed, rhetorical models drawn from other public spheres may have tacitly encouraged it. There is a long tradition of catechetical and mystagogic preaching that refers to the liturgy for its content, but that is different from an approach that turns to liturgy for its means.

In the last few decades, however, teachers of liturgy and preaching have shown significantly increased interest in making a much greater interplay and synthesis of liturgy and preaching.[56] It is not only the formal

---

56. See, for example, Charles Rice, *The Embodied Word: Preaching as Art and Liturgy* (Minneapolis: Fortress Press, 1991).

liturgy as commonly conceived that is being integrated with preaching. At the same time (with particular thanks to the work of Henry Mitchell and Frank Thomas), the interweaving of preaching and celebratory worship in African-American traditions has excited interest in the preaching practices of that community.[57] In feminist work, the role of creative ritualization has been an important aspect of the interpretive process, including preaching.[58] Pentecostal preaching, which frequently incorporates different means of prayer and praise, has also attracted interest from preachers beyond that tradition.

This has made for a greater awareness, at a pragmatic level, of the sequence of the liturgy and preaching's place in it. How does preaching *depend on* the liturgy, *respond to* the liturgy, and *lead to* the liturgy? How can liturgical elements be shaped more explicitly for proclamation?[59] How can preaching more directly incorporate liturgical elements (responses, refrains, sacramental or symbolic action)? What do the basic modes of public prayer — thanksgiving, adoration, confession, intercession, and petition — have to teach us about preaching? Calvin insisted that the sacraments present us with an even clearer communication of the gospel than does preaching, because they speak to us not only through the ear but through all the senses. If that is true, perhaps there is something preaching can learn from the liturgy.

Our various traditions, of course, bring highly varied assumptions to the table when it comes to what we mean by liturgy, and we often seem to be speaking different languages. Perspectives from ritual studies can help us find areas of key commonality and difference. Ted Jennings has proposed that in ritual we engage in an embodied way of knowing: learning, teaching, and demonstrating knowledge that we can learn, teach, and demonstrate in no other way.[60] Just as we learn to eat by eating and to

---

57. Henry H. Mitchell, *Celebration and Experience in Preaching* (Nashville: Abingdon Press, 1990); Frank A. Thomas, *They Like to Never Quit Praisin' God: The Role of Celebration in Preaching* (Cleveland: United Church Press, 1997).

58. See Elisabeth Schüssler Fiorenza, *Bread Not Stone: The Challenge of Feminist Biblical Interpretation* (Boston: Beacon Press, 1984), pp. 15-22. "The hermeneutics of creative actualization" includes a wide range of arts and performance forms — liturgy among them — in a feminist interpretive approach.

59. See Charles L. Rice, *The Embodied Word*; F. Russell Mitman, *Worship in the Shape of Scripture* (Cleveland: Pilgrim Press, 2001).

60. Theodore W. Jennings, Jr., "On Ritual Knowledge," *Journal of Religion* 62 (1982): 111-

dance by dancing (not by reading books or attending lectures on those activities), we acquire ritual knowledge through our embodied participation. This means that ritual knowledge is not a secondary or derivative kind of knowledge, with the real meaning or knowing to be found in the explanation. It is itself a primary knowledge, about which we may reflect, to be sure, but which we know only through participation.

If this is the case, then what is it that a Christian community's ritual life — which will be larger than the formal liturgies — is seeking to do? Following Jennings, we could say that the function of Christian ritual is to enact the essential shapes of Christian life.[61] Ritual and liturgical forms are powerfully condensed symbolic actions that teach us how to live. They point beyond their own enactment in the ritual context toward an enactment in the life of the community. We eat and drink at Jesus' table to learn how to eat and drink at every table.

This suggests wide-ranging implications for preaching. One would be the relationship between the priestly and the prophetic. It is a commonplace notion to assign to the liturgy the priestly function and to preaching the prophetic. What happens if we look at the liturgy and say that the community itself has a prophetic vocation? We could then ask how our liturgy enacts this identity—how it can become a prophetic liturgy. And we could ask how preaching could provide priestly care for a prophetic people. What is the priestly and pastoral care of those who are called to prophetic life?

Another line of reflection could focus on what preaching itself models. If, indeed, the purpose of liturgy is to model possibilities for Christian life, could we say that, similarly, a central purpose of preaching is to model possibilities for Christian speech? If preaching is something that can only be done by "experts," and if the hearer's response to great preaching is awe at the preacher's eloquence ("I could never do that!"), then something seriously wrong has happened. If preaching takes on modes and vocabularies that only make sense in the context of the gathered community, how does that equip the community for its speech vocation in the world? Seen in this way, the questions of liturgy and preaching then become the ques-

27; reprinted in Ron Grimes, ed., *Readings in Ritual Studies* (Upper Saddle River, NJ: Prentice-Hall, 1996), pp. 324-34.

61. See Theodore W. Jennings, Jr., *Life as Worship: Prayer and Praise in Jesus' Name* (Grand Rapids: Eerdmans, 1982); Jennings, *The Liturgy of Liberation: The Confession and Forgiveness of Sins* (Nashville: Abingdon, 1988).

tions of preparation for Christian praxis. By form and content they demonstrate and model essential shapes for Christian life, including our life of interpretation and speech in the world.

From Reaching That Is Governed by the Dynamics of Writing/Reading *Toward* Preaching That Is Governed by the Dynamics of Speaking/Hearing

While it may seem self-evident that preaching is an oral event — speaking and listening — the dominant preparation for preaching has been reading and writing. The educational process itself, especially higher education, prepares persons in the modes of thought and expression that writing provides. When we are asked to demonstrate what we know, it is most commonly through some process of writing. This has led to preaching that takes the form of the oral essay, as we have discussed above, and it does so chiefly through the means of the written essay (which is then read, or repeated from notes, or memorized). Even when preaching moves in some of the directions we have been describing, it can do so in ways that unconsciously reinforce the writing mode. Indeed, for those who have undertaken graduate education, it is enormously difficult even to recognize how thoroughly we have been formed in this way. Robin Meyers says: "Perhaps the single biggest failure of the teaching of preaching is that young ministers are not fully impressed with the difference between textuality and orality."[62]

Without denying the immense value of writing, homileticians have been increasingly concerned to understand the distinctive dynamics of orality and its implications for preaching. The work of homileticians such as Tex Sample, Lucy Rose, Henry Mitchell, Fred Craddock, Eugene Lowry, Thomas Troeger, Richard Jensen, Jana Childers, David Buttrick, Robin Meyers — and the list could be much longer — provides wide-ranging examples of that concern. Some of the issues are about basic dynamics of oral communication: how language is used, how storytelling works, how images function in imagination, memory and mnemonic patterning, emotional feeling and tone. Other issues concern deeper dynamics of mind, such as forming consciousness by the ear rather than the eye, concretion,

---

62. Quoted in Lowry, *The Sermon: Dancing on the Edge of Mystery,* p, 115.

speaking-thinking rather than writing-thinking. Still other issues concern the relational dynamics of orality between speaker and hearer, and between hearer and hearer, and the dimension of mystery that the human voice evokes.[63]

One aspect of the shift toward understanding the process of speaking is of special importance. Good writing takes the place of the writer. It must be able to stand alone and communicate with the reader without the author standing by, saying, "Here's what I meant." Good writing presupposes absence and the self-sufficiency and autonomy of words themselves: whatever needs to be there has to be on the page. Good speaking, on the other hand, needs the speaker to say what it has to say. Write it down on the page, as you might write down notes for a song, and it will probably look and feel wrong, incomplete, awkward. Good speaking needs the voice, the face, the body, the particularity, the presence, the relationship, the community, the situation, the time, the moment — it needs all that makes up the actual event of speaking and listening to say what it has to say. As listeners, we know if and when we are actually being spoken with, if and when we are actually part of the event, if and when something is happening between and among us and not just in front of us. This characteristic of the orality of preaching leads to our final shift.

From Preaching as "Talks about Religion" *Toward* Preaching as Testimony

On the *from* side, preaching is often characterized by "objectivity," distance, control, formalization, authority, anonymity, office. The "modern" sermon may be interesting, informative, instructive, as a good lecture often is. On the *from* side, preaching may also be vivid, lively, informal, colloquial, artistically or aesthetically pleasing — seemingly a world apart from those other characteristics. And it may still amount to just another "talk about religion." Talks about religion are not the same as witness and testimony.

Witness and testimony are ancient terms we know well, both from

---

63. The work of Walter Ong has been enormously influential in shaping homiletical understanding of orality; see Ong, *Orality and Literacy: The Technologizing of the Word* (London and New York: Methuen, 1982); Ong, *The Presence of the Word* (New Haven: Yale University Press, 1967).

Scripture and from history. Jesus and John bear witness, prophets and apostles and martyrs bear witness, and the Holy Spirit bears witness and gives words to those who are called before the powers. In Acts, the risen Jesus' final words to the apostles before his ascension are: "You will be my witnesses . . . to the ends of the earth" (Acts 1:8). That is, indeed, the commission of those who are sent, the authority of those who are sent, the essential speech-act of those who are sent by Jesus. None of this sounds much like "objectivity," distance, control, formalization, authority, anonymity, office — or even like vivid, lively, informal, colloquial, and aesthetically pleasing talks about religion.

It is ironic, perhaps, that in the dislocations and deconstruction of the modern world the ancient terms of witness emerge with new energy; but there are special qualities to those terms that do indeed take on renewed significance now.[64] In ancient and contemporary usage alike, the terms "witness" and "testimony" come from the juridical realm. A witness is a person who testifies in a dispute about the truth.

> By testifying a witness does more than simply express an opinion. A witness makes an outward attestation of an inward conviction, indeed, an inward faith. What a witness testifies to, however, is something known in the visible and tangible life of the world. Conviction or faith is inward, but their risk is that they make a claim about something true in the world we share. Integrity is the binding together of this inward and outward dimension, and integrity is what makes a true witness. One may ultimately be mistaken, outweighed by the testimony of other witnesses or rejected, and still not be a false witness, for the integrity of the witness does not depend upon the outcome of the trial. It is not being mistaken, outweighed, or rejected that makes one a false witness, it is the lie.[65]

The person of the witness and the testimony of the witness are inextricably bound together. The witness is not the judge determining the law, not the forensics expert presenting the "facts." The witness is not the prosecuting or defense attorney arguing about both. The witness is not the jury or assembly who must decide, nor the onlookers, whatever their interests may

64. This conception of the witness is based on Ricoeur, "The Hermeneutics of Testimony," in *Essays on Biblical Interpretation*, pp. 119-154.

65. Edgerton, *Speak to Me That I May Speak*, pp. 189-90.

be. These all play vital but different roles. The place of the witness is to attest to what he or she understands to be true from his or her own experience — and why.

Although the theme of testimony focuses attention on the role of the witness, it is essential to remember that testimony is presented for a reason. In the dispute about the truth there are those who must decide what they themselves will attest on the basis of what they have seen and heard. The role of the witness is essential because there are those who must decide themselves what witness they will bear in the world. If a witness must testify for the sake of the truth, the witness must also testify for the sake of those who must decide for themselves.

Contemporary theoretical reflection on the nature of witness has been particularly developed in the work of Emmanuel Levinas and Paul Ricoeur (with significant prior history), and their thought has been appropriated in the work of Rebecca Chopp, Walter Brueggemann, and Anna Carter Florence.[66] But the theme of witness has long been part of African-American preaching, as well as evangelical and Pentecostal preaching. It has been at the heart (explicitly or implicitly) of every theology of liberation, and of homiletical approaches that orient themselves toward the praxis of the speaker and hearer. It is, after all, an ancient commission.

A particular effect of the role of testimony has been preaching that names and claims the person, place, and stake of the preacher's identity much more clearly. The preacher is not anonymous, impersonal, authoritative, omnicompetent, universal in scope; rather, he or she is present, partial, incomplete, and particular. Gender, race, age, class, sexual orientation, social location, and personal history are inseparable from the event of witness. If an earlier homiletical practice urged the preacher to become "invisible" in the sermon, the contemporary concern is quite the reverse. If an earlier concern was to set aside the "earthen vessel" of the preacher for the sake of the "treasure" of the message, now the earthen vessel is indeed an essential part of the message, without which the message is no longer a treasure.

---

66. See McClure, *Other-wise Preaching*, p. 123. For a discussion of the theme of witness going back to Kierkegaard, see Edgerton, *Speak to Me That I May Speak*, ch. 5.

Conclusion

The homiletical and hermeneutical shifts of the last decades have been profound and far-reaching. They have affected foundational understandings of Scripture, tradition, reason, and experience; they have affected foundational understandings of what it means to be a community of faith; and they have affected foundational understandings of what the gospel is, and how it can be communicated. In this time of transition in homiletics and hermeneutics, we wish to consider a communal practice of "dynamic translation" and what it might have to offer preachers and their communities. As we shall see, dynamic translation embodies in its own particular ways various dimensions of the *toward* side of the shifts; at the same time, it honors certain values and interests of the *from* side. We shall consider these connections with the current homiletical scene at the conclusion of the next chapter, which introduces the method of "incarnational translation."

CHAPTER TWO

Introduction to Incarnational Translation

From early times the church has read Scripture aloud in worship and preachers have talked about the meaning of Scripture. Recital (reading aloud) and commentary (talking about) are mainstays of Christian teaching and preaching. Sometimes preachers have also restated a passage of Scripture in a contemporizing way, such as retelling the parable of the Good Samaritan in a modern setting. This kind of retelling stands between recital and commentary, sharing features of both. It is not a common way of communicating Scripture — at least for most preachers — and its nature and logic have never been thoroughly examined. It tends to be used, if at all, only with certain kinds of narrative (such as parables). The present book focuses on this mode of communicating the message of Scripture, which we call incarnational translation. A brief description of recital and commentary will set the stage for our discussion.

Much modern worship distinguishes recital from preaching, making recital a separate ceremonial reading before the sermon proper. But in the ancient church, recital was treated as a preaching event in its own right. This is suggested in Acts by the following mention of the reading of the law in the synagogue as a form of preaching: "For in every city, for generations past, Moses has had those who proclaim him, for he has been read aloud every sabbath in the synagogues" (Acts 15:21). This description probably reflects both Jewish and Christian views of the reading of the law in synagogue worship. Evidence that many Christians considered reading aloud of Scripture in church a form of preaching is found in a passage from Justin Martyr's *First Apology*. Dating to Rome in the middle of the second century, it is our earliest description of Christian worship in which Scripture reading figures as part of the service. Justin tells us that before the "president" gets up to speak, there are readings from the Gospels or the Jewish scriptures "as long as time permits" (67.3). In other words, these are not short lectionary texts, as in many churches today, but extensive readings. Once the readings were completed, Justin says, the president gave an exhortation in which he encouraged the congregants to imitate "these examples," that is, the examples set forth in Scripture. Apparently, the president's address was not an explanation of the readings but a reinforcement of them.

By contrast, most contemporary preaching is conceived and practiced as commentary of one kind or another, that is, a speaking about Scripture in the third person and in the form "this means that." The commentary form of preaching has a venerable tradition stretching back to the very early days of the church. We find bits of commentary in Paul (e.g., in his use of *pesher* and allegorizing exegesis), and 2 Clement exemplifies an early sermon style in which many different passages are adduced and commented upon using the rhetorical form "this means. . . ." Later, Christian preachers would expound whole books paragraph by paragraph. Thus, our earliest biblical commentaries (e.g., those by Chrysostom and Origen) are sermons.

Incarnational translation combines features of both recital and commentary. Like recital, it is a performance of Scripture in translation, a contemporizing translation. This contemporizing aspect aligns incarnational translation with the purpose of homiletical commentary, the effort to connect the ancient text with a contemporary time and place. Moreover, some uses of illustration in homiletical commentary display features of incarnational translation. Narrative preaching, when it involves contemporizing the biblical text, can be a form of incarnational translation.

In what follows we present a model of incarnational translation for preaching, drawing on the modern science of translating and taking a fresh look at genre and medium in preaching. At points we also highlight the symbiotic relationship between incarnational translation and recital, demonstrating how the two can be used fruitfully in tandem.

Translating the Translations

Historical translation means rendering the Bible into linguistic expressions that accurately convey the original sense. We rely on professional biblical translators to do this work, and the most respected modern Bible translations are the work of scholarly teams. Today, however, Bible translation by people other than biblical scholars is on the increase in privately and commercially published forms as well as electronic formats (on disc and online). Then there are the unpublished occasional translations that ministers make: some of these are acts of direct translation from the original languages, which may be aided by sophisticated computer software;[1] others take their cues from comparing published translations. The democratizing or "flattening" cultural effect of postmodernity, epitomized by the Internet, creates a climate in which those so inclined are emboldened to do their own translating from scratch or by "retranslating" the published translations into forms better suited to their needs and settings. Scholars in this postmodern environment have less authority than they used to; through the commercial publishing houses, scholar-translators are retailers of presumably reliable goods. Preachers, as buyers of these goods, assume authority for how to use them, which may involve transforming them. The age of officially and unofficially authorized translations is over, despite continued pleas by some that churches or whole denominations should officially adopt a single translation for everything. Not only is this impractical, it is also based on a faulty notion of translation. There is no such thing as a universal translation. Every translation reflects some social location, some limited cultural experience. Seen in this light, the democratization of translation is a good thing, if it means informed use of many translations to reformulate Scripture for different times and places. Professional translators are not the only ones who understand the modern (or postmodern) cultures into which they translate. In fact, they are not always the best interpreters of the cultures for which they translate. They need the help of the rest of the church. Retranslating the published translations of scholars is something we can all do.

This retranslating falls along a continuum from the more historical to the more contemporizing. The more one shapes the translation to speak to one's own time and place, the further one is moving in the direction of incarnational translation. But all translation, including the historical form that professional Bible translators practice, has contemporizing elements because it involves conveying in a modern language a message originally

---

1. Notable Bible Study software packages are *GRAMCORD*, *Accordance*, *Bible Windows*, *Bible Works for Windows*, and *Logos*.

couched in an ancient language.[2] Therefore, it will be helpful to begin our discussion of translation on the historical end of the spectrum.

Incarnational translation is a kind of "dynamic" translation. The concept of dynamic translation comes from Eugene Nida, whose work on cross-cultural issues of translation led him to a theory of translation that values "functional equivalence" over "formal correspondence." Formal correspondence in translation means seeking to represent each word by its literal equivalent in the receiver language and to reproduce the syntax of the original as far as the receiver language permits without awkwardness. The New American Standard Version is a good example of this kind of "literal" translation. Dynamic translation or functional equivalence, which Nida also called "dynamic equivalence," seeks to render the original meaning with language (words and syntax) in the receiver language that has the *same function* as the original, even if this means departing significantly from a literal rendering.[3] Achieving dynamic equivalence calls for finding an idiomatic way of speaking in the receiver language to convey the same sense as the original. For example, the Hebrew expression "for three transgressions . . . and for four" is an idiom. Its functional equivalent (dynamic translation) in English is "time after time." A functional equivalent of another sentence, "I will give you cleanness of teeth"(Amos 4:6), might be "I will starve you" (or "I will give you famine").[4]

In appropriating the concept of dynamic translation from the science of translation, we have modified and developed it in certain crucial ways. To distinguish it from historical dynamic translation, we have termed it "incarnational" translation, a way of imagining what the text might have

2. For example, the traditional English Bible translation terms for the instruments of Psalm 150 include trumpets and cymbals, making us think of the trumpets and cymbals we know, not the ancient instruments.

3. See Eugene A. Nida and C. R. Tabor, *The Theory and Practice of Translation: Helps for Translators* (Leiden: E. J. Brill, 1969), pp. 5, 173, 202; Jan de Waard and Eugene A. Nida, *From One Language to Another: Functional Equivalence in Bible Translating* (Nashville: Thomas Nelson, 1986), pp. 36-40.

4. There is considerable debate among professional translators about which is better in Bible translation — formal correspondence or functional equivalence. Our opinion is that both have merits, depending on the purpose of the translation. For a balanced treatment of functional equivalence theory relative to formal correspondence, see D. A. Carson, "The Limits of Functional Equivalence in Bible Translation — and Other Limits Too," in *The Challenge of Bible Translation: Communicating God's Word to the World*, Glen G. Scorgie et al., eds. (Grand Rapids: Zondervan, 2003), pp. 65-113.

looked like if it had been produced in our own culture, time, and place.[5] Moreover, we are concerned with not only the sense but also the form (genre) of the text.

Incarnational translation for our modern cultural contexts involves contemporizing, taking account of the differences between then (the ancient world) and now (the modern world) in ways that recontextualize Scripture in the concrete terms of our everyday lives. For example, an incarnational translation for a modern urban context of Jesus' triumphal entry into Jerusalem would not have Jesus riding on a donkey since this is not a mode of transportation in the modern city. Recontextualization is also cross-cultural translation. For example, in the contemporary North American context, an incarnational translation of "one who gives an honest answer gives a kiss on the lips" (Prov. 24:26) would have to substitute a functional equivalent for the kiss on the lips, which almost inevitably evokes romantic/sexual connotations for us, instead of the mark of friendship that an ancient Hebrew would have heard.

The transformative nature of recontextualization means that incarnational translation is not translation in the ordinary sense of that word. It is a kind of contemporizing paraphrase or illustration that imitates the form and content of the text. Whether we speak of incarnational translation or incarnational paraphrase, we have in mind a transformation of the text through the lens of the analogical imagination (or what some might prefer to call "sanctified imagination"). "Incarnational" is a theological way of thinking about recontextualization; "translation" (or "paraphrase") refers to a logic of recontextualization that aims at holistic functional equivalence of form and content (and even medium) in a new cultural setting.

We see traces of recontextualizing in Scripture itself. The Bible abounds in what historians call anachronisms because those who preserved the biblical stories continually updated them (consciously or unconsciously) so that they would speak with freshness and directness in new times and places.[6] For example, the Gospel of John uses a term for "excom-

---

5. "Our own" is a pluralistic descriptor here, since "we" (preachers today) are from many cultures. In this book, however, contemporary refers especially to "modern" (or "postmodern"), and our examples will be culturally Western and to a large extent North American.

6. On the reinterpretation of Scripture through retelling, with modification and expansion, for a new time and place (rather than through commentary and explanation as a

munication" from the synagogue (ἀποσυνάγωγος) that fits the late-first-century synagogue but not the pre-70 CE synagogue. In fact, the word itself was probably first invented at the end of the first century to denote a new kind of institutional act. The narrative in John 9, where this word is used, appears to retell a story of Jesus healing a blind man in ways that also describe typical experiences of the community from which the Fourth Gospel comes.[7] Likewise, Deuteronomy presents the law in a new and updated version of the Mount Sinai legislation, an updated version that probably reflects a much later period in Israel's history.

Therefore, when we carry out cross-cultural, contemporizing translations, we are doing something similar to what the biblical writers (and the bearers of the oral tradition before them) also did with the sacred tradition. We can illustrate this by considering how we might recontextualize a story that already passed through some modest recontextualization within the biblical tradition. When Mark narrates the story of the healing of the paralytic, he tells how the man's friends dug a hole in the roof (Mark 2:4). This makes sense in a rural setting, where houses had thatched roofs. But when Luke tells the same story for an urban audience, he says that the friends removed tiles to make an opening (Luke 5:19). City dwellings had tile roofs, so Luke makes a cross-cultural adjustment, recontextualizing the story for an urban setting. How might we retell this detail if we were to set the narrative in a modern suburb? Taking apart a roof would be impractical and seriously destructive of property. We have to find another resourceful approach by which the friends of the paralyzed man can get access to Jesus — not a literal but a functional equivalent. Perhaps we could have the friends discover a back basement door unlocked, have them carry the man through the basement to a set of stairs leading up to the kitchen.

---

way of connecting with a later situation), see Michael Fishbane, *Biblical Interpretation in Ancient Israel* (Oxford: Clarendon Press, 1988); James Sanders, "Adaptable for Life: The Nature and Function of Canon," in *Magnalia Dei: The Mighty Acts of God: Essays on the Bible and Archeology in Honor of G. Ernest Wright,* F. Cross et al., eds. (Garden City, NY: Doubleday, 1976), pp. 531-560; Bruce Norman Fisk, *Do You Not Remember? Scripture, Story and Exegesis in the Rewritten Bible of Pseudo-Philo,* Journal for the Study of the Pseudepigrapha Supplement Series 37 (Sheffield: Sheffield Academic Press, 2001).

7. See J. Louis Martyn, *History and Theology in the Fourth Gospel,* rev. and enlarged ed.(Nashville: Abingdon Press, 1968); Martyn, *The Gospel of John in Christian History: Essays for Interpreters* (New York: Paulist Press, 1978). One does not have to be persuaded by every detail of Martyn's reconstruction of the contemporizing shape of Johannine stories to be convinced that he is on to something.

Let's put Jesus at the kitchen table. When the friends reach the door to the kitchen at the top of the basement stairs, they find it locked. No one answers their knocking, so, finding a hammer and screwdriver in the basement, they remove the door from its hinges and carry in their friend.

Some elements of incarnational translation are found in *The Message,* Eugene Peterson's popular paraphrase of parts of the Bible. Here's a sample passage:

> Then he told them what they could expect for themselves: "Anyone who intends to come with me has to let me lead. You're not in the driver's seat — I am. Don't run from suffering; embrace it. Follow me and I'll show you how. Self-help is no help at all. Self-sacrifice is the way, my way, to finding yourself, your true self. What good would it do you to get everything you want and lose you, the real you? (Luke 9:23-25, *The Message*)[8]

Peterson uses not only contemporary idioms ("in the driver's seat") but also, to a modest degree, contemporary cultural references ("self-help," "true self," "real you") in this example. Thus his translation goes beyond what is usually understood as functional equivalence among scholars. Nevertheless, incarnational translation for preaching aims to be even more comprehensive in contemporizing and recontextualizing a text than is *The Message,* as our example above of retranslating the story of the healing of the paralytic shows. This is not a criticism of *The Message;* it is simply an observation about its different purpose.

The aim of an incarnational translation is to say and do in our time and place something like what the text once said and did in its ancient settings. That "saying and doing" is a function of content, genre, and medium. Hence, we define functional equivalence as including not only "sense" (Nida's focus) but also *genre* and *medium.* Translating the sense into another language might be called "translingualization." In its fullest expression, incarnational translation entails not only translingualization but also "transgenrelization" and "transmediatization."[9]

---

8. Eugene H. Peterson, *The Message: The New Testament, Psalms, and Proverbs in Contemporary Language* (Colorado Springs, CO: NavPress, 1993), p. 144.

9. Standard translations such as the NRSV and NIV offer us translingualizations from Greek and Hebrew into English. They follow a modest functional equivalence approach, but they do not aim to be contemporizing or recontextualizing. This makes them useful as study

Incarnational Translation as Transgenrelization

Open the Bible and put your finger on the page. Perhaps what you find are words such as these: "Thus says the Lord: Maintain justice, and do what is right, for soon my salvation will come, and my deliverance be revealed" (Isa. 56:1). Perhaps what you find is the story of King Nebuchadnezzar in a rage, ordering that Shadrach, Meshach, and Abednego be brought before him (Dan. 3). Perhaps you find: "To you, O Lord, I lift up my soul" (Ps. 25:1). Perhaps it is: "You foolish Galatians! Who has bewitched you?" (Gal. 3:1). Perhaps "Jerusalem, Jerusalem, the city that kills the prophets and stones those who are sent to it! How often have I desired to gather your children together as a hen gathers her brood under her wings, and you were not willing!" (Matt. 23:37). Perhaps "Whoever loves discipline loves knowledge, but those who hate to be rebuked are stupid" (Prov. 12:1).

On a given page you may find an oracle, a narrative, a hymn, an argument, a lament, a wisdom saying, a parable, a teaching, or a vision. The verses will themselves be combined with still other forms of writing, and they in turn will be part of a larger work such as an Epistle, a historical chronicle, a Gospel, an apocalypse, a collection of oracles or sayings. What difference does it make that when we open the Bible we find so many forms of writing?

One important difference it makes is that *form* is part of the message. Form is not just a container; it does something. It has effects—"rhetorical effects," we may call them. Or to put it another way, the overall impact of any communication is a result not only of what is said but also how it is said. Genre (form) is a large part of this how. For example, one kind of rhetorical effect happens when the sense of the message is conveyed in the form of poetry, a different kind when the genre is a form of didactic prose. The sense itself, as part of that rhetorical effect, is dependent on the form. Just as the tone in which words are uttered affects their sense, so does the genre shape their meaning.

Holistic incarnational translation aims to do justice to these effects by re-creating not only a functionally equivalent *sense* but also a functionally

---

Bibles, for recital, and for preaching as commentary. Nevertheless, the preoccupation of these translations with translingualization issues fosters the misleading impression that questions of genre (except when it comes to "poetry") and medium are not important considerations in translating.

equivalent *form,* so that the translator can achieve something like the same rhetorical effect of the original.[10] Of course, we cannot know exactly what those effects were and we can only approximate them in our own time and place. All we can do is make our best effort at transgenrelization, recasting the biblical text in contemporary rhetorical forms that are analogous to those of antiquity.

It is difficult to define ancient genres, especially when one considers genre in terms of rhetorical function. Formal correspondence theory appears to take for granted that genre translates automatically when translators render words and syntactical relationships more or less literally. This assumes that genre as form is in the words and syntax as form. But genre is as much a "system of expectations" resident in readers as it is specific linguistic patterns.[11] Better, the rhetorical patterns are cues in the discourse that trigger cognitive and affective experiences in readers based on social conventions about what is funny, tragic, frightening, ennobling, comic, ironic, and so forth.[12] Is Jonah a realistic historical narrative or a satire making a serious point through humorous cardboard-character role reversals?[13] To what extent does Paul's "fool's speech" in 2 Corinthians 11 involve parody, irony, or hyperbole? And what might functionally equivalent transgenrelizations of these texts look like for, say, contemporary Americans who have grown up with *Saturday Night Live* and *The Simpsons?*

We will examine different genres more closely in subsequent chapters.

---

10. A similar point is made by Thomas G. Long in his groundbreaking book *Preaching and the Literary Forms of the Bible* (Philadelphia: Fortress Press, 1989). His understanding of the significance of literary form (we will speak of "rhetorical forms" and "genres") has informed our thinking. Fred Craddock also speaks briefly (and cautiously) about the value of learning to preach from the genres of the Bible; see Craddock, *As One without Authority,* 3rd ed. (Nashville: Abingdon, 1981), pp. 153-54; see also Don M. Wardlaw, ed., *Preaching Biblically: Creating Sermons in the Shape of Scripture* (Philadelphia: Westminster, 1983), pp. 21-23.

11. E. D. Hirsch, *Validity in Interpretation* (New Haven, CT: Yale University Press, 1967), pp. 80-81. Frank Kermode speaks similarly of "probability systems" in *The Classic: Literary Images of Permanence and Change* (New York: Viking Press, 1975), p. 140.

12. On genre as a sociocultural formation, see William A. Foley, *Anthropological Linguistics: An Introduction* (Oxford: Blackwell, 1997).

13. On the genre of Jonah, see Jack M. Sasson, *Jonah,* Anchor Bible 24B (New York: Doubleday, 1990), pp. 321-352. Sasson lists some of the possibilities that have been suggested for categorizing Jonah: myth, fable, folktale, allegory, midrash, legend, parable, satire, parody, theodicy. Sasson points out that the enduring power of Jonah through the centuries testifies to its amenability to more than one way of grasping its genre and message (p. 326).

Here it is enough to give a few examples of transgenrelization. The work of Walter Wangerin can assist us. Although Wangerin's "Bible as Novel" is not incarnational translation in our sense — because it does not contemporize and recontextualize the stories it retells — it does give an idea of one approach to transgenrelization. For example, Wangerin offers the following retelling of 1 Samuel 15:1-3:

> Samuel, the white-haired priest of God, now traveled down from Ramah to Saul in Gibeah. They met in the gate of the city. Samuel sat down to rest before he spoke. As long as the old man kept silence, so did the king. He stood, his dark hair brushed glossy for the sake of the priest, his tall frame like a column, waiting.
>
> Finally, Samuel raised his eyes and said, "You remember that it was the Lord who sent me to anoint you king over Israel."
>
> "Yes, I remember."
>
> "Then listen to the words of the Lord who made you king. *Amalek is harassing the tribe of Judah. He has never changed his ways, nor have I forgotten how he opposed Israel when they came up out of Egypt. Now I will punish him. Saul, son of Kish, go and smite Amalek. Utterly destroy all that he has. Spare no person and no thing, but kill both man and woman, infant and suckling, ox and sheep and camel and ass.*"[14]

If Peterson's *The Message* is contemporizing in its use of idioms, Wangerin's Bible is contemporizing in its use of genre. Wangerin uses a popular novelistic style to recast the ancient narrative genre. Does he go far enough? Some of the language sounds a bit stilted to us, especially in Samuel's speech at the end. There is perhaps too much non-contemporary language with phrases such as "changed his ways," "go and smite," and "spare no person or thing." This is not how characters speak in modern novels. A better transgenrelization of this speech might go something like this:

> Finally, Samuel looked up and said, "You remember that it was the Lord who sent me to anoint you king over Israel."
>
> "Yes, I remember."
>
> "Then listen to what God has to say to you. *Amalek is terroriz-*

---

14. Walter Wangerin, *The Book of God* (Grand Rapids: Zondervan, 1996), p. 245.

ing Judah. He hasn't changed one bit. And I haven't forgotten how he treated Israel when they came up out of Egypt. Now it's payback time. Here's what I want you to do. Kill him. Wipe him out. Destroy his property, his family, everything he has."

We learn something about the content of the divine speech in 1 Samuel 15:2-3 from this experiment with translating its genre. The more traditional biblical language in Wangerin's version — taken from the old King James tradition — has the effect on our ears of softening and perhaps also ennobling the direct and brutal statements of the original. Today the words "changed his ways," "smite," and "spare no person or thing" sound like religious language in elevated style. In other words, the rhetorical form of the language may have the same kind of sanitizing effect that the euphemisms "collateral damage" and "surgical strike" do in contemporary military jargon. Asking the question of genre forces us to consider not only the literal sense but also its rhetorical expression, which modifies the sense. On the other hand, one may ask whether our incarnational translation of God's message is too colloquial. Maybe it should be couched in more dignified (but not archaic) language. Maybe we should not have God using contractions. A more substantial question is whether the Hebrew verb in verse 3, the word translated "utterly destroy" in the NRSV, carries the connotation of "dedicate to God through destruction" (such as a whole burnt offering). Perhaps this calls for a religiously tinged translation, something like "Wipe him out. Sacrifice his property, his family, everything he has."

We can think of transgenrelization as a continuum from more literal to more transformative imitation. For example, if we retell in our own words the story of Jacob at the well by sticking close to the narrative style and technique of Genesis 29, then we are imitating the biblical genre in a more literal way. But we may find that our retelling can be more effective if we use a more modern style and technique of narrative. Finding the right balance between imitation and transformation can be called *genre adaptation*, a creative imitation of biblical forms in which we transform what we imitate by using contemporary rhetorical strategies. Those contemporary ways of retelling are also reshaped as we bring them under the logic of the original, ancient forms.

A group of our students produced the following incarnational translation of Amos 5:21-24, one that achieves an effective genre adaptation:

I hate your Christmas trees with their brightly colored lights
      and glimmering tinsel;
   I despise your Advent wreaths
  with their candles celebrating the passage of time.
I do not enjoy your solemn Christmas eve services,
      candles lit in every window, manger scenes with misbehaving
      toddlers in
  sheep and donkey outfits.
I can't stand to look at them.
And just because you give one percent of your income to the church,
     all on December 31 so you will get the maximum tax break,
Don't think this makes *me* proud of you.
Take away the noise of the guitar playing "Silent Night"
    or the paid tenor belting out "O Holy Night."
I refuse to listen to your cute children singing "Away in the Manger."
Instead of a Christmas Eve service, I want justice.
Let justice pour down like water and righteousness like an
      everflowing stream.[15]

This incarnational translation ends with a bit of recital, illustrating how contemporizing translation can be combined with traditional recital in a compelling way.

The more tightly a translation tracks with verbal functional equivalents at the sentence-to-sentence level (what the text says), the less functionally equivalent it may be in rhetorical effect (what the text does). On the other hand, as we move toward greater functional equivalence in rhetorical effect by using genre adaptations that are more transformative (contemporizing), we often lose the precision of equivalence at the sense level. Consider again Wangerin's translation of 1 Samuel 15:1-3, this time in comparison to the NRSV:

NRSV:

And Samuel said to Saul, "The Lord sent me to anoint you king over his people Israel; now therefore listen to the words of the Lord. . . ."

---

15. From a group presentation by David Anderson, Judy Angleberger, Ron Brown, Tim Dugan, and Judy Rois; used by permission.

Wangerin's retelling:

Samuel, the white-haired priest of God, now traveled down from Ramah to Saul in Gibeah. They met in the gate of the city. Samuel sat down to rest before he spoke. As long as the old man kept silence, so did the king. He stood, his dark hair brushed glossy for the sake of the priest, his tall frame like a column, waiting.

Finally, Samuel raised his eyes and said, "You remember that it was the Lord who sent me to anoint you king over Israel."

"Yes, I remember."

"Then listen to the words of the Lord who made you king. . . ."[16]

The NRSV conveys the sense with great accuracy, but it lacks features of modern storytelling: detail of setting, action, appearance, emotion, and so on. Wangerin's translation expands the detail of the original in a very contemporizing way, but in the process he alters some of the sense. The additional detail cannot help but affect the meaning.

Seeking a union of sense equivalence and rhetorical equivalence calls for a judgment about where on the continuum from imitation to transformation we can best approach our incarnational paraphrase of the genre. Doing justice to the text as a whole also calls for using more than one translation. The closest we can get to genuine functional equivalence of the whole text, in all its dimensions, is by experiencing the text in multiple translation forms. We will keep these challenges in mind in later chapters as we consider the opportunities for incarnational translation in different biblical genres.

Incarnational Translation as Transmediatization

Most published translations set up the biblical text in visual form as prose or poetry. This reflects our modern notion of the Bible as a printed text. Modern Bibles print parts of the Bible as poetry by breaking the text into separate lines set off with varying degrees of indentation. This is an effort to do justice to the genre of the Psalms, prophetic oracles, and other parts of the Bible (e.g., the Song of the Sea and the Magnificat) judged to exhibit the marks of poetry. Nevertheless, the print medium of the modern Bible is a

16. *The Book of God,* p. 245.

manifestly different form (different semiotic system) from the handwritten (chirographic) medium of the ancient biblical manuscripts. The ancient scribes did not present poetry for the eye the way our modern English Bibles do. Moreover, the biblical world was a predominantly oral culture in which what little reading took place was done out loud, usually in group settings. Thus, ancient books were like musical scores, designed for performance out loud. The shift from Bible as handwritten manuscript to Bible as printed book reflects the shift in the West from oral culture to print culture. This raises at least three important questions for incarnational translation. First, is print the functional equivalent in a print culture of manuscript in an oral culture? Second, since print culture does not displace oral communication but only modifies its character and role, should incarnational translation consider how the medium of ancient orality can be reproduced in contemporary orality? Third, are there other media besides speech and print that may serve as functional equivalents to the ancient medium of oral communication? These are all questions of transmediatization.

The term "transmediatization" was coined by Thomas Boomershine to describe translating the Bible into contemporary media.[17] In the electronic age, books compete with audio-visual media — film, TV, video, and other digital forms of communication. Are these appropriate media for Bible translation? This is not simply a question of how to make movies and multimedia presentations "based on" the Bible. To imagine that the Bible could never "be" a movie or multimedia presentation is to make the mistake of assuming that the Bible *is* the printed book. But the Bible as printed book is itself already a transmediatization of the original chirographic form of the Bible. Unless we are ready to say that our familiar modern printed Bible is not the Bible but is only a modern media presentation "based on" the Bible, we should be willing to consider the possibility that

---

17. Thomas Boomershine, "A Transmediatization Theory of Bible Translation," *Bulletin — United Bible Societies* 170/171 (1994): 50; others use the term with a slightly different spelling — "transmediazation." See Scott S. Elliott, "'The Word' in Text, Sound, and Image: The American Bible Society's New Media Bible and the Research Center for Scripture and Media," *Council of Societies for the Study of Religion Bulletin* 30 (2001): 65-67. See also Robert Hodgson and Paul A. Soukup, eds., *From One Medium to Another: Basic Issues for Communicating the Scriptures in New Media* (Kansas City, MO: Sheed and Ward; New York: American Bible Society, 1997); Hodgson and Soukup, eds., *Fidelity and Translation: Communicating the Bible in New Media* (Kansas City, MO: Sheed and Ward; New York: American Bible Society, 1999).

other media — that is, media other than the printed book — might also serve as vehicles for translations of the Bible.[18]

A caution to the preceding logic is the plausible argument that print is analogous to chirograph, while audiovisual (television, video, film, etc.) is not.[19] Perhaps. But we should not underestimate how profound the shift to print was in shaping people's experience of Scripture. Moreover, we should not overlook certain similarities between audio-visual communication in an electronic age and the rhetorical enactment of texts in antiquity. The ancient chirograph was to be read aloud by a skilled reader. Skilled readers dramatized with their voices and gestures when they read. In reconstructing the oral performative nature of ancient Christian enactment of Scripture, we can probably learn from the practices of the rhapsode or Homerist in the Greco-Roman world,[20] from study of ancient storytelling, and from what the rhetoricians and other ancient writers say about the use of voice and gesture in reading. Moreover, the Bible contains marks of the oral performance practices by which it was read aloud.[21] This

---

18. Bernard Brandon Scott makes a similar point in emphasizing that "full fidelity" in translation requires that we translate the theatrical oral medium of Scripture into the new media of the electronic age rather than treating the Bible as a modern book and translating only what we take that book to mean (the "signified"), apart from attention to the "signifier" (the ancient medium of communication, which was oral performance); see Scott, "A New Voice in the Amphitheater: Full Fidelity in Translating," in Hodgson and Soukup, eds., *Fidelity and Translation*, pp. 101-118.

19. J. Ritter Werner suggests that translating the Bible into contemporary audio-visual media is best thought of as a form of *midrash*, a thesis that involves both the recognition that new media translation is necessarily creative and also the argument that the ancient norms governing Jewish midrash should guide new media translation; see J. Ritter Werner, "Midrash: A Model for Fidelity in New Media Translation," in Hodgson and Soukup, eds., *Fidelity and Translation*, pp. 173-197. Joy Sisley maintains that it is inherent to new media translation that it displaces the text and produces something new that is not functionally equivalent; see Sisley, "Power and Interpretive Authority in Multimedia Translation," in *Fidelity and Translation*, pp. 203-217.

20. For a foundational article on the rhapsode, see Donald E. Hargis, "The Rhapsode," *Quarterly Journal of Speech* 56 (1970): 388-97. In the later Roman period we no longer hear about rhapsodes, but specialists in the recitation of Homer are carrying on the tradition, perhaps using some dramatic techniques. For an introduction to ancient storytelling, see Alex Scobie, "Storytellers, Storytelling, and the Novel in Graeco-Roman Antiquity," *Rheinisches Museum für Philologie* 122 (1979): 229-259.

21. On clues in the biblical text for oral performance, see Scott, "A New Voice in the Amphitheater," pp. 110-118.

"theatrical" aspect of ancient reading distances ancient oral performance of Scripture from silent reading in a print culture, as well as from the ways Scripture is typically read from behind the lectern in most churches today. Ancient reading performance has greater affinities with the modern art of oral interpretation. Moreover, ancient oral reading also has certain affinities with audio-visual communication, since the ancient oral reader combined aural and visual effects in rendering the text.[22]

These similarities between ancient reading and contemporary audio-visual media probably explain why some students of biblical media are especially concerned not only to explore new media for presenting and translating the Bible but also to recover ancient oral forms of Scripture presentation. This dual interest is especially evident in Boomershine's work, where he describes silent reading of the Bible as anachronistic, a kind of "media eisegesis."[23] He reasons that, "[i]f the medium does significantly influence the meaning of a biblical tradition . . . historical interpretation requires an effort to experience the tradition in its intended medium."[24] Fidelity to the original medium requires translations that do justice to the orality of Scripture with sensitivity to contemporary oral expression. At the same time, Boomershine has also been an advocate of the use of new media: he sees audio-visual electronic media as analogous to oral performance and appropriate for a postmodern age.

Incarnational translation for preaching is not likely to use film as a medium, but other forms of electronic media — including video and computer-based multimedia formats — are feasible. At the same time, ancient forms of performance communication — not only oral recitation but also drama — have their counterparts in postmodern culture as vehicles for transmediatization. It may be that biblical stories were dramatized in antiquity, but this is a historically obscure subject. In the wider Hellenistic world, storytellers dramatized stories in their oral performances. The Homerists, who succeeded the ancient rhapsodes as reciters of Homer, became increas-

---

22. A recent study looks at a wide evidence of dramatic storytelling and argues that the Gospel of Mark was originally performed dramatically by a speaker — with audience interaction; see Whitney Shiner, *Proclaiming the Gospel: First-Century Performance of Mark* (Harrisburg, PA: Trinity Press International, 2003).

23. Thomas E. Boomershine, "Peter's Denial as Polemic or Confession: The Implications of Media Criticism for Biblical Hermeneutics," in *Orality, Aurality, and Biblical Narrative, Semeia* 39 (1987): 48, 65.

24. Boomershine, "Peter's Denial," p. 50.

ingly dramatic in the centuries before the birth of Christ. They mimed the scenes they were describing — even used props.[25] Moreover, in addition to the staging of dramas in the theaters, there were also troupes of actors who would perform skits before a street crowd or in a wealthy person's home.[26] Sacred stories and revered legends were also dramatized in religious cults and mystery religions,[27] as well as at dinner parties.[28]

But some Jews (like some later Christians) opposed the pagan theater. Perhaps they were also averse to any comparable staging of biblical stories. Unfortunately, we have no direct evidence for biblical drama in the synagogues and very little for biblical drama in the church of the first several centuries. One can speak only loosely of a "dramatic" shaping of the liturgy.[29] But there is evidence that Christian students were taught to craft and enact "personifications." The personification was a Greek rhetorical practice in which one acted the role of a character from a story by imagining that character's response in a particular set of circumstances in that story. Thus we find in a Christian school setting in fourth-century Egypt the assignment to

25. See Gregory Nagy, *Poetry as Performance: Homer and Beyond* (Cambridge, UK: Cambridge University Press, 1996), pp. 162-72; see also Hargis, "The Rhapsode," p. 394.

26. Scobie, "Storytellers, Storytelling, and the Novel in Graeco-Roman Antiquity," p. 234.

27. For example, Pausanias relates how Megarian women "hold a performance that is a mimic representation" of a legend associated with the naming of a rock in Megara (Pausanias, *Description of Greece*, 1.43.1). At the annual festival of the goddess Flora, young girls performed mimes *(ludi scaenici)* in front of her temple. See John Stambaugh, "The Function of Roman Temples," in *Aufstieg und Niedergang der römischen Welt* 2.16.1 (Berlin and New York: Walter de Gruyter, 1978), p. 57. On liturgical-ritual pantomimes of founding myths in the mystery religions, see Hans-Josef Klauck, *The Religious Context of Early Christianity: A Guide to Greco-Roman Religions,* tr. Brian McNeil (Edinburgh: T. & T. Clark, 2000), pp. 51, 102-03, 131.

28. In describing an ancient dramatic musical text, William Johnson imagines its performance at a private party, where a solo singer would act out the dramatic parts and simulate dialogue; see Johnson, "Musical Evenings in the Early Empire: New Evidence from a Greek Papyrus with Musical Notation," *Journal of Hellenic Studies* 120 (2000): 59, n. 11. Theological dramas were performed at banquets in the Greek and Roman clubs; see Dennis E. Smith, *From Symposium to Eucharist: The Banquet in the Early Christian World* (Minneapolis: Fortress Press, 2003), p. 179. Dramas and pantomimes were also performed at private dinner parties of the well-to-do (Smith, *From Symposium to Eucharist*, pp. 117-18, 121).

29. On the dramatic shaping of Christian liturgy, beginning in the fourth century, see Christine Catharina Schnusenberg, *The Relationship between the Church and the Theatre: Exemplified by Selected Writings of the Church Fathers and by Liturgical Texts until Amalarius of Metz, 775-852 A.D.* (Lanham, MD: University Press of America, 1988) and the relevant literature cited there.

create a personification in response to the question, "What would Cain have said when he killed Abel?"[30] The *kontakia* of Romanos of Constantinople in the sixth century were poetic paraphrases of biblical stories, intoned by a homilist-soloist and punctuated by congregational refrains.[31]

Direct evidence for full-fledged dramatic enactments of Scripture does eventually appear, beginning with the medieval tropes or mystery plays out of which the passion play tradition evolved. The cantata is another example of dramatic transmediatization of Scripture. Cantatas and passion plays are still performed in our time.[32] They also have their contemporary counterparts in Christmas pageants, Christian musicals, denominational and other church-related films, and bibliodrama.

Bibliodrama, a recently developed approach to Bible study,[33] is especially suggestive for dramatic incarnational translation. A bibliodrama is an enactment of a biblical story in which the actors combine verbatim or paraphrased quotations of words from the biblical text with their own scripted or spontaneous embodiments of the characters. A well-crafted bibliodrama is not only a way for actor-participants to explore the biblical story; it is also a dramatic proclamation of the text. When a bibliodrama also recontextualizes the story in a contemporary life setting, it becomes a holistic incarnational translation.

Many parts of the Bible contain story, even those that are not cast as narratives. The oracle from Amos 5, presented above in incarnational translation, assumes a particular historical and cultural setting. One way to contemporize that setting and history, as a way of framing the oracle, is to dramatize it. The students who produced the above contemporized version of the Amos 5 oracle also prepared a bibliodrama as a setting for the

---

30. See Jean-Luc Fournet, "Une éthopée de Caïn dans Le Codex des Visions de la Fondation Bodmer," *Zeitschrift für Papyrologie und Epigraphie* 92 (1992): 253-66.

31. The great composer of *kontakia* was Romanos of Constantinople. See R. J. Schork, *Sacred Song from the Byzantine Pulpit: Romanos the Melodist* (Gainesville, FL: University Press of Florida, 1995).

32. In addition to the long-running and famous passion play at Oberammergau, there is also an American Passion Play, which was still running as of 2004. See Louis L. Williams, *The American Passion Play: A Study and a History* (Bloomington, IL: The American Passion Play, Inc., 1970).

33. On bibliodrama, see *Body and Bible: Interpreting and Experiencing Biblical Narratives*, Björn Krondorfer, ed. (Philadelphia: Trinity Press International, 1992); Hans-Ruedi Weber, *The Bible Comes Alive: New Approaches to Bible Study Groups* (Valley Forge, PA: Judson Press, 1996), pp. 29-40.

words of the oracle. They invited us to imagine a woman, one of the newly wealthy, relaxing at a cluttered table on Christmas Eve, with a cigarette and drink, reading a tabloid newspaper and talking out loud to herself and to us, the audience. Her family is getting ready to go to church. As the scene unfolds, it becomes clear that the woman is simultaneously from Amos's time and our time.

Off you go now, girls! Can you make the beds and make those corners straight. Oh, and get the children ready. Make sure they look *real nice.* We're leaving in an hour — solemn assembly for Christmas Eve. *You can look ten pounds thinner.* Oh look, this week's *celebrity recipe.* Michael J. Fox makes sugar cookies. Girls! Girls! Come get this recipe. I want some Michael J. Fox sugar cookies. Where are they, anyway? Can't get good help these days. Always wanting more money and doing less. Oh, an *anti-aging breakthrough. Better than Botox. $5000 for five treatments.* Maybe my handsome darling can give me that in my stocking for Christmas. *Late-night jokes make mincemeat out of Martha Stewart.* Well, she deserves it, doesn't she? All that insider information. Maybe her subpoena should be served with a nice appetizer! I hate her. *Horoscope. Beware of religious leaders, they're not always what you think.* Must be referring to those late-night TV types. Never can trust them. We do our duty. We go to church every Sunday, and send the children to Sunday School, me and my babycakes, we know what is right. We do our solemn duty, even give to a local charity. Well, that's after we build the pool. The kids gotta have a proper playtime right here in our own home. Oh, I love it here in Beverly Hills! So much better than that dump Bashan. Living the good life, sleeping in satin sheets, big oak bed, ivory on the bed post. And it's all thanks to our new governor, Jeroboam. What a name! Who in their right mind would name their child *Jeroboam?* Whatever. He's a fine governor. Good lookin', too. He's made life good, bringing all that copper into town, perfumes, precious stones, luxuries we deserve. Making Christmas good this year. He says it's a sign of God's favor — wealth, that is — even our minister says so. He says the Good Book declares God's favor on us by giving us wealth and good living. We're teaching our kids that, too. . . .

The preceding drama is not an incarnational translation of any words of the text. Instead, it dramatizes in a contemporizing way the sociohistorical setting of the judgment oracle of Amos 5:21-24. The satirical cameo of a Christmas Eve domestic scene provides a context for the incarnational translation of the oracle we presented earlier in this chapter. Having dramatized the contemporary setting for the oracle, the students performed the oracle as a response:

> I hate your Christmas trees with their brightly colored lights
> > and glimmering tinsel;
> > I despise your Advent wreaths
> > with their candles celebrating the passage of time.
> I do not enjoy your solemn Christmas Eve services. . . .

Incarnational Translation and Analogical Imagination

Our example of incarnational translation of an oracle from Amos 5 shows analogical imagination at work: an ability to imagine a situation that is like the situation presupposed by the biblical text and to create a form of speech that is like the original speech of the Bible. Producing this likeness is a challenge because it must stretch across centuries and vast differences of culture.

In our concern for the unity of form and content in the biblical text, we think of incarnational translation as an effort to let the text say and do with us, through contemporizing recontextualization, what it said and did with its ancient hearers. Connection with the situation of the audience is typically analogical for an audience today — as it was for ancient hearers. It is easy to fall into the misconception that the Bible speaks directly, not analogically, to its original hearers and only analogically to us because we are removed in time and place. There is some truth in this when it comes to some parts of the Bible. For example, the original function of the letters of Paul and of prophetic oracles in their original form (when they were first delivered) was to speak directly and not analogically. But many passages never had this original function (e.g., the patriarchal narratives and the Gospels). Moreover, even in those parts of Scripture that contain material originally intended as non-analogical, directly situational speech has been shaped and edited as part of the traditionizing and canonical processes that led to the form in which these traditions now stand in the Bible. Speech that is as apparently direct and situational as the oracles of the prophets has undergone editing. Even some of the Pauline letters probably possess a canonical form that differs from their original form.[34] Moreover, it is the nature of the Bible *as Scripture* to be for later generations. The canon has an analogical intention.

These observations provide a context for understanding what it means to speak of incarnational translation as seeking to say and do with us what the text said and did with its original hearers. By original hearers we do not mean the very first audience that heard the very first form of the text in question. We mean that incarnational translation seeks to translate the texts so that they do with us modern (or postmodern) hearers what they did with ancient Mediterranean hearers. In the case of some texts, we have clues to historical situations that can help us imagine one kind of original hearing and thus guide a new hearing in our time. But even when we have clues to original historical occasions, reconstructing those occasions leads quickly to multiple possibilities.

It will be important to keep all of this in mind. Sometimes it is possible to create an incarnational translation out of current experiences of our audience (the congregation we serve). In these instances we may speak with the kind of situational directness that the historical Paul used with the Corinthians or the historical Jeremiah used with Judah. But usually our incarnational paraphrases are drawn from the larger fabric of life experience in our world, sometimes using real events as subject matter, other times turning to the inventiveness of our imaginations. Hence, in most cases our incarnational translations speak analogically to our hearers. And we contend that analogical speaking is already the primary mode of scriptural speech.

Incarnational Translation and the New Homiletics

We can now describe the relationship of incarnational translation to the shifts toward a new homiletics outlined in Chapter One. Incarnational translation reflects shifts to new interests and orientations in homiletics but also preserves valid concerns and values of traditional approaches.

---

34. Many scholars judge that 2 Corinthians is composed of two or more letters that have been stitched together for preservation and use by other churches. If that is true, then the present form of 2 Corinthians in our Bibles includes the intention that it be taken by analogy in different times and places than those of Corinth in Paul's day.

Incarnational translation exemplifies the shift from preaching that treats rhetorical forms as irrelevant for meaning to preaching that takes rhetorical forms as essential shapers of meaning and as revelatory in their own distinctive ways. The attention to media of communication and to the emphasis on oral performance of Scripture in incarnational translation reflects the shift from preaching as informed by the process of writing to preaching informed by the process of speaking, including its dramatic aspects. (Hence, we are acutely aware as authors that we face a limitation when we give examples in this book, examples that obviously can appear here only as text.) Incarnational translation aims to create a contemporary experience of the text through performance rather than through commenting on or explaining concepts in the text. But we do not claim that incarnational translation obviates commentary. This venerable form of communication has an important place in preaching. We also do not claim that incarnational translation does not deal with the propositional or the conceptual. It does — but in a way that is different from commentary and explanation. Where biblical texts present propositions and concepts, incarnational translation seeks to re-present and recontextualize them. In this way incarnational translation also reflects the shift from preaching as discourse about the text to preaching as displaying the icons, an aspect of proclamation in which a revitalized practice of Scripture recital also has a vital role to play. In this way, incarnational translation resonates with other modes of liturgical communication. When we take up liturgical forms of Scripture in incarnational translation, we enhance the liturgical integration of preaching with worship. At the same time, we learn and model the ways in which liturgical forms are proclamatory.

Incarnational translation also partakes of the shift from the priority of reasoned argument toward the priority of constructive imagination. It does not conscript every scriptural text to the genre of homiletical argument, whether that means locating Scripture in the warrants for arguments or making arguments for what the preacher sees as the point of the text. Not all Scripture texts make their appeal through argument. Incarnational translation means re-presenting argument as argument, poetry as poetry, story as story, proverb as proverb, and so forth. Therefore, the concern in incarnational translation for the form of the text means that imagery and story are not decorative but constitutive. Incarnational translation also tends to expose our interpretive choices and their connections with our lives in ways that are especially transparent and self-involving, because following the form (genre) often leads us away from distancing, objectifying, and explanatory speech toward restatements of Scripture that show exactly where we make the connections with contemporary life. These connections, by their particularity, broadcast that we have chosen *this* way and are accountable for it.

Incarnational translation has a unique way of joining interpretation of the text and interpretation of life. The process of placing the text in a new life setting by translating the text into contemporary terms makes us both subjects and objects of interpretation. We are in control of the interpretive translation process because we use our own analytical and creative powers to reproduce the text in fresh words. But we are also objects, because wherever we place the text in life as we know and experience it, incarnational translation for that time and place is a way of letting the text say and do something to us.

The Uses of Incarnational Translation

Incarnational translation is both a process and a product: it is a way of interpreting Scripture and a way of communicating Scripture.

As a process, incarnational translation offers a discipline for sermon preparation that keeps our hermeneutical gyroscope in close touch with the pattern of the text. In the work of incarnational translation we cannot simply abstract a theme or aspect of the text and ignore the rest. We are compelled to wrestle with the text as a whole, considering the parts of the text in their interrelationship and asking how we might hear that pattern today — in our own time and place. Now it may happen that sometimes we decide not to preach the pattern as we have reimagined it, that we leave our incarnational paraphrase in the study. In some cases there are sound hermeneutical reasons for such a decision. But incarnational translation makes our responsibility for these decisions transparent. What we will do in a sermon comes after our effort to reimagine the text as a whole in contemporary terms that are attuned to our time and place. Hence, in addition to inspiring possibilities for appropriating the text in preaching, incarnational translation is a method of interpretive exploration that keeps us honest.

Even expository preaching, as a form that encourages comments on each component of the text, does not require that the preacher say how the parts — in their application to life — fit together to form a pattern like the pattern of the text. The preacher is free to translate each part separately and to convert it into a sermonic point (declarative statement or imperative); a series of points *may* form a pattern that reflects the pattern and genre of the text. More often, it makes an entirely new pattern and genre or no integrated pattern at all. For example, in treating a biblical story verse by verse, expository sermon preparation calls only for finding a point in each verse and discovering an illustration for it. A sermon made up of four points might illustrate those points with four very different stories. Or one illustration might be a story, another a simile, another a proverbial saying, still another a concept. Since the sermonic form (making points and offering illustrations) reflects the process of sermon preparation (identifying points and inventing illustrations), sermon preparation does not require that one wrestle with the connections between the parts or their unity of form.

In non-expository preaching that selects a theme or aspect of the text, sermon preparation properly involves consideration of the theme in its original textual context. But developing the sermon involves recontextualizing the theme, not the text as a whole. It is easy to leave the text behind and treat the theme on its own. That is usually not the preacher's aim, but it is a common result.

The preceding is not meant to disparage expository preaching or preaching that is thematically focused on a dimension of the text. Rather, it is to suggest that incarnational translation as an interpretive process can assist these forms of scripturally focused preaching and make them more honest. Through incarnational translation we confront more directly not only what we are eager to preach — what immediately strikes us as relevant — but also what we find hermeneutically difficult and what we might otherwise simply overlook. The discipline of incarnational translation helps us take responsibility for our homiletical decisions because it exposes those decisions so vividly.

As we have already said, the use of incarnational translations as a process of interpretation does not necessarily assume that one will use an incarnational translation in any given sermon. Sometimes the role of incarnational translation is to do its work on us, so that we can speak a word that is informed by that experience but does not seek to reproduce it. Other times, our incarnational translation is the best word we have to offer our hearers. Nonetheless, the aim of incarnational translation as a process of interpretation is to restate the text in words we *can* share, in words that embody our own witness to how the text might speak to us today.

There are any number of ways to share an incarnational translation in a sermon. The sermon may prepare the listeners for the giving of the incarnational translation at the end of the sermon. Or we may offer the translation at the beginning of the sermon and then analyze it as a way of sharing and exploring our struggles with the text. We may present more than one incarnational translation as ways of reimagining the text from different vantage points. We may position ourselves and our hearers in different relationships to an incarnational translation, depending on its genre. It is also possible for an incarnational translation to be a sermon in its own right.

The medium of incarnational translation may be an oral restatement of the text in a conventional sermon. Or it may be expressed in other media. It may be a contemporizing bibliodrama. Or it may be an oral or visual (textual) communication in an audio-visual presentation that involves music and images. It may be a film, and it could be accompanied by dance or mime.

Incarnational translation can also have a place outside the sermon, whether as an independent form in the liturgy (perhaps a companion to recitation), as a teaching method in group Bible study and Christian education (with children, youth, or adults), or as a spiritual discipline. It is a mode of interpretation that those not trained in seminaries can also learn and share in various settings. It is well suited to a collaborative process that draws on the analytical skills and creative imagination that exist in a group.

Incarnational Translation as Illustration

We have said that incarnational translation is a form of sermon illustration. To be more precise, it is illustration that restates a passage of Scripture as a whole in ways that reflect the content of the text in unity with its form. To understand the nature of incarnational translation as a kind of illustration, we should be clear about the forms that illustration can take.

There are basically two kinds of illustration: example and metaphor. Consider the stories of faith in Hebrews 11. In expounding these in a sermon, one might give contemporary examples of faith: the faith of Nelson Mandela in the struggle against apartheid in South Africa; the faith of Alexander Solzhenitzyn in surviving a Soviet gulag; the faith of a congregation venturing into a new ministry; the faith of a child bringing her allowance as an offering in Sunday School. Each of these is a conceivable example of the kind of faith Hebrews 11 describes when it talks about Abel presenting his offering by faith, Abraham leaving his home by faith, Noah heeding God's warning and building the ark by faith. One might also interpret the teaching about faith in Hebrews 11 by comparing faith to a key that starts the ignition of a car, a bridge that spans a canyon, the water in an ocean that keeps an ocean liner afloat. These are not examples but metaphors: they are not additional *instances* of what Hebrews 11 describes; they are nonliteral *parallels* to other kinds of things.

In some cases, the line between example and metaphor becomes fuzzy. If we illustrate faith in Hebrews 11 by comparing it to the trust it takes to sit down on a chair in the belief that it will support us, this comparison involves faith and to that extent resembles an example. But it speaks of faith in connection with something very different from trusting God (it is not an instance of trusting God) and in this respect resembles a metaphor.

The Bible speaks about some things literally and other things metaphorically. Incarnational translation answers literal speech with literal speech, metaphor with metaphor; it answers according to the form (genre) of the biblical speech it seeks to represent. Some forms typically display mixtures of literal and figurative speech. The Gospels, for example, use literal speech in narrative descriptions of movement, places, time, persons, and things; but they also show Jesus using figurative speech — parables, similes, metaphors. The Psalms describe suffering, joy, thanksgiving, complaint, hope, and celebration in literal terms and also in metaphorical language. Incarnational translation pays attention to the kind of language used in the text as a guide to restatement through contemporary illustration.

There are some cases, however, when overriding hermeneutical reasons call for answering literal biblical speech with figurative translation. Some of the language that biblical writers understood literally, many moderns can understand only metaphorically. In such cases incarnational translation deviates from its ordinary rule and offers metaphor — figurative speech — as a way of restating literal speech. For example, all biblical speech related to a three-storied cosmology requires hermeneutical adjustment in contemporary incarnational translation. "Up" and "down" were literal, absolute directions for all but a few ancient people. The cosmos was imagined as consisting of three domains stacked in layers and ordered according to this absolute "up" and "down": an underworld (a realm of underworld gods and, in some cosmologies, of punishment), a middle world (the scene of everyday human life), and an upper world (a divine domain partly visible in the stars but otherwise inaccessible to human beings through any ordinary means). Where biblical speech assumes this cosmology in literal terms, incarnational translation appropriately reaches for nonliteral ways of speaking or takes over such biblical language figuratively.

Conclusion

Incarnational translation for preaching seeks to recontextualize biblical texts so that they say and do in new times and places something like what they said and did in ancient times and places. This calls for functionally equivalent translation of the language, genre, and medium of the text. Paraphrasing the language means "translating the translators" so that the text speaks in contemporary terms fitted to the preaching moment. Translating the genre means finding rhetorical forms in our own world that can help produce the kinds of rhetorical effects that the original biblical genres likely evoked. Translating the medium means exploring oral, dramatic, and even electronic modes of communication in conversation with the ancient oral and dramatic media, as ways of performing Scripture rather than merely commenting on it as print in a book or reciting it in traditional lectionary reading.

No doubt many readers will discover that they have already heard or done incarnational translation in some form or other. It has become especially popular in narrative preaching to retell biblical stories in contemporizing terms, which amounts to incarnational translation of the story genres in Scripture. We hope to encourage incarnational translation in other genres of Scripture as well and to bring hermeneutical clarity and discipline to the practice of incarnational translation. The following chapters serve that aim by describing incarnational translation of various genres, beginning with poetic genres, moving on to story forms, and concluding with genres that fall under Wisdom literature and Law. Along the way we address questions of faithfulness in incarnational translation — faithfulness to both the text and the hearers. A concluding chapter explores in a more systematic way the hermeneutical dimensions of incarnational translation.

CHAPTER THREE

Psalms, Hymns, and Oracles

This chapter (and the two following) will examine possibilities for incarnational translation of various genres in the Bible. We understand genre as carrying theological, hermeneutical, and homiletical significance. Our notions of how God is made known to us, our conceptions of the nature and authority of Scripture, our approaches to the task of interpretation, and our strategies of communication are all profoundly affected by the forms of the texts we read — and how these forms are "translated" into our own communications. Speech genres use a variety of different forms of address: narrative, teaching, dialogue, argument, poetry, oracle, and so on. We may call these *strategies of address* because they are different ways of seeking to influence hearers. Each strategy has its own particular ways of making an appeal to its listeners. For example, each one may make different claims to authority and position the reader (or hearer) in different roles and relationships. A strategy may invite different kinds of participation, validation, and ways of knowing. Moreover, within a genre, the particular composition and content of a text can create variations and surprises that upset or even reverse what hearers are otherwise led to expect. Genres are always undergoing development, creating expectations and subverting them. For this reason — and because the biblical writers mix genres — we should not imagine that they come to us in the Bible in neat, distinct, or static forms. Nevertheless, it pays to organize them in rough categories that bear important family resemblances. We begin with the poetry of the Psalms.[1]

---

1. This chapter treats psalms, hymns, and prophetic oracles, all of which are forms of poetic speech. We might have included other parts of the Bible here as well, including parts

Psalms

The Settings of Performances of the Psalms

We have to consider a variety of settings and performers of the Psalms. The following, somewhat overlapping list gives an idea of these: the gathered congregation; special liturgies of communal or individual worship; the daily Temple service with its professional singers; the individual engaging in personal devotion; and the family. From ancient times up through at least the Second Temple period, the congregation of Israel gathered on special occasions and sang. The story of the Exodus includes a number of such gatherings, including one featuring the famous "Song by the Sea" in Exodus 15. Centuries later, we have a description of a spontaneous celebration that brought the whole population of Jews in Alexandria into the streets and down to the beach singing "hymns and songs of praise" all night (Philo, *Flaccus* 122). This singing presumably included psalms. Some psalms were connected with specific liturgies: processions, offerings, washings, pilgrimages, rituals of lament (with tearing of clothing, weeping, cutting of hair), or entrance into the temple. The Temple liturgy also included daily psalm-singing by the Levites, who sang from collections of psalm books and eventually received permission to memorize the Psalms and perform them without books.[2] Some of the psalms speak in the first person, which suggests an original personal and individual use — in the temple or in some other setting. These and other psalms would have lent themselves to personal devotion by individuals at prayer. By the first century, at least some pious individuals used the Psalms devotionally.[3] It may be that families used certain psalms when they celebrated feasts such as Passover. Eventually, the Hallel Psalms (Psalms 146–150) became part of the domestic Passover celebration. We are not sure how early this happened, perhaps sometime during the Second Temple period. The reference

---

of Job and Ecclesiastes, which also display poetic forms. Instead, we have grouped these under Wisdom literature, which is, admittedly, only a broad genre in the loosest sense. What we say about the poetic form of the Psalms also applies to Hebrew poetry in the Prophetic books and Wisdom literature.

2. See Josephus, *Antiquities of the Jewish People* 20.216-18.

3. 4 Maccabees 18:15 refers to the seven martyred brothers' pious father, who sang the Psalms to them.

to a closing song by Jesus and his disciples at the end of their Passover meal is suggestive (Mark 14:26).

Poetic Form

Ancient Hebrew-speaking Israelites had no word to differentiate poetry from prose. Hence we must be cautious in drawing distinctions between these two styles, and we should be especially careful not to differentiate too sharply between them.

A line of Hebrew poetry is typically made up of two parts *(cola)*. The relationship of these parts may be a form of synonymous parallelism: "[The wicked] are not in trouble as others are; / they are not plagued like other people" (Ps. 73:5). Or the two parts may be set in contrast: "All the horns of the wicked I will cut off, / but the horns of the righteous shall be exalted" (Ps. 75:10). The second *colon* can also expand the first, adding detail to it. Or it may introduce a logical relationship (a reason or explanation). Although analysts of Hebrew poetry have often developed categories for these different kinds of relationships, they are not always easy to separate. Nor does a line always consist of only two parts.[4] For incarnational translation, the important thing is to be alert to how lines of Hebrew poetry are constructed in patterns of two, three, or more parts, which are set in a variety of relationships. The beauty and power of Hebrew poetry arise from these forms of construction, together with rhythm, sound (assonance and euphony), and imagery.

In an incarnational translation of the Psalms, we engage in free imitation. We aim to re-create not only the sense but also the form, doing so in a contemporizing way that achieves not only the meaning but also the aesthetic effect. The question is not only, What does the psalm say? but also, How does it say it? For example, Psalm 102:3 reads, "For my days pass away like smoke, and my bones burn like a furnace." In idiomatic contemporary English we would say "my life" instead of "my days," and we would probably not refer to "our bones" in a metaphor of suffering (although the reference to the bones may be literal here). But when we choose a contemporary way of speaking, it is not enough to be idiomatic; we want to do justice to the

---

4. On Hebrew poetry, see James L. Kugel, *The Idea of Biblical Poetry: Parallelism and Its History* (Baltimore and London: Johns Hopkins University Press, 1998).

poetic force of the line. So we need to create contemporary metaphors or images that do justice to the ancient ones. "Smoke" in the original is part of everyday experience in ancient Israel — cooking on an open fire. An experience in the "bones" was a way of talking about something deep, at the core, inescapable — the bones being more permanent than the flesh. Notice also the association of "smoke" and "furnace" through their common (but unstated) term "fire." Perhaps we might retranslate: "For my life is rushing away like water down a drain; / I'm drowning inside." One might object that this incarnational translation is not as "elevated" as the original, which sounds more "poetic." Of course, the original may well be better poetry, but we should be careful not to confuse the archaic with the poetic. The original line (as rendered above from the NRSV) sounds archaic to us because "my days" is an old-fashioned way of speaking, and the figures of smoke and furnaces of fire are ancient metaphors. For the Hebrews, however, the imagery of the line belonged to everyday speech and experience: the smoke of the everyday dirty fire over which one cooked (not some romantic smoke of campfires on a canoe trip), the furnace of the local blacksmith or smelter (not an unfamiliar furnace rarely encountered in everyday life). And it is also likely that the metaphors of this line were already figures of speech — comparable to "water down a drain" or "drowning inside" in contemporary English language. Thus the aesthetic power of Psalm 102:3 comes from the use of the everyday elements of experience in a poetic way.

Hebrew poetry uses plays on words, acrostics, vivid imagery, rhythm, and other devices that make for elevated speech. There is no bold line separating exalted prose from poetry and no need for us to employ the categories of prose and poetry in sharply defined ways. The important thing is to be alert to the various ways in which the biblical writers craft elevated speech. Often these devices are evident only in the original language. For example, the oracle of Isaiah 5 uses two nice word plays in verse 7: God "expected *mishpat* (justice) but saw *mispah* (bloodshed); *tsedaqah* (righteousness) but heard *tse'aqah* (a cry)!" The commentators provide an indispensable guide to these artful uses of language.

The Genres of the Psalms

The genre of the Psalms is not one but several. The following is a typical categorization: complaint, thanksgiving, praise, and instruction (wisdom psalms).[5] This list is somewhat artificial, and one could include separate categories for psalms of lament and penitential confession. We should also keep in mind that from early times a given psalm could be used for multiple purposes. An autobiographical psalm could be used corporately, an originally cultic psalm could be used in private devotion, and so forth.

The Complaint Psalm

Complaint psalms are plentiful. They ask God for help in the midst of some extremity (illness, misfortune, threat of enemies, drought, flood, etc.). Most of the complaint psalms probably arose out of specific situations of distress. However, their incorporation into Scripture and their regular use in personal and corporate devotion set them loose from these original contexts and gave them broader meanings and new functions. They could now speak for any individual or community in trouble. As Scripture, these psalms express typical moments of life, giving the congregation traditional words to speak of distress, petition, and hope. Individuals in extremity can read themselves into these prayers and be encouraged and sustained by the great voice of the community, past and present, speaking in the Psalms.

Complaint psalms provide a ritual expression of suffering. They are *spiritual containers* for violent emotions and despair, safe places in which we can speak without restraint before God and others. Jesus provides a model for this. On the cross he cries out, "My God, why have you forsaken me?" These words give honest vent to the anguish he feels and express the absence at the crucifixion of any sign of God's presence or help. Jesus' cry from the cross also quotes the first line of Psalm 22, a complaint psalm. By expressing his alienation and isolation from God in the words of a biblical psalm, Jesus encloses his complaint in a sacred container, a form of God's presence with us and around us. Jesus puts his own experience of God's absence into this form of God's presence, the psalm through which one can doubt God, rail at God, despair of God within the spiritual container

5. For discussions of the genres, forms, and uses of the Psalms, in addition to Kugel's study (cited above), see Hermann Gunkel, *Introduction to Psalms: The Genres of the Religious Lyric of Israel*, completed by Joachim Bergrich, trans. James D. Nogalski (Macon, GA: Mercer University Press, 1998); Hans-Joachim Kraus, *Psalms 1–59: A Commentary*, trans. Hilton C. Oswald (Minneapolis: Augsburg, 1989); Erhard S. Gerstenberger, *Psalms: Part 1 with an Introduction to Hebrew Poetry* (Grand Rapids: Eerdmans, 1998).

of a divinely sanctioned word. A contemporary translation of a complaint psalm can be a spiritual container in which the body of Christ can speak with utter honesty, without fear of being overwhelmed or destroyed by the content of that speech, whether by grief, anger, or despair.

Liturgical space or a given liturgical ritual becomes a sacred container when the symbols of the faith are rightly handled by the community of faith. One of these symbols is Scripture. Its power as a vehicle for creating sacred space to contain dangerous speech depends on the community recognizing its words as Scripture. Thus one could argue that a lament psalm, for example, can be an effective sacred container for us only if we recite it in a familiar translation, so that we recognize by its style and by our memory of its content that *this is Scripture.* But achieving an immediacy and directness of expression of our lament through a biblical psalm calls for an incarnational translation, which will almost inevitably obscure the familiar scriptural style and language and make the psalm sound like our own words and not those of Scripture.

In view of that, there is a strong argument for enclosing the performance of an incarnational translation (or multiple incarnational translations) of some scriptures (such as the complaint or lament psalms) with recitals of the same text using a familiar translation. In this way the verbal container has clear biblical boundaries, and the recontextualization of the text in our own style and language sits within these boundaries as both container and contained. For example, the oral presentation of a series of incarnational translations of Psalm 22 might be framed by opening and closing recitals of the psalm in its KJV or NRSV versions. Another approach is an incarnational translation that mixes traditional recital and contemporizing language. The spiritual container in this kind of translation offers familiar old words that link us with the many generations before us who have testified by speaking this psalm in these traditional words and also new words that express our feelings more directly, specifically, and concretely in our present circumstances. Here is an example of an incarnational translation of Psalm 42 that contains bits of recital as links with the tradition:

> I long for you, God, the way a lost backpacker longs to stumble
>   onto a well-trafficked highway.
> I long for the wide, paved,
>   homebound way of you, O God.

When will I see a sign, a marker
    that you are near?
Inside I am all tears, night and day.
My crisp-collared colleagues at the office
    want to know where my reports are;
    they don't care where my God is.
I keep thinking about last December,
    that clear snow-dusted day when I walked to church
holding my eight-year-old daughter Sarah's hand,
    leaving behind in the kitchen cabinet,
      tucked behind the dinner plates,
    Friday mail's surgical strike from my husband,
      calculated shock and awe.
Sarah and I lit the Advent candles in the service that day.
    There, in front of the congregation, I thought,
    Everything is going to be okay.
    And I wanted to shout it out to everyone.
    We're all going to be okay!
But we're not okay.
Why am I trapped in this darkness,
    gasping for breath in this air-sucking
      hole of depression?
    I tell myself, *You have to have faith.*
I'm so depressed I could scream,
    but I have no energy to scream.
I think about the past, all those yesterdays
    when God was like a melody in my life,
    when I believed every preacher's buttered promise
      about the Lord's mighty and minute acts of salvation,
all the big and little ways that God
    is with us in our lives.
I still believe those things, God.
    But deep calls to deep
      and before I know it
    your deep waters are washing over me,
      piling on top of me.
Is this a deadly or a cleansing sea you've sunk me in?
    By day the Lord commands his steadfast love;

and by night his song is with me, a prayer to the God of my life.
God, you're my rock. Why have you abandoned me?
Why am I seeing a therapist?
Why have you turned my life against me?
The one I loved has become my enemy,
the flesh of my flesh and bone of my bone
has become a cancer, eating me from the inside out.
And he's not even here. His absence is a deadly wound.
So is yours, God.
But I keep telling myself, Don't give in to this emptiness.
Hope in God.
You will find the melody again. The song of God is on the way.

In form, this translation uses a style of contemporary poetry (free verse) that shares features with elevated prose and in this way resembles Hebrew poetry, which does not sharply distinguish itself from prose. There are rhythm and imagery but not rhyme or meter. As for content, each set of lines translates something in the original, and these translations range from more imitative to more transformative correspondence of sense. For example, "I long for you, God, the way a lost backpacker longs to stumble onto a well-trafficked highway" is highly imitative of the original first line of the Psalm, which the NRSV renders, "As a deer longs for flowing streams, so my soul longs for you, O God." A more transformative translation is the following: "My crisp-collared colleagues at the office want to know where my reports are; they don't care where my God is," which renders, "while people say to me continually, 'Where is your God?'" A justification for this transformation is that the translation assumes a modern Western secular setting in which people usually do not ask each other directly, "Where is your God?" Rather, they challenge faith by marginalizing it. Another way to handle the verse would be to have the woman pose the question to herself, "Where is your God?" Whatever possibility for translation is chosen, the challenge is to be faithful to the realism of the Psalm by finding functional equivalents in contemporary experience.

One way to present this incarnational translation of Psalm 42 in a sermon (or elsewhere in the liturgy) would be for two readers to present an alternating recital, section by section, of the original version (using, say, the NRSV or NIV) and the contemporizing translation. In this way, the connection between the two can be experienced directly. Providing a narrative context would also be important. The incarnational translation suggests a moment in the life of a woman who has just been served divorce papers. Her story could be filled out in the sermon to set the stage for the incarnational translation. This approach would involve thinking of the sermon as a strategy for ushering hearers into an experience of Psalm 42 *as a psalm,* a poetic form that deals with the themes of divine presence and absence, doubt, suffering, memory, and hope, not simply by discussing them in relevant ways, but also by offering a poetic, psalmic incarnation of the themes that is analogous to their expression and interconnection in the poetry of Psalm 42.

The Thanksgiving Psalm

Thanksgiving psalms belong originally to acts of sacrifice in fulfillment of vows made in distress (the kinds of vows we encounter in some of the complaint psalms). The thanksgiving song used to accompany sacrifices and was identified over time as a kind of sacrifice in its own right. Thus, "[a] thanksgiving song was promised by the supplicant at the height of distress and delivered when the salvation had occurred or was in sight."[6] The one who had been rescued or cured would give a feast for friends and neighbors, offering the thanksgiving psalm at an appropriate point during the dinner, which might include other elements of liturgical ceremony. It is possible that there were also liturgies for communal expressions of thanksgiving.

Thanksgiving songs typically display some of the following elements: (1) an invitation or call to give thanks or praise to God, (2) a description of the trouble from which one has been delivered, (3) praise to God for deliverance, (4) an offertory formula to accompany the presentation of the sacrifice, (5) blessings on participants in the ceremony, and (6) exhortation.[7] Although the Psalms cannot be neatly classified into categories that sharply distinguish thanksgiving psalms from other types, biblical songs typically included in this category are Psalms 30, 32, 41, 66, 118, 138; Isaiah 38:10-20; and Jonah 2:3-10 (RSV 2-9). Some scholars also include Psalms 18, 34, 40:2-12 (RSV 1-11), 92, 116, and Job 33:26-28.[8]

6. Gerstenberger, *Psalms, Part 1,* p. 14.
7. Gerstenberger, p. 15.
8. Gerstenberger, pp. 13-14.

The following is an example of an incarnational translation of a portion of one of the thanksgiving psalms, Psalm 66:13-20, set in parallel with the NRSV:

13 I will come into your house with burnt offerings;	I will come to your sanctuary with an offering of thanksgiving;
I will pay you my vows,	I will make good on the promises
14 those that my lips uttered	I made when I was in trouble,
and my mouth promised when I was in trouble.	I will offer true words of gratitude from my heart,
15 I will offer you burnt offerings of fatlings,	a gift of gratefulness and praise.
with the smoke of the sacrifice of rams;	I will be generous in my giving, to my church and to those in need
I will make an offering of bulls and goats.	as an expression of devotion to you.
16 Come and hear, all you who fear God,	Listen, all you who reverence God,
and I will tell what he has done for me.	and I will tell you what God has done for me.
17 I cried aloud to him,	I cried out to God,
and he was extolled with my tongue.	I praised God.
18 If I had cherished iniquity in my heart,	I resisted the seduction of bitterness and to hate.
the Lord would not have listened.	
19 But truly God has listened;	Therefore God listened to me,
he has given heed to the words of my prayer.	and answered my prayers.
20 Blessed be God	Blessed be God
because he has not rejected my prayer	for listening to my prayers
or removed his steadfast love from me.	and surrounding me with a love
Ps. 66:13-20 NRSV	that holds tight and never lets go.

Psalm 66 is a generic thanksgiving psalm in that no specific circumstances are given. The psalm begins with the history of Israel's redemption in which all the people share, then moves to an individual expression of thanksgiving for deliverance from trouble. The psalm does not name the trouble or give any other details specific to an individual situation. Any Israelite who has every experienced an answer to prayer can pray this psalm.

Likewise, the community as a whole can pray the psalm, taking the "I" collectively. Our incarnational translation retains this generality but interprets certain elements of the psalm in a spiritualizing way. The literal sacrifice of fat bulls, rams, and goats becomes a sacrifice of gratitude. This translation is perhaps less a matter of contemporizing and more a reflection of the way the church, beginning with the earliest Christian writers, appropriates the worship traditions of Israel and spiritualizes them.

The idea of spiritual sacrifices is also found already in ancient Judaism, although it is rarely seen as a substitute for animal sacrifice. One of the effects of spiritualizing is the loss of the material expense of sacrifice. The fatlings, rams, bulls, and goats in Psalm 66 constitute a substantial material outlay. Thanksgiving is costly! In consideration of this, we have in our incarnational translation paired offerings of gratefulness with the generosity of giving. At this point both the original psalm and our translation raise the question of whether the ritual of thanksgiving assumes a quid pro quo. Can one make tangible promises without falling into the spiritual trap of bargaining with God? Should an incarnational translation for use in personal or corporate worship edit this implication out of Psalm 66?

Liturgical use of the incarnational translation raises the question of a psalm's perspective. The closing stanza of this psalm (vv. 16-20) suggests that the time of difficulty is over. God has delivered the psalmist. The use of the future tense in verses 13-15 could imply that the psalmist, grateful for God's deliverance, speaks in anticipation of making a sacrifice in God's house in the near future. But is the occasion of the psalm really the time between deliverance and worship in the temple? It seems better to interpret the use of future tense as a literary device that creates the sense of a narrative: prayers in the midst of trouble accompanied by vows; God's answer to those prayers (deliverance); a renewed promise to fulfill the vows; the act of fulfillment by offering a sacrifice in the temple. The psalm would have its natural place at the time of sacrifice, but given the very general character of the psalm, we can also assume that it served not only as part of a liturgy of thanksgiving for specific answers to prayer but as a typical thanksgiving that was not tied to particular times or circumstances. In this usage, the psalm is both thanksgiving and teaching: it tells the story of Israel's great redemption; it binds the small stories of individuals in trouble to that pattern of redemption (God acts for them as God acted for Israel as a whole); and it exemplifies the right way to approach God, to hope in God, and to thank God.

In Christian liturgy, an incarnational translation of Psalm 66 could include a moment for naming specific answers to prayer between verse 19 and verse 20. This liturgical use could be included as part of a sermon on the psalm or at another place in the order of worship.

Although we have presented an incarnational translation of only the second half of this psalm, fidelity to the form argues for including the first half as well. One theological question that confronts the task of rendering the first half of the psalm is whether the narrative of God's redemptive acts might appropriately include reference to God's act of redemption through Christ as well. The psalm assumes that later generations of Israelites belong to the generation that experienced God's deliverance from Egypt so that in every generation the people of Israel can say, "*We* went through the fire and the water" (v. 12). Redemption through Christ's death and resurrection, which Christians have often linked typologically with the Exodus, has a similar character. Every generation of Christians says, "*We* have been crucified with Christ and raised with him to new lives."

The Praise Psalm

Closely related to thanksgiving psalms are praise psalms, songs extolling God's character and deeds. Typical elements of the form are invocation, a call to praise, a litany of praise, and concluding blessings.

Praise psalms were performed as hymns that were sung by choirs to the accompaniment of musical instruments. At festivals these psalms were typically performed in processionals and also with dance. They were also often sung responsively, with the congregation providing "hallelujahs," "amens," and other brief refrains. We do not know how these psalms were performed in the regular temple liturgy. Presumably, the daily psalmody was less exuberant than the psalm-singing at a festival, although the temple psalmody also used instrumental accompaniment and may have been quite rhythmic.

Today there is a lively tradition of contemporary praise songs based on biblical texts of the Psalms. Choruses of this kind lend themselves to highly rhythmic performance with contemporary instrumentation (in the jazz, rock, and black gospel tradition). Many of them are transmediatizations that use traditional English Bible translations with only slight modifications or have their own freely composed lyrics that incorporate a few traditional lines from the Psalms.

Here is an example of a contemporary praise chorus based on Psalm 8:

O Lord, our Lord, how excellent Your name is,
How excellent Your name in all the earth.
Your glory fills the heavens beyond the farthest star,
How excellent Your name in all the earth.
When I think about the heavens, the moon and all the stars,
I wonder what You ever saw in me.
But You took me and You loved me, and You've given me a crown,
and now I'll praise Your name eternally.[9]

Transgenrelization in this example entails the use of meter, rhythm, and rhyme. This brings the psalm into a poetic form familiar to us. It has antecedents in the long tradition of English psalters, which also converted the Psalms into forms of English meter. This kind of transgenrelization also facilitates transmediatization: the conversion of the psalm as an ancient musical form into a contemporary musical expression.

The praise chorus quoted above includes a significant change of focus, turning the psalmist's contemplation of humanity's value and status in the grand scheme of creation into a contemplation of one's own individual value and status in creation. This shift of focus does not break any hard-and-fast rule of incarnational translation, but it is important to ask whether the individualizing and personalizing is a good rhetorical strategy for incarnational translation of Psalm 8. The line "I wonder what You ever saw in me" is especially open to criticism since it suggests that God found and elevated the psalmist the way an agent or film director discovers a Hollywood star. The individualizing of the exaltation — "given me a crown" — also seems to violate the corporate anthropology of the original.

The following is a very different translingualization of Psalm 8, more economical and image-laden, like much modern poetry.

O God, our beginning and end,
    extraordinary in everything,

9. Peter Jacobs, "How Excellent Your Name," in *Maranatha! Music Praise Chorus Book*, 3rd ed., compiled by George Baldwin et al. (Nashville: Word Maranatha, 1993), no. 80.

voice in a child's voice,
    silencing the killers.

Lost, surely, we, in the monitor of your consciousness,
    amidst the billions upon billions of galaxies,
found, strangely, we, in your mirror,
    glittering there —
makers, shakers, moon-walkers, space-dancers.

O God, our beginning and end,
    extraordinary in everything.

Perhaps the middle stanza of this translation is too cryptic. It calls for re-reading and might not communicate well if heard only once in a sermon. But before giving the translation, a preacher might first present and develop the individual metaphors of translation. This could serve as a preparation for a closing recital of the incarnational translation in which the metaphors reappear, integrated poetically but not cryptically, because they have already been made familiar in the body of the sermon.

We know that praise psalms, as well as many other types of psalms, were used not only in formal liturgical settings but also for private devotion. The most famous of all psalms in the Christian tradition is Psalm 23. Certainly it is not only the sense but also the beautifully poetic language of Psalm 23 that brings comfort when we have nowhere else to turn. In these private moments of personal distress, we often speak the words of that psalm not in the jubilant cry of rhythmic song but in the quiet intonation of the subdued poetic voice. Ancient Israelites probably often did the same.

The tradition of recourse to Psalm 23 in times of personal need, including its recital by a friend or minister at the bedside of one who is dying, invites special consideration of what a highly personal, situation-specific incarnational translation of this psalm might look like. An incarnational translation of this kind does best if it achieves something of the poetic power, in a contemporary poetic style, that the psalm accomplishes in its ancient style. Below is one effort at this kind of poetry. We have placed it side by side with the RSV for comparison. Notice that, despite the very different language and imagery of the incarnational translation, each line of the original Psalm 23 is represented in the incarnational translation and often with a metaphor or image that echoes in some way the original figurative speech of the psalm.

The Lord comes early morning
before I am fully awake, before I
am fully able to distinguish the
bone ache of dreams from the bone
ache of day that never goes away.

The Lord is my shepherd, I shall not
want. He makes me lie down in green
pastures. He leads me beside still
waters. He restores my soul. He leads
me in paths of righteousness for his
name's sake.

Like Sally, my old friend, bringing
my medications and painkillers, a
quiet gentleness with cool hands,
humming sometimes, soothing,
smiling, reading to me, sometimes
just sitting, her hand on mine,
feeding me little bits of her own
soul. My soul can hardly keep
anything down except these morsels
from her. I don't think she realizes
it, but she is teaching me how to
die well, a righteous death, if there
is such a thing, and she's about the
only one from whom I'll accept this
lesson.

Yea, though I walk through the valley
of the shadow of death, I will fear no
evil, for Thou art with me. Thy rod
and thy staff they comfort me.

Light hurts my eyes; the curtains
are drawn; my room is dark. But
you are there, Lord, present in her
hands, busy with sheets, pillows,
tubes. The sight of these quiet
hands puts me at ease somehow.

Thou preparest a table before me in
the presence of my enemies.

You bring me a tray of food. I eat
very little these days; everything
tastes bitter. But you make my
lunch colorful anyway: slices of
orange, bright green kiwi, yellow
banana — all in a pretty ring
around the broth I can probably
just get down. A feast for my eyes
at least, a celebration of my life in
the presence of my enemies, in the

	presence of my body that keeps me alive against my will and in the presence of death itself, who has not yet become my friend.
Thou anointest my head with oil. My cup overflows. Surely goodness and mercy shall follow me all the days of my life; and I will dwell in the house of the Lord for ever. RSV	You dab my cracked lips with ointment, my tears overflow in the darkness, because you are here. Today and tomorrow you come early morning before I am fully awake. Before I am even able to be afraid of an empty house or silence without presence or the end of my life, you are there.

Special challenges greet any effort to create an incarnational translation of something as familiar and beloved as Psalm 23 in its English-language tradition that reaches back to the beauty and dignity of the King James Version. Our incarnational translation seeks to do justice to the poetic quality of this psalm through transgenrelization in a contemporary style of poetry to create a comparable rhetorical effect of simple beauty and dignity. Perhaps the most difficult obstacle to rewording Psalm 23 is the metaphor of God as a "shepherd." What contemporary metaphor can convey what "shepherd" has come to mean to us in and through this psalm? Our incarnational translation substitutes a *simile* ("Like Sally. . .") for the psalm's original *metaphor* ("The Lord is my shepherd"). From this point on, the description of Sally's care functions as an extended metaphor for God as the shepherd. The incarnational translation depends on an incarnational theology, the conviction that God comes to us in certain persons who become agents and living icons of divine care and presence.

The Wisdom Psalm

Wisdom psalms may stem from scribal circles and have been intended originally for instructional use outside of worship, or, more likely, they may be psalms for worship that reflect the heightened interest in wisdom traditions after the exile. In either case, they display an instructional purpose, incorporating the original wisdom forms (proverbs, sayings, examples, admonitions, etc.) into larger structural units. It may be that their primary home was the synagogue, where some of these psalms served as prayers and others as words of teaching and exhortation.

Here is an example of an incarnational translation of a wisdom psalm, in this case the first six verses of Psalm 90:

Lord, you have been our dwelling place
    in all generations.
Before the mountains were brought
      forth
    or ever you had formed the earth
      and the world,
from everlasting to everlasting,
    you are God.

Lord, we call you home,
    just as our mothers and fathers did,
and the generations before them.
Before anything existed,
    before the moment of creation itself,
from the time before time
    to the time after time,
    you are God.

You turn us back to dust
    and say, "Turn back, you mortals."
For a thousand years in your sight
    are like yesterday when it is past,
    or like a watch in the night.

You turn us back to dust
    and say, "Go back where you came
      from."
For a billion light years
    are like a single yesterday for you,
    like an evening's work for a security
      guard.

You sweep them away. They are like
    a dream,
    like grass that is renewed in the
      morning;
in the morning it flourishes and is
      renewed;
    in the evening it fades and withers.
NRSV

You make the years fly by.
They are like a dream,
like the movie screen
filled with sound and light
    one moment,
empty and silent the next.

In this translation and in others, we take over the traditional "Lord" from the original. A good deal of theological discussion has considered whether traditional descriptions of God as Lord, king, ruler, and so forth carry connotations of divine despotism that ought to be avoided in preaching and other forms of liturgical language. There is also an interest in avoiding the suggestion that God is literally masculine or has, even metaphorically speaking, typically masculine character traits, whatever these might be in a given culture. At the same time, it could be that, for many modern listeners, the word "Lord" in application to God amounts to a proper name that has lost its original meaning from everyday speech. In any case, incarnational translation can appropriately seek alternate renderings for such terms, which are, after all, metaphors based on language conventions of ancient Mediterranean social life. In the case of Psalm 90, one might simply render the first address as "God."

Psalm 90 also uses a bit of creation theology, with typical ancient notions of how the world came into being. Our translation recasts these in more modern terms. But the point is not to substitute science for the ancient mythopoeic language. In subsequent chapters we will consider this matter in greater detail, when we come to Genesis 1 and to the descriptions of the created order in the book of Job.

The Lament

Closely related to the complaint psalm is the *lament,* and some scholars treat the complaint psalms under the broader category of the lament.

Laments were often performed as chants (dirges) with tearing of clothes, self-flagellation, wearing sackcloth and ashes, and other symbolic bodily expressions of the awful depths of the inner experience. We have evidence that, in the Greek tradition, laments were uttered in the high vocal register with an attenuated voice.[10] This may reflect a wider Mediterranean practice. In the Jewish tradition, dirges and lamentations sometimes had a limping poetic meter of five stressed syllables (3 + 2) per line. Some of the laments in Lamentations use an acrostic poetic technique. In content, laments typically move from complaint and expressions of pain to hope and praise.

The ancient traditions of lament suggest that there is something primordial in the human need to express grief through ritualized symbolic actions and rhythmic chanting of traditional words. Laments are passionate expressions of mourning about death, destruction, and disaster. They contain the following typical features: moaning and wailing, descriptions

---

10. See Egert Pöhlmann and Martin L. West, *Documents of Ancient Greek Music* (Oxford: Clarendon Press, 2001), p. 10; M. L. West, *Ancient Greek Music* (Oxford: Clarendon Press, 1992), p. 45.

of catastrophe, recollections of former happiness, calls to weep and wail, sometimes an expression of guarded hope. Like complaint, lament provides a spiritual container for expressions of profound grief and despair.

In North America today there are few robust grieving rituals that involve body and song or chant in this way. Music from our Western tradition that traditionally expresses mourning includes funeral dirges, but our collective memory knows these not as shared ritual practices but only as parts of classical music (e.g., the dirge in the second movement of Beethoven's Third Symphony and the funeral march from Chopin's Piano Sonata in B-flat minor). The closest many of us come to experiencing the emotions of lament in musical form is when films present tragic scenes accompanied by Samuel Barber's Adagio for Strings. The opening bars of this hauntingly beautiful music have become a familiar musical background to scenes of soldiers fighting and dying in slow motion. But again, this musical expression of tragedy belongs not to a ritual form of lament but to an artistic expression in which we are spectators — audience, not participants. Nor does most contemporary North American Christian liturgy supply us with adequate traditions of lament. The church usually turns to familiar and comforting hymns in times of loss or disaster. We have few songs of lament. And even the few we possess tend not to be used as laments. For example, the spiritual "Nobody Knows the Trouble I've Seen" may be sung from time to time, in both African-American churches and in non-African-American churches, but almost never as part of a ritual of lament.

North American churches also tend to move immediately to comfort and hope in the face of disaster and loss. We give little if any time to grieving, even though our professional therapists have been telling us for years that giving time for a "grieving process" in the face of loss is necessary to human health.

Comfort, encouragement, and memorializing all have their place in response to loss, but they are not lament. Biblical lament, which has such a conspicuous place in Scripture, is virtually absent from our own lives as individual Christians and communities of faith. We rarely preach on lament passages, and when we do it is usually not in the context of a liturgy of lament. In a very important essay on lament, Walter Brueggemann suggests that the absence of a lament tradition in the Western church owes to a tendency toward triumphalism combined with a scholastic conception of God's omnipotence, omniscience, and omnipresence. With the rise of modernity, "*self-sufficient selves* in communion with an *all-managing God* had

81

no room for lament, and that theological premise is now powerfully replicated in so-called 'praise hymns' in which 'never is heard a discouraging word.'"[11] Brueggemann also suggests that the events of 9/11 have "awakened consumer America from its narcoticized notion of self-sufficiency." Suddenly the opening lines of Lamentations sound close to home.

> How lonely sits the city
>> that once was full of people!
> How like a widow she has become,
>> she that was great among the nations!

(Lam. 1:1)

Of course, in modern times cities such as Dresden, Hiroshima, and London harbor memories of destruction more comparable to the widowhood of Jerusalem laid waste by Babylonians than was New York's. Nonetheless, the attacks of 9/11 have left a wound in New Yorkers and in Americans generally that deserves a lament. But how many churches in the United States held grieving rituals after 9/11? The dominant Christian response in Sunday services following that fateful Tuesday was to emphasize comfort and hope. And special memorial services have focused on encouragement and honoring the memory of the dead and the heroes of 9/11. All of that is appropriate, but it has been carried out without rituals of lament. Perhaps calls to display courage and to "show the terrorists that we are not afraid" have led Americans to suppress any urges they have to lament.

Not all lament is immediate, public ritual in response to events; there are also private laments that only later become public. The laments ("confessions") of Jeremiah present puzzling questions in this regard. William Holladay believes that Jeremiah did not publish them immediately, but only after his vindication by God.[12] Other scholars see the present canonical form of Jeremiah as a product of later redaction that makes it impossible to know if and when a historical Jeremiah published his laments.[13] A substantial number of scholars hold that Jeremiah reflects exilic and/or

11. Walter Brueggemann, "Necessary Conditions for a Good Lament," *Horizons in Biblical Theology* 25 (2003): 19-20.

12. William L. Holladay, *Jeremiah 1: A Commentary on the Book of the Prophet Jeremiah, Chapters 1-25*, Hermeneia (Philadelphia: Fortress Press, 1986), pp. 358-361.

13. See, for example, Robert P. Carroll, *Jeremiah: A Commentary*, Old Testament Library (Philadelphia: Westminster Press, 1986).

postexilic preaching. In any case, Jeremiah's laments were made public not as an immediate response to the personal experiences they describe but only later as *memory*. They assume a substantial interval of time (in the prophet's life or in the history of Israel) between the events of which they speak and the ritual of public expression — whatever form that took. Here is a famous example of one such lament:

> 7 O LORD, you have enticed me,
>   and I was enticed;
> you have overpowered me,
>   and you have prevailed.
> I have become a laughingstock all day long;
>   everyone mocks me.
> 8 For whenever I speak, I must cry out,
>   I must shout, "Violence and destruction!"
> For the word of the LORD has become for me
>   a reproach and derision all day long.
> 9 If I say, "I will not mention him,
>   or speak any more in his name,"
> then within me there is something like a burning fire
>   shut up in my bones;
> I am weary with holding it in,
>   and I cannot.
> 10 For I hear many whispering: "Terror is all around!
>   Denounce him! Let us denounce him!"
> All my close friends
>   are watching for me to stumble.
> "Perhaps he can be enticed,
>   and we can prevail against him,
>   and take our revenge on him."
> 11 But the LORD is with me like a dread warrior;
>   therefore my persecutors will stumble,
>   and they will not prevail.
> They will be greatly shamed,
>   for they will not succeed.
> Their eternal dishonor
>   will never be forgotten.
> 12 O LORD of hosts, you test the righteous,
>   you see the heart and the mind;

let me see your retribution upon them,
    for to you I have committed my cause.

13 Sing to the Lord;
    praise the Lord!
For he has delivered the life of the needy
    from the hands of the evildoers.

14 Cursed be the day
    on which I was born!
The day when my mother bore me;
    let it not be blessed!
15 Cursed be the man who brought the news to my
    father, saying,
"A child is born to you, a son,"
    making him very glad.
16 Let that man be like the cities
    that the Lord overthrew without pity;
let him hear a cry in the morning
    and an alarm at noon,
17 because he did not kill me in the womb;
    so my mother would have been my grave,
    and her womb forever great.
18 Why did I come forth from the womb
      to see toil and sorrow,
    and spend my days in shame?

Jer. 20:7-18

From a form-critical standpoint, verses 7-12 are often taken as a complete unit of tradition, a lament to which other traditions have been added, including an out-of-place word of praise in verse 13, which leaves the song of praise in verse 13 outside the lament; but the final form of the text presents a single speech in which both lament and praise appear. Moreover, as we have noted, the lament form typically moves from complaint to praise. Hence, we can see verses 7-13 as a typical lament form; the addition of what follows in verses 14-18 is atypical. The traditional language of praise, which in the lament form ought to be the final word, is drowned out by curses. The rhetorical effect is a word of praise conditioned in a peculiar way by its placement, rendered ambiguous and open to competing readings of its tone. Is Jeremiah's praise an expression of confident trust? Is it mere doxological reflex? A desperate effort at faith? An ironic or sarcastic statement of mock hope? It may be all of these and more. Jeremiah is in a funk, and this cannot be described or expressed simplistically.

With the preceding in mind, the following incarnational translation of Jeremiah 20:7-18 transposes the prophet's experience into that of a minister serving a middle-class congregation.

Lord, you have seduced me and I was seduced.
    You swept me off my feet with visions of pretty vestments,
        gorgeous outfits in basic black, crowds riveted to my
            every word.
I gave up a career for you.
    I even went into debt for you.

You called and called again, and would not let me go,
    until that day in Lent when I gave up,
when you wore down my resistance and I said yes.
Since then, I have become a curiosity, a kind of joke
    to my successful friends from college.
Their patronizing eyes say, "Loser."

But I had no choice. I had to speak,
    to carry the Lord's word —
    not always a pretty word.
Sometimes it was "Violence and destruction!"
    There is something wrong here. Doesn't anyone else see?
    But not to see it, not to speak of it would make me complicit.
        I would know my guilt.
    It would be nagging at me all day long.

If I say, "I'll cool it with the justice sermons.
    I'll preach soothing sermons on the value of faith,
        the power of positive thinking,
    the glory of the flag and family values" —
then from deep within me there is something like a volcano,
    building pressure, preparing to erupt.
    I try and try to hold it in.
    I suppress it with every ounce of my being.

But it explodes.
After the Sunday morning service, they huddle in the parking lot
    and say:
    "Church was too long again today."
    "Another church conference tomorrow."
    "Money, money, money. That's all we hear about around here."
    "We've never done it this way before."

My members think I'm crazy. They're calling the bishop.
My close friends are watching to see me lose it!
They take me to Starbuck's for a latte and a decadent brownie
    to remind me of the good old days
      when the mentally ill had to sit in the parlor
        and listen through the loudspeaker.
    The service was peaceful then.

They take me to lunch to remind me
    that if the Africans wanted African music
      they would go to an African church.
They invite me to their condos to convince me
    to keep the homeless off the front steps of the church.
They take me to a concert
    to point out that gentrification is our future.
The old faction says, "One more time and we'll get her out.
    Withhold your pledge. Call the bishop."

But the Lord stands by me like a Jedi knight.
Zap the complainers and the bigots!
    Embarrass my persecutors! Stun the whiners!
      And really give it to the holier-than-thou's!
They don't have the votes!
    They'll go down to defeat.
The bishop says *stay.*
    The faction is humiliated.
There will be a buzz at coffee hour this week!
    Even the newcomers will hear about it.

O Lord of hosts, you tested the church
    and those who hear your lively word.

It is clear who wants the church to grow,
    who wants the status quo.
It is clear whose hearts and minds are open,
    and who needs a reprimand.
Let the others be sidelined.
Let them retire from altar guild and treasury,
    from the women's groups and greeters.
For I have laid it on the line for you.

Praise God from whom all blessings flow.
Praise God, all creatures here below.
God rescues the weak and vulnerable
    from the hands of the evildoers.

Damn!
Rip May out of the calendar, the month in which I was born.
Smash the pink rattle; toss the cigars into the gutter.
Shoot the nurse who brought the news to my father,
    "You have a beautiful little girl!"
Shred the baby album.
    Tear out the page of my baptism from the church register.
        Cut my face out of the family photographs.
        Burn my report cards and diplomas.
Damn my mother's OB/GYN.
Take away his license to practice.
Let him he be like the cities wasted by tsunamis and hurricanes.
Let him fear car bombs in the morning and sirens at noon
    because he did not abort me,
    a simple D & C at three months.
Why was I born for this —
    to work and weep, to struggle and fail,
        to risk everything and be humiliated?[14]

It would probably be neither prudent nor altogether innocent for a minister fresh from the experiences here described to deliver an incarnational translation like this one as a first-person complaint to a congregation broiling

14. Incarnational translation by David Drebert, Michele Matott, Fred Mueller, Tony Alford, and Barbara Cathey; used by permission.

with these conflicts! As an autobiographical confession based in actual experience, this lament would have its place in private liturgy or as a memory shared only well after the time of the pain it describes has subsided, preached perhaps only to "later Israelites." Of course, an incarnational translation of this kind can also be a fictitious re-embodiment of Jeremiah's confession in contemporary form and clearly represented as such to hearers.

New Testament Hymns

A scholarly tradition inaugurated early in the twentieth century identified various examples of hitherto unrecognized early Christian "hymns" in the New Testament (such as the Christ Hymn of Philippians 2). These hymns use very traditional biblical imagery and language, and some of them have put their mark on the creeds of the church. Along with passages long treated as hymnic by the church (e.g., the Magnificat of Luke 1:46-55), New Testament scholars have identified the following passages as hymns or fragments of hymns: Philippians 2:5-11; John 1:1-14 (with editorial insertions); Colossians 1:15-20 (with editing); Ephesians 5:14; 1 Timothy 3:16 and 6:15-16; 2 Timothy 2:11-13; Titus 3:4-7; Revelation 22:16.

Let's look more closely at one of these. The words of the Christ hymn of Philippians 2:5-11 strike us twenty-first-century Christians as elevated and dignified, but those words probably did not strike their first hearers that way, with their references to the Son becoming a *slave* and dying on a *cross,* a word that sounded almost like profanity in the ancient world (at least in "cultured" circles).[15] It is difficult to re-create this original rhetorical effect. Here's one non-poetic effort:

> Christ in the image of God did not count life at the top something to be held on to but climbed down the social ladder and took the job of bus boy, checkout girl, garbage collector, hospital orderly. And he kept faith with God every day of his life, right up to the end, dead in an electric chair in a federal penitentiary, wrongly convicted of treason. Therefore, God made him CEO of the universe and assigned him a title above all titles, that at the name of Jesus, hats will

---

15. See Martin Hengel, *Crucifixion in the Ancient World and the Folly of the Message of the Cross* (London: SCM Press; Philadelphia: Fortress Press, 1977).

come off and hands will cover hearts, all over the world, from boardrooms to waiting rooms, in honor of God, so that we will be patriots no longer of "God and country" but only of God.

The closing sentence of this recontextualization assumes that the hymn has anti-imperialistic overtones, which people in Paul's day would have heard as an implicit critique of the religio-political pretensions of the Roman Empire to world sovereignty.[16] Those overtones would no doubt have pleased some and disturbed others. The incarnational translation is also provocative and troubling in a way that early Christian preaching was provocative and troubling for first-century people. Without good information about Jesus, they would have been just as dubious that a man crucified by the Romans for treason could be God's emissary as modern Americans would be dubious if confronted with the claims made in our translation about a convicted and executed felon.

A more poetic version of the hymn might run as follows:

Form of God
Son above
God's shining star
Christ of cosmic praise
immune from pain
beyond all weakness
took these things
made fragile human life his life
death row man
ghetto man
AIDS man
forgotten —
but not by God
who made him Son above
God's shining star
Christ of cosmic praise
our praise
our shining star

16. On Paul and Roman imperialism, see Richard A. Horsley, ed., *Paul and Empire: Religion and Power in Roman Imperial Society* (Harrisburg, PA: Trinity Press International, 1997).

This translation is less political and interprets the movement into servanthood and death in terms of social humiliation, estrangement, and poverty.

The Musical Aspect of the Psalms and Other Biblical Songs

The history of the Psalms and other biblical songs shows that at some points in their history and in some settings many of them were sung, and at other points and in other settings they were not. Evidently, the singing of the Psalms in the ancient congregation of Israel could be melodic or at times might take the form of a shout (Ps. 33:3). Psalms were performed with string, wind, and percussion instruments (Pss. 33:1-3; 149:3; 150)—and accompanied by dancing (Pss. 149:3; 150:4). Unfortunately, we do not know what the melodies sounded like.[17]

In Israel, many of the Psalms were performed musically before becoming part of Scripture. Once incorporated into the collection of Psalms as part of the Hebrew Bible, they were sung primarily in the Temple, although some continued to be sung on other occasions. Other songs of the Hebrew Bible, such as the songs of Moses in Deuteronomy 32 and Exodus 15, were probably originally independent songs performed at particular feasts. We do not know how long these songs continued to be performed musically in Israel after becoming part of the Pentateuch. The Psalms were probably not sung in the ancient *synagogue* liturgy, although they might have been recited from time to time as part of ancient lectionaries. Nor is there any evidence that they were sung in the earliest church.

In the third and fourth centuries, the Christian monasteries — and eventually the church as a whole — began singing the Psalms in worship.[18] As for the ancient musical form of Christian psalmody, it is very unlikely that the church knew and used the traditional melodies of the Temple,

17. Some twentieth-century scholars, notably Eric Werner, have argued that melodies known to us from later church and synagogue traditions preserve the melodic forms of the ancient tradition of psalm-singing that was established in the synagogue and taken over directly by the first-century church. But this theory has been discredited; see, for example, James McKinnon, "On the Question of Psalmody in the Ancient Synagogue," *Early Music History* 6 (1986): 159-191.

18. James W. McKinnon, *The Advent Project: The Later-Seventh-Century Creation of the Roman Mass Proper* (Berkeley, CA: University of California Press, 2000), pp. 19-59.

whose liturgy came to an end in 70 CE. The church undoubtedly produced its own musical tradition of psalm-singing; unfortunately, there is no record of this music.

In view of the evidence as a whole, it seems appropriate (but certainly not necessary) to use musical settings for incarnational translations of the Psalms. In so doing we cannot imitate or adapt ancient psalm melodies to contemporary musical forms since we have no knowledge of these melodies; thus we have to make our own musical decisions based on the content of the Psalms.

New Testament hymns present another set of problems for those interested in music as a medium of Scripture. If we consider these hymns from the standpoint of the Greek musical tradition, they do not look like songs: the verse of Greek songs was metrical; none of the New Testament hymns are. Perhaps they are prose hymns, for which we also have examples in wider Greek literature. Or perhaps they are instances of elevated prose, rather than quotations of traditional hymns. Or perhaps they are hymns in a nonmetrical Jewish style of poetry. It seems certain that Greek-speaking Jews, in addition to learning Greek music and composing in it, would also have preserved traditional Jewish melodies and styles of singing. Hence, Greek-speaking Christian Jews might have created songs for the new faith in a traditional Jewish musical style. But we don't know whether the identified hymns of the New Testament are examples of this kind of song because none of them is explicitly introduced as a song.

Prophetic Oracles

The words "Thus says the Lord. . ." alert the reader that what follows is a prophetic oracle. The formula announces the form as a kind of double speaking, a voice behind the voice. The prophet speaks, but behind the prophet is the speech of God. The listener hears the prophet (or reads the prophet's words) but is directed to understand not the prophet but the One who speaks through the prophet. We can lay out the basic model this way:

$$\text{God} \rightarrow \text{Prophet} \rightarrow \text{Speech} \rightarrow \text{Audience}$$

The import of this model is that the prophet is transparent (or "transaudient") to the Word that comes from beyond. The prophet is inspired by God to speak and thus is a herald or messenger. The model of the oracle makes the strongest theological claim about the authority of the words themselves. In some cases, prophets are depicted as compelled to prophesy, even against their own desires (e.g., Jeremiah and Jonah); in other cases, prophets are depicted as welcoming or cooperating in — even delighting in — the oracles entrusted to them (e.g., Isaiah and Ezekiel). In either case, the words of the prophet claim divine authorization.

This is a mode of revelation that many have treated as a model for all of Scripture, expressing what it means for Scripture to be inspired or holy.[19] In such an understanding, Scripture itself (as a whole and in all its varying genres) is placed in the position of the prophet, presenting a word that is "breathed out" by the Holy Spirit. This notion of the inspiration of Scripture comes in a wide range of conceptions, from divine dictation theories to those that include the activity of the human understanding under the guidance of the Holy Spirit. These theological models of the nature of divine communication in Scripture evoke corresponding models for the interpretation of Scripture.

The Bible itself, however, shows many different approaches to authority reflected in different speech models, each with its own particular means of communication and persuasion. The prophetic model of authority, belonging properly to the nature of the prophetic oracle, is distorted and distorting when pressed into service as the paradigm for all of Scripture and all interpretation of Scripture (including preaching). When the model of the prophetic oracle serves as the model for Scripture as a whole, it creates a strong logic that positions the interpreter in the role of the prophet, the oracle's oracle. As Scripture (regarded as oracle) is to God behind it, so the interpreter is to Scripture. The role of the interpreter is to repeat what God has said. As a homiletical concern, the speech model of the prophetic oracle brings forward in a stark way the question of the authority of what is written and spoken and what it means to respond. The authority of the divine word establishes the authority of the scriptural word, which in turn establishes the authority of the interpreter's word. Since the communication is transparent, the chain of authority is direct and unqualified, and the interpreter is not understood as interpreting but only as delivering. The claim on the reader is to accept or reject the interpreter's (preacher's)

---

19. Paul Ricoeur, "Toward a Hermeneutic of the Idea of Revelation," in *Essays on Biblical Interpretation*, ed. Lewis S. Mudge (Minneapolis: Fortress Press, 1980), pp. 75-76.

message. As we have seen and will observe further in connection with other genres of Scripture, this model does not work well with biblical genres that are not oracular. Indeed, we must be cautious about treating prophetic oracles as places in Scripture where the oracular mode of address speaks directly to us, since prophetic oracles usually have narrative frameworks of some kind and are in other ways linked to particular times and places.

In one sense, the form of the prophetic oracle presents a self-authenticating claim to authority: 'X' is so because God says it is so. One might reasonably suppose, therefore, that its claim is authoritarian in nature. But, in another sense, a given oracle may function in an anti-authoritarian way, in that it appears from outside the structures of authorization (law, tradition, custom, reason, experience, argument, etc.). The oracle appears as a testimony to the divine overthrowing of expectations based on presumed limits of what is real, possible, and right — including expectations about God. One could argue that the form of the oracle emerges as a countertestimony provoked by unjust (or otherwise illegitimate) human authority. If that is the case, then it would be all the more ironic if the anti-authoritarian dynamic of the oracle were hardened into authoritarian modes of human speech, which would constitute an *inversion* of oracular address. The process of incarnational translation of an oracle makes these issues of revelation and authority especially vivid.

Let us consider how these issues emerge in a particular text, Isaiah 56, an oracle that is commonly accepted as postexilic. Granting that historical assumption, we can view it in a social setting where the exiles are returning from Babylon to discover that, in their absence, the imperial policies of the conquerors have brought great changes — social, political, and religious. The resettlement of Jews and other subjugated peoples led to the presence in the Temple of foreign proselytes and eunuchs. Eunuchs were excluded by Levitical law from divine service (Lev. 21:16-24) and by Deuteronomic law from the assembly itself (Deut. 23:1). Foreigners also had a problematical status, whether because of particular national origins (e.g., Ammonites and Moabites) or the simple fact that they did not belong to Israel by lineage or marriage. No matter whom they descended from, the covenant did not include them. Yet the exiles have returned to find these outsiders not only in Jerusalem as neighbors but worshiping in the temple. What are the exiles to do?

Four parties appear in the oracle of Isaiah 56, each of whom offers a viewpoint on the postexilic situation: God, the prophet, the returning exiles (insiders), and the foreigners/eunuchs (outsiders). Each party has a different role, interest, and orientation in this oracle. God's role in the action, let us propose, is to say and do a new thing: in the great vision of Isaiah 56, God's house is to be a house of prayer for all peoples, a vision that goes beyond those already gathered to include yet unknown others. In the implied narrative of the oracle, God has listened to the lament of the eunuchs and foreigners, whose presence in the assembly is threatened. The eunuchs and foreigners who love God and keep God's covenant are given place, name, and monument within God's house. Setting aside even the words of the law, God points to those who had been outside — and to those who are still outside — and declares that the promises and covenant of God are for them. Here are the words of Isaiah 56:3-8 in the NRSV:

> Do not let the foreigner joined to the LORD say,
>> "The LORD will surely separate me from his people";
> and do not let the eunuch say,
>> "I am just a dry tree."
> For thus says the LORD:
> To the eunuchs who keep my sabbaths,
>> who choose the things that please me
>> and hold fast my covenant,
> I will give, in my house and within my walls,
>> a monument and a name
>> better than sons and daughters;
> I will give them an everlasting name
>> that shall not be cut off.
>
> And the foreigners who join themselves to the LORD,
>> to minister to him, to love the name of the LORD,
>> and to be his servants,
> all who keep the sabbath and do not profane it,
>> and hold fast my covenant —
> these I will bring to my holy mountain,
>> and make them joyful in my house of prayer;
> their burnt offerings and their sacrifices
>> will be accepted on my altar;
> for my house shall be called a house of prayer for all peoples.
> Thus says the LORD GOD,

who gathers the outcasts of Israel,
I will gather others to them
    besides those already gathered.

The role and interest of the prophet in this oracle are oriented toward two different directions of responsibility. First is the responsibility to God; second is the responsibility to the ones God seeks to address. Unlike a call narrative, in which the reader is given to overhear the dialogue between God and the prophet, we find no instruction for the prophet to carry out, no words to pronounce. In this oracle there is only the most austere beginning: "Thus says the Lord." How did the word come to the prophet? The text does not say. What sign does the prophet have to show the origin of the new word? What authority or argument does the prophet show to overturn the law? The text refuses all of these and presents only the bare word itself: *Thus says the Lord.* We conclude, therefore, that the relationship between God and prophet, the issue of the call, the struggle and obedience of the bearer of the message—all these stand outside the oracle and are not part of its drama.

Whom, then, does the prophet address in the name of God, and what is their role? The text offers two different possible audiences. On the one hand, God seems to be speaking to the outsiders; yet the text speaks of them in the third person. Who is being admonished when the prophet says, "Do not let the foreigner joined to the Lord say. . ."? Who is it that must be instructed about the new thing God has already done (and intends to continue doing)? The grammar suggests that the oracle is addressed not to those who already know what God has done but to those who do not yet know (or do not yet believe) that the presence of the foreigners and eunuchs is the work of God. The oracle, then, is addressed to insiders who have the responsibility as gatekeepers of the house of God.

If the preceding interpretation is correct, how can we understand the position of the outsiders in this oracle? If the oracle is addressed first of all to insiders, yet concerns those who are already present, we might conceive of these outsiders as those who *overhear.* We might also imagine them as those who are being defended or justified by the oracle. We can see them as those whose laments (v. 3) have been heard, like the cry of the Hebrews in Egyptian bondage. Their laments are in the mouth of the prophet. But we should also consider that in verse 8 there may be a warning for them to overhear: "I will gather others to them, besides those already gathered to

Israel." If the insiders are being instructed and admonished in verses 1-7, then the outsiders are being instructed and admonished in verse 8 — not to become new insiders who reject the "yet others" still to come. In this case, there is a multi-directionality of the oracle: it is a word to both insiders and outsiders.

Within the text, then, we find four implied standpoints: those of God, prophet, insiders, and outsiders. The standpoint of the prophet virtually collapses into that of God. The prophet, speaking for God, initiates no dialogue. Although there are references to the laments of the outsiders and an invitation to the insiders to respond, the only actual speaking in the oracle is that of the prophet speaking for God. To take one's hermeneutical and homiletical cues from this position means to take up the task of prophetic speech oneself. That is certainly a common choice that preachers make. Whether through inspiration, knowledge, imagination, or intuition, the preacher reads and speaks as the prophet, and the congregation is positioned as the community to whom the oracle is addressed. As Isaiah was a prophet, the preacher is a prophet and claims prophetic authority for what she says. This could happen in a literal sense: the preacher makes an explicit claim that her words are those of the Holy Spirit. It could also happen in a dramatic sense: the preacher enacts the role of prophet, and the listeners enact the role of the community. In this case, what we have is a kind of theater in which the preacher adopts the persona of the prophet (which is not the same thing as pretending to be Isaiah) and speaks *as if* she is a prophet: "God says. . . ."

For those who would speak from the standpoint of the prophet, what possibilities does the text propose? The first is the very condition that makes this an oracle: that there is a word from the Lord. This is what makes a prophet, after all; in the absence of such a word, one's speech may be many things — but not prophetic. The second is the requirement of public speech: one is not given a public word for one's own sake but so that it will be spoken to those whom God intends to address (and in the hearing of those God intends to overhear it). So Moses, the prophet par excellence in Israel, is given a word to say but pleads for divine signs to accompany his words because he knows that, no matter what God has said to him, no matter how much he intones "Thus says the Lord," only Moses will be visible and audible. The standpoint of the prophet poses the question, Can *I* say "Thus says the Lord" in my own speech? By what authority? What does it mean to be overtaken by the word of God so that one is utterly identified with it? To be overtaken yet still be nothing more than one-self, with nothing more to show than the words themselves spoken in a human voice? The second requirement, public speech, poses a different question: Will one actually *be* the prophet of God by saying what he has been given to say? To whom will I prophesy? How do I know to whom God intends to direct this word? Even if I ultimately say exactly what the oracle says — if I simply recite — to whom will I say it so that they know that it is specifically they (in their particularity and responsibility) who are being addressed? If neither of these questions is the subject matter of this partic-ular oracle, both are nonetheless real questions for the genre itself — and real questions for the preacher.

Another viewpoint (perhaps less audacious but no less demanding) is that of the insider. Here the interpreter takes up a position with no special access to either the condition of the prophet or the mind of God. Instead, it is the position of one who is confronted by what the prophet says and must seek to understand what it means and how one is to respond (speak). In the speech model of Isaiah 56, this requires a further decision: To whom will one speak? Am I hearing as an insider who must speak to other insid-ers? If so, what is the message? In the story-world of the text, perhaps it goes something like this:

> There is a hard word from God that the prophet has spoken. It seems that God is doing a new thing. The eunuchs and foreigners among us are God's idea. Even though the law has said one thing, something greater than the law is here, and we are face to face with it in the faces of the outsiders. Yes, we have chapter and verse on our side. No, we were not wrong. And yet . . . God has done a new thing. We must decide if we will go into the new future with God or not.

Another possibility is to hear as an insider who speaks to the outsider. Perhaps something like this:

> A prophet has spoken to us. There is a word of the Lord, and it con-tained your own words, your cry of lament because of us. You whom the law shut out have been heard by God, and God has taken your side. This new word from God says that this house shall be a house for all peoples. God has said "yes" to you, and now we say "yes." We welcome you.

Yet another possibility is to hear as an outsider who speaks to the insider. Perhaps something like this:

The God who heard your cries in Egypt and in Babylon has heard our cries in Jerusalem; as God answered you, so God has answered us. Your God has spoken to you by a prophet and has thrown open the doors of the Temple to all who come to serve God and keep God's commandments. Do not harden your hearts. Accept us as God has accepted us.

A final possibility in the speech model of this oracle is that of the outsider who speaks to other outsiders. Perhaps something like this:

God has spoken! God has heard our cries and taken our side. Have the insiders heard? We do not know. Will they listen? We cannot say. Will they recognize that a new time has come? That God is doing a new thing? That we (and others still to come) belong in the house of God? The answer to all these questions lies with them, but the answer to all *our* laments has been given by God, who has spoken by the prophet and has said, "Welcome."

All of these possibilities for address may be found within the frame of the oracle. The standpoint we adopt shapes the homiletical form and content of what we say. Deciding on which standpoint to adopt depends on the place in the midst of life where the preacher places this oracle for incarnational translation in terms of contemporary insiders and outsiders.

What might an incarnational translation of our oracle look like if we set it in a contemporary life setting where "insider" and "outsider" categories are about participation in leadership and authority, among other things? The following story is fictitious but describes a phenomenon that is known to patriarchal churches that have faced a shortage of male leadership.

Once upon a time, in the ancient 1970s, Shiloh Baptist Church called a young man named Kevin Olsen, just out of seminary, to serve as its pastor. Two years later Kevin received a short-term missionary appointment in Cambodia under the auspices of the Macedonian Missionary Agency and Tract Society. He and his family would be gone for three months in the summer of 1975. Kevin left the Shiloh church in the hands of a twenty-three-year-old pastor-in-training named Don Kramer. The church at the time had about a hundred members.

Several very active women in the church were extremely unhappy that an inexperienced young man was assigned pastoral responsibility for the congregation, even if it was only for three months. They felt that they knew more about running the church and more about the Bible than Don did, who had never been to college, much less to seminary — and, on top of that, he was a relatively new convert. Sheila Stanger and Ann Johnson were both college graduates, and Sheila had a master's degree in English Literature. Both had grown up in the church and had taken turns over the years as superintendents of the Sunday School department. Sheila also led a women's Bible study group and a reading circle. Both women were better equipped to assume pastoral duties than the inexperienced Don Kramer was, but the church had never had a woman minister. Tradition was against it. What's more, no one — least of all Kevin — had even considered one of the women as a possible stand-in for preaching and other pastoral duties.

A coup in Cambodia in the summer of 1975 led to a changed government and a changed attitude toward foreigners, especially missionaries. Kevin was jailed and his family placed under house arrest. Back at Shiloh Church, Don was completely unprepared to deal with the shock and emotional trauma these events created for the church. After six chaotic months, he took a job in another part of the state and left the church. There were no other men in the congregation willing to take on the pastoral duties of preaching and visitation. The deacon board tried to find an interim minister, but to no avail. It sought to secure at least minimal pastoral service from ministers in neighboring towns, but this also led nowhere. Two Sundays went by without a sermon. One of the deacons, Bob Strauss, volunteered to read a sermon from a book he had found in the local library. That reading was so agonizingly poor, however, that people said afterward they would rather stay home or have no sermon than listen to that again. Bob himself was glad to be relieved of the duty. On the fourth Sunday, with no pastor and the prospect of no sermon, Sheila Stanger stood up after the reading of Scripture and before the selection of six hymns that were to take the place of a sermon, and asked if she could say something. She went to the lectern, not the pulpit, and talked about the difficult time the church was in. She told a story from the Bible and related it to the church's experience. Everyone liked this "talk"; no one called it a sermon. It was suggested that others might give such talks. The only other person to volunteer was Ann Johnson. Soon Sheila and Ann were taking turns "giving talks" from the lectern during the Sunday morning service. The deacons also agreed to have another woman, Grace Linscomb, help with visitations, which the deacons were getting a little tired of. The sick and the shut-ins would have preferred to have a "real" pastor visit them, but they did not seem to mind having Grace visit instead of one of the deacons. It turned out that Grace had a knack for this ministry.

And so the church settled into a new pattern of life. And a funny thing happened. Most people became so accustomed to the new arrangement — though of course there were some grumblers — that the work of finding a new minister never got off the ground. This was due mostly to the fact that the economy was failing in the Shiloh area and an unusually high percentage of church members were out of work. The deacons and trustees did not think the church could afford a new minister. So it was agreed that, at least for the time being, the church would make do without a pastor. So Sheila, Ann, and Grace became the de facto pastoral team — without the titles or compensation, of course.

In June of 1976, Kevin Olsen and his family were released from Cambodia, and they returned to Shiloh. The deacons and trustees met with Kevin to talk about the church's changed financial circumstances. Kevin agreed to take a large reduction in salary. He found a job at an auto plant fifty miles away, and he became the church's part-time pastor. But what about Sheila, Ann, and Grace? They were still needed — since Kevin was no longer available full-time. Not only that, his work hours in the auto plant varied from month to month and would sometimes keep him from Sunday services. Kevin's opinion was that one of the men of the church, whom he would train, should take on preaching responsibilities when he was away and that the deacons should resume the task of visitation. In a congregational meeting after one Sunday's worship, Kevin made his opinion known. Not everyone agreed. Some people took the view that, since the church had not ordained Sheila, Ann, and Grace, had not called them as ministers, and had not asked them to preach from the pulpit but only expected them to share meditations on some Sunday mornings — when Kevin was not there to preach a sermon — and to help with visitation, there was nothing wrong with having them serve the church as they had been doing. Others, including Kevin, argued that the women were assuming pastoral roles, roles that belonged properly to men, not women — and in particular to ordained men.

Sheila, Ann, and Grace sat quietly, feeling perhaps that it was not their place to speak on behalf of themselves. They could sense that the circle of leadership and authority was being redrawn to shut them out again. Finally, Sheila was no longer able to bite her tongue. She stood in her pew seat and spoke directly to Kevin, who had assumed a position at the pulpit. She talked about the events of the past year. She shared the anxiety of the church over the welfare of Kevin and his family after they were arrested. She talked about how hard it had been for the church to find a pastor and how the new arrangement had come about. She spoke of how much it had meant to her to share her gifts and how she had watched Ann and Grace blossom in their new roles. She said that she believed the deacons had been very wise in guiding the church through a difficult time and calling on all to give more of their time as they were able. She mentioned the contributions of others, both men and woman, toward keeping the church going. Then she spoke of her sense that God had called her and Ann and Grace to their "new forms of service," and she concluded with these words:

> Pastor Kevin, God heard your prayers in Cambodia and our prayers for you, and God heard our prayers for our church and your prayers for our church here in Shiloh. God answered you and us. And God told me not to say, "The Lord will surely take this job away from you; you have no business doing it." God told me not to say, "I am just a woman who can bear children and teach them but not bear any fruit of the Word for men." God told me: "You have been my faithful servant." No, I am not perfect! All of you know my faults and shortcomings. But I have done what I could when my church needed me. I have used my gifts. I have purchased commentaries on the Bible, with my own money, so that I would not lead you astray in my Sunday talks. Ann and I together have been studying commentaries and talking things over — and praying. And God said to us: "You have chosen something that pleases me, and it won't be taken away from you. I will give you a place in my church to speak my Word, not just to children in the Sunday School program, but to the whole body of Christ. I accept your service on my altar, because my church is a place of ministry for everyone — not just for men but for women, too." And maybe out of the tragedy and terrible events that took our pastor away, God has found a way to do something good, giving him back to us but also giving some of us a chance to share what *we* have to give. You know, when I hear some

people talk, I feel like an outcast when it comes to ministry. But when I hear God speak, I know I am not an outcast. I am one of those daughters who will prophesy — yes, preach. I would never take that away from you, Pastor Kevin. Don't try to take it away from me or Ann.

Sheila's speech recontextualizes the oracle of Isaiah 56:1-8 by adopting the standpoint of the outsider speaking to outsiders and insiders, where these designations have to do with the circle of leadership and authority. The message of the oracle might also have been recast as a prophetic word from one of the deacons in the congregation, an insider speaking to outsiders and insiders. Other configurations are also conceivable. The narrative framework leading up to the speech by Sheila suggests how a sermon might contextualize such an incarnational translation.

Judgment Oracles

A familiar type of prophetic oracle is the judgment oracle (sometimes called the "disaster oracle"). It typically consists of an indictment (reasons for the judgment), an announcement of divine judgment (what God is doing or is about to do), and the consequences of that judgment. Sometimes a promise of salvation is included. The language of these oracles borrows from other genres, notably the speech of the Law court and Wisdom literature, as well as from the funeral lament.

Judgment oracles pose special challenges for incarnational translation because they are inherently political, that is, they take sides on national and international issues. This presents a challenge for translating judgment oracles in settings where there are tacit social agreements not to voice political opinions, which is often true of church gatherings (for worship, Bible study, etc.). In their ancient settings also, the judgment oracles of the Hebrew prophets probably sounded politically extreme to most people, which is why prophets were often alienated or harassed and sometimes treated as political subversives. Consider the following oracle from Amos 8:2-8:

> "The end has come upon my people Israel;
> I will never again pass them by.

The songs of the temple shall become wailings in that day,"
    says the Lord God;
"the dead bodies shall be many,
    cast out in every place. Be silent!"
Hear this, you that trample the needy
    and bring to ruin the poor of the land,
saying, "When will the new moon be over
    so that we may sell grain;
    and the sabbath, so that we may offer wheat for sale?
We will make the ephah small and the shekel great,
    and practice deceit with false balances,
buying the poor for silver
    and the needy for a pair of sandals,
    and selling the sweepings of wheat."
The Lord has sworn by the pride of Jacob:
    Surely I will never forget any of their deeds.
Shall not the land tremble on this account,
    and everyone mourn who lives in it,
    and all of it rise like the Nile,
    and be tossed about and sink again like the Nile of Egypt?

Amos 8:2-8

An incarnational translation of Amos 8:2-8 aiming at cultural and temporal immediacy for Americans at the beginning of the twenty-first century might sound like this:

"That's it! I want nothing to do with the United States.
Go ahead and sing 'God Bless America' from the steps of the capitol;
    make it a funeral hymn," says the Lord God.
"Your dead shall be piled up,
    they deserve no decent burial. Shut up!
I'm not listening to your defenses, explanations,
    or patriotic litanies of how good and brave you are,
    'the greatest country on the face of the earth.'"
Now hear this, nation of twenty million children below the
        poverty line,
    you who say, "When will the weekend be over
    so we can trade on the NASDAQ again?"
and "Let's deregulate every industry we can, from banking to airlines,

so that no one will be looking over our shoulders to see what
    we're up to,"
and "It's time for an end to welfare as we know it (but not for
    corporate welfare
    or middle-class welfare)."
The Lord has sworn by your Bible and your flag:
    Surely I will never forget any of your deeds.
Shall not the land tremble on this account,
    and everyone mourn who lives in it,
and all of it rise and fall like San Francisco real estate
    when the earthquake of God comes,
when the great California earthquake of God
    comes and shakes the earth?

This effort at immediacy carries loaded political freight like that in the original oracle of Amos's time; but not everyone will agree with its politics, and many will therefore doubt that it fairly and aptly translates Amos 8:2-8 as a prophetic word for contemporary America. There is also the theological question of whether one should analogize ancient Israel to any modern people or country. Nevertheless, our incarnational translation of this oracle illustrates how one might rephrase a judgment oracle to achieve something like the prophetic directness and punch of the original. It helps to create in us something of the political emotions that ancient Israelites must have felt in listening to Amos's prophecies.

The political freight of prophetic speech becomes even more pronounced if we seek to translate Amos 8:2-8 as part of the larger rhetorical strategy of Amos, which begins with prophecies against surrounding nations. Retaining the Israel/America analogy and representing that larger strategy would call for a series of oracles against nations that most Americans consider hostile to U.S. interests and values, culminating with an oracle against the United States. One might construct oracles against China, North Korea, Iran, and Syria, for example. No doubt many Americans would object to including the United States in that list, claiming that the sins of the United States do not rise to the same level as do those of these undemocratic states. But others might point out that most Israelites would also likely have objected to Amos's implication that Israel was in the same moral boat with the other nations.

In any event, the exercise of incarnational translation helps us understand the risks and burdens of prophetic judgment oracles. If the oracle makes our patriotic blood boil so that we would almost like to kill the prophet, maybe it has struck a nerve of truth!

Distance and Immediacy Effects

We have been treating judgment oracles as words spoken with immediacy and directness. But we should also remember that the prophetic writings passed through processes of redaction before they became part of Israel's Scripture. These processes included both preservation and updating of historical references. Over time, preservation of references to specific events and participants in those events produced a *distance effect*. The oracles became marked as belonging to the past. By contrast, the process of updating made the oracles current. Nevertheless, once the oracles were fixed as Scripture, passage of time made older editorial updates obsolete. For example, by the time the book of Isaiah took its final form, many of the historical circumstances assumed in its oracles lay in the past. This means that the first audiences of the book of Isaiah (as we know it) did not hear Isaiah speaking directly about their own time. Already, the relevance of Isaiah for them was indirect and analogical, as it has necessarily remained for all subsequent audiences of Isaiah (except for misguided apocalyptic literalists who take Isaiah to speak predictively of their own time). Nevertheless, the canonical form of the text (by virtue of its narrative portions) implies that the prophecies are immediate and direct, even though we are aware that, thanks to the traditioning process, these prophecies are edited versions of the originals and refer to occasions that are long past for readers of Scripture.

We are often better able to receive a message of judgment when it comes to us indirectly: the judgment oracle is less confrontational in its distanced form. Sometimes we may wish to mix immediacy and distance effects in our recontextualizations of judgment oracles, based on a calculus of how best to negotiate the need for a direct prophetic word and the hearers' willingness to hear such a word. One way to accomplish such a mixture of effects is to combine recital with contemporizing references. For example:

"The end has come upon my people;
    I will never again pass them by.

The songs of the temple shall become wailings in that day,"
     says the Lord God.
"I will close my ears to their patriotic songs;
Hear this, you that trample the needy,
    and bring to ruin the poor of the land,
saying, "When will the new moon be over
    so that we may sell grain;
when will the sabbath be over, so that we may offer wheat
    for sale?
When will the weekend be over
    so we can trade on the NASDAQ again?"

This kind of blending of the original oracle with references to the present makes the indictment in a less heavy-handed way that cues hearers to ways of receiving the original oracle as a word for their time and place as well.

The "Woes" of Matthew 23

The woes of Matthew 23 also belong to the genre of the judgment oracle. Here Jesus indicts scribes and Pharisees. Scribes were teachers of the law, only some of whom belonged to the theological sect of the Pharisees. There are contemporary concerns about the possibility that unqualified recitals of Matthew 23 and like texts (such as the blanket statements about "the Jews" in John's Gospel) may continue to encourage anti-Semitic attitudes, and these concerns are well placed, given the history of Christians' relationships with Jews. The church has tended to hear Jesus' prophetic speeches against scribes and Pharisees as a Christian attack on Jewish religion — an attack resented by Jews and embraced by Christians as a general criticism of the essential nature of Judaism and Jews. This long-dominant Christian reading ignored the specificity of the polemic and disregarded the real variety of ancient Judaisms. It also failed to see Jesus' speech as prophetic speech that stood in a long Jewish tradition. Any criticism by Jesus of his contemporaries would not have amounted to an attack on "Jews" or "Judaism." It would have been an instance, with many precedents, of one Jew summoning other Jews to greater fidelity to God, and giving that summons in a venerable style of address — the prophetic mode. But with the breach between the church and the synagogue and the formation of the Christian way as a religion separate from Judaism, the conditions were created in which the church would hear the voice of Jesus as a divine revelation speaking against Judaism. Therefore, we must be careful not to repeat this way of appropriating the Gospels.

It is important to keep in mind that the effectiveness of the judgment oracle, like that of political satire today, owes much to its use of stereotypes and hyperbole. It typically generalizes and makes its charges in blunt, unqualified, even exaggerated terms. The judgment oracle is not the discourse of dialogue, diplomacy, pastoral care, or political tact and civility. It is not "fair" in the way a judge must be fair in a courtroom or a journalist must be fair in a news report or a counselor in a conjoint family therapy session. The judgment oracle also shares another feature with most political satire: it targets the powerful, not the weak. There are oracles against nations; there are no oracles against oppressed groups within a nation. There are oracles against scribes and Pharisees; there are no oracles against lepers and paralytics. There are oracles against the wealthy; there are no oracles against widows and orphans. The judgment discourse of Matthew 23 is directed against religious elites who exercised considerable influence over the interpretation of the law and the relationship of the individual Jew to the law. In the "woes" of that passage, Jesus, himself a teacher and a Jew, speaks to other Jewish teachers. His discourse is not a Christian indictment of Jewish religion but a Jewish indictment of a dominant religious tradition within first-century Judaism. Within the Matthean redaction of the tradition, the scribes and Pharisees probably also stand for Christian teachers whose understanding of the law conflicted with that of Jesus in Matthew.

The following is an incarnational translation of a portion of Matthew 23; it transposes verses 2-23 into a judgment oracle against preachers today:

> The preachers tell you what the Bible teaches. Listen to them, but don't follow their example. For they do not live what they preach. They impose huge expectations on their congregations, implying that their parishioners should spend almost every moment of their free time serving in programs of the church while the preachers are paid to talk and orchestrate from the sidelines. They practice their piety on a stage. Their clerical collars make them look noble and saintly. Their sermons include plenty of stories about themselves, their own ministry, their acts of giving, their comfort to the bereaved, their advice to the perplexed. They like to be called Pastor or

Father or Reverend and especially Doctor. Don't be like them and live for titles. Only God deserves a lofty title. The greatest among you will be the one who lives for others. All self-promoters will be humiliated. The humble will receive honor in the end.

Shame on you, preachers![20] Hypocrites! For you shut out of the kingdom of heaven anyone who does not fit your formula for being a Christian. Truth be told, you don't belong to the kingdom yourselves, and you prevent others from entering the kingdom.

Shame on you, preachers! For you cross hundreds of miles of cable TV to win a convert, and you make your convert twice as much a child of hell as you yourselves.

Shame on you, preachers! You find loopholes in the call to discipleship. When you meet something in the Bible that strikes you as inconvenient or too demanding for you and your congregations, you make special distinctions between how things were in biblical times and how they are now. Or you read minds, saying, "I don't think Jesus meant for us to . . ." or "I don't think Paul was telling us to. . . ."

Shame on you, preachers! You are scrupulous about the elements at the eucharist, exacting about the order of service, so intent on finding a moving illustration for this week's sermon, but you have little energy for what really counts. For you justice is nothing more than a theme in one of your "most courageous" sermons, not something you and your congregation actually practice. Mercy is a concept in your theology of the atonement, not part of your habitual way of relating to others. Faith is beliefs you don't have to prove, not a risk of discipleship that proves whether you live by what you believe.

In the effort to construct this incarnational translation, we learn firsthand several important things about engaging in the style of prophetic judgment. First, whatever examples we devise to illustrate hypocrisy and moral blindness, they inevitably appear to be only partially true — of any typical preacher or of preachers (clergy) as a group. And yet we feel, as preachers,

---

20. It is difficult to find a good equivalent for the archaic "woe" to you, which reflects the Greek οὐαί, which is in turn a transliteration of the Hebrew *hoy* (or *'oy*). "Shame on you!" is probably too soft a rendering of "woe." Would "Damn you!" be too strong or out of place?

the sting of the elements of truth in the charges that touch us. If the oracle succeeds with us, its uncompromising, unqualified voice compels us to search our souls by making us uncomfortable. But the oracle might simply alienate us. This brings us to a second point, already discussed in the case of the Amos oracle: sometimes it is difficult to avoid partisanship in prophetic speech — in this case theological partisanship. Wherever we stand on the theological spectrum, we tend to see those to the theological "right" of us as exhibiting stereotypical traits of overly strict legalism and to see those to the "left" of us as displaying a penchant for watering down the faith with various loopholes and exceptions to God's demands. Jesus' speech in Matthew 23 addresses both tendencies.

The question of whether our incarnational translation is likely to sound partisan brings us to a third point. Is the oracle "for" its targets? Is Jesus seeking to win over those whom he criticizes? Or is the oracle for others, for an audience meant to overhear the woes, perhaps an audience that is sympathetic to what Jesus has to say? In that case, the point is perhaps not to compel the overhearing audience to respond with personal soul-searching but to affirm them, encourage them, strengthen their convictions and resolve, and comfort them.

Of course, the judgment oracle of Matthew 23 can and does serve multiple functions at once. The tradition history of the sayings and the editorial work of Matthew make for a multiplicity of audiences within the narrative: the scribes and Pharisees who are addressed in the second-person plural in the woes of verses 13 and following; the crowds and the disciples to whom Jesus is speaking (see 23:1); the city of Jerusalem, which is addressed directly in verses 37-39; and, more generally, "this generation" in verses 34-36. But the audience is also the readers of Matthew's Gospel, living at least a generation after the time of Jesus, after the destruction of Jerusalem and during a time of conflict between the church and the synagogue. In working out an incarnational translation, we must be clear about what *we* are doing with the audiences in our own setting and how we position ourselves in delivering the translation.

Salvation Oracles

When we discussed incarnational translation of judgment oracles, we considered the question of whether (and in what ways) it is appropriate to analogize from the Jewish people (Israel/Judah) of the oracles to the church, other nations, or any other group. The same question arises with the salvation oracle. Related to this is another issue. Early Christian writers tended to read the prophets not only Christologically but also apocalyptically, that is, as speaking about the future judgment and new world that is to appear with Christ's return. In time, much of this apocalyptic expectation was transferred to Christian expectations of "heaven." With the rise of modern historical interpretation of the Bible, an era of reading the Hebrew Bible on its own terms was begun, often with the theological implication that Christian theology should honor the historical nature of prophetic writings.

Biblical scholarship generally holds that prophecy in the Bible typically has the following features: (1) it is not predictive but conditional, presenting the people with alternatives and their consequences; (2) it is concerned with the present, historical forces (social, economic, national, etc.) that shape the life of the people and that pose moral questions about how to live corporately before God; and (3) it assumes that history is shaped in the interaction of human and divine agency, so that the future is relatively (but not absolutely) open. By contrast, apocalyptic thinking and writing, which begins to appear in some of the later prophetic literature of the Bible, has a different orientation. In its full-blown forms, apocalyptic thinking has the following traits: (1) it is concerned with describing the past and predicting the future course of history as determined by God's secret plan; (2) it looks to an ultimate end of the world and the creation of a new world that is fundamentally different from the present world; (3) it often expects that new world to appear within the generation of the apocalyptic seer; and (4) it despairs of human agency to shape the present world for good, pinning all hope on God's other-worldly intervention to bring history to a close, establish a final judgment, and transform the present world into a glorious new form of existence.[21]

For Christian theology — and thus for preaching — the question is whether to follow the New Testament's apocalyptic hermeneutic in reading Old Testament prophecy or to interpret prophetic texts in their original "historical" sense. This is not necessarily a forced choice. It is possible to give a double reading, keeping prophetic and apocalyptic readings in di-

---

21. For a discussion of these tendencies of the prophetic and apocalyptic forms, see Paul D. Hanson, *The Dawn of Apocalyptic* (Philadelphia: Fortress Press, 1975).

alectical tension. And we may be encouraged in this direction by the evidence that some oracles are themselves a mixture of prophetic and apocalyptic vision, perhaps because they reflect the transition from prophetic to apocalyptic in the history of Jewish eschatology.

The relationship between the oracle of Isaiah 65:17-25 and the visions and oracles of Revelation 21–22 is instructive. Isaiah 65 reads like a prophetic-apocalyptic text: it celebrates God's cosmic sovereignty but does not speak the language of secret divine determinism. It promises a new order (a new heaven and earth) but does not speak of cosmic cataclysm. In the new heaven and earth, people live out long lives, but they do not live forever. By contrast, Revelation 21–22, which clearly builds on the vision of Isaiah 65, has the new Jerusalem coming down out of heaven, which signals its other-worldliness, and the oracle in 21:3-4 announces the end of sorrow and death. The visions go on to describe the splendor of the city. Later we hear that the tree of life will be in the city and that there will be no more night because God's presence "will be their light." It appears that Revelation has more thoroughly apocalypticized the prophetic-apocalyptic hope of Isaiah 65.

Reading Isaiah 65 through a Christian hermeneutics shaped by the apocalyptic lens of Revelation 21–22 may lead us to see Isaiah's vision of a new heaven and earth as an other-worldly hope lacking implications for Christian responsibility for social justice in the here and now. But one can also read Revelation 21–22 from the perspective of Isaiah, viewing Isaiah 65:17-25 as connected to the social justice themes of Isaiah. Reading reciprocally, so to speak, from Isaiah to Revelation and from Revelation to Isaiah, so that the Hebrew prophet shapes our reading of Revelation and Revelation shapes our reading of the Hebrew prophet, encourages us to develop a Christian theology of hope that is prophetic-apocalyptic. One cannot read Isaiah 65 in the context of Isaiah as a whole without feeling that we, God's people, should be doing what we can now to create the conditions of well-being and peace described by the oracle about God's new creation. Therefore, reading the Christian hope of Revelation in the light of Isaiah 65 (on which it is based) links the Christian hope with an ethic of corporate social responsibility, the prophetic concern of the Hebrew prophets.

In his book *Amazing Grace*,[22] a study of poverty-stricken children

---

22. Jonathan Kozol, *Amazing Grace: The Lives of Children and the Conscience of a Nation* (New York: Crown, 1995).

growing up in the South Bronx, Jonathan Kozol tells the story of a thirteen-year-old named Anthony who has a gift for writing and loves the poetry of Edgar Allan Poe. At one point, Anthony writes down his own vision of heaven, which he calls "God's kingdom" and which is connected in his mind with the description of the new heaven and new earth at the end of Revelation. We think Anthony's vision of God's kingdom can be regarded as a free incarnational translation of Revelation 21–22 and the salvation oracle in Isaiah 65:17-25 on which the visions of Revelation are based. Anthony's heaven is a city that is free of the gloom, suffering, violence, and misery of the city in which he lives:

> God's kingdom. God will be there. He'll be happy that we have arrived. People shall come hand-in-hand. It will be bright, not dim and glooming like the earth. All friendly animals will be there, but no mean ones. As for television, forget it! If you want vision, you can use your eyes to see the people that you love. No one will look at you from the outside. People will see you from the inside. All the people from the street will be there. My uncle will be there and he will be healed. You won't see him buying drugs, because there won't be money. Mr. Mongo will be there too. You might see him happy for a change. The prophets will be there, and Adam and Eve, and all of the disciples except Judas. And, as for Edgar Allan Poe, yes, he will be there too, but not like somebody important. He will be a writer teaching students. No violence will there be in heaven. There will be no drugs or guns or IRS. You won't have to pay taxes. You'll recognize all the children who have died when they were little. Jesus will be good to them and play with them. At night he'll come and visit at your house. God will be fond of you. How will you know that you're there? Something will tell you, "This is it! Eureka!" If you still feel lonely in your heart or bitterness, you'll know you're not there.[23]

Anthony's vision is prophetic-apocalyptic in the sense that it describes a world beyond this world that at the same time resembles our own in ways that call us to prophetic social action. Who can read Anthony's vision without feeling that we ought to be doing what we can now to create the conditions of well-being and peace that he imagines for heaven?

23. Kozol, pp. 237-38.

CHAPTER FOUR

Story

It may be impossible for Christians to recognize how deeply they have been formed by the narrative shape of their Scripture.[1] Story is not something incidental to the Bible, but constitutive of it, and all the various genres may be seen as celebration, interpretation, extension, lamentation, codification, and so forth, in response to the "Story in the stories" at the Bible's core.[2] This means that the various genres bear within themselves a narrative trace. The trace may be implicit or explicit; it may be primarily formal (that is, story-like in its workings) or primarily material (that is, using the

1. It is helpful to distinguish "story" and "narrative" as category and sub-category. A narrative is a story put into words; a story can be a narrative or can be thought of as existing apart from narrative in the sense that one can tell the "same" story in more than one way. In what follows, however, we do not make a strict differentiation in our use of these two words.

2. We say "may" because construing the Bible as having a "Story in stories" at its core is a perception, a way of conceiving the Bible as a whole. But it is not the only way to characterize the Bible. We think it is a good perception, one that does justice to essential features of Scripture in an integrative way and has meaningfully shaped the life of the church through the centuries. But we do not claim that the use of non-narrative categories for conceiving Scripture as a whole cannot also be good perceptions, and we affirm that it is wise to use more than one model of Scripture. Scripture can be seen as stories in a Story, also as many-faceted words of teaching in a book of Wisdom, or as a kind of grand Psalm in which every genre of Scripture appears as so many different gestures toward what is ultimately unutterable and available only through metaphor and symbol. On different models for conceiving Scripture, see John Goldingay, *Models for Scripture* (Grand Rapids: Eerdmans, 1994); Daniel Patte, "Scriptural Criticism as a Practice of Biblical Studies," in Charles H. Cosgrove, ed., *The Meanings We Choose: Hermeneutical Ethics, Indeterminacy and the Conflict of Interpretations* (London and New York: T. & T. Clark/Continuum, 2004), pp. 74-75.

elements of particular stories). But a story will always be present. Prophecy, lamentation, praise, thanksgiving, instruction, wisdom, argument — all the different genres are connected in some way *to* a larger story, and within the Bible all may be seen as connected *by* a larger story.

The very movement from Creation to Fall to Redemption lays out an all-encompassing plot in which everything else finds its place. Of course, these are theologians' terms for interpreting the Bible's story, not a scheme that the Bible presents explicitly in just these categories. Yet whatever language we use to describe the movement from Genesis 1 and 2 to Genesis 3 to everything else that follows is likely to have the character of a plot, a dramatic unfolding, a story. The way the Christian canon begins (a beginning bequeathed to Christians by Israel) makes a claim that goes beyond the story of particular individuals, tribes, nations, and religions and affirms a common and universal history shared by all of creation. This beginning determines how we interpret what follows, makes it a story about the God who created the world. In that story even refusal to recognize the universality of the scope of God's dealings with all of creation is part of the biblical story. Thus, for example, in Isaiah 19 we find reminders that the Story is about God's redemptive intentions for other peoples (not just Israel) and in Paul a word to Christ-believers that the Story is not just about them but continues to be about God's commitments to Israel (Rom. 9–11) and God's liberating hope for the whole of creation (Rom. 8:19-23).

Stories can stand on their own, without commentary and explanation from us; but it is also natural for us to interpret them. They provoke response and in this sense want to be interpreted. It is important, however, not to confuse interpretation with the story. Theological affirmations about the Story/stories of the Bible are not the same as the stories themselves; nor are expressions of doctrine that claim a foundation in the scriptural story simple equations in which the story and its interpretation are equivalent. Story and commentary are two different genres or strategies of address, distinguished by a formal incommensurability that precludes the reduction of one to the other.[3]

---

3. W. Dow Edgerton, *The Passion of Interpretation* (Louisville: Westminster/John Knox Press, 1992), p. 14.

The Narrative Strategy of Address

The stories in Scripture are of many different kinds and vary in scope, weight, and authority. Although they may share common features, they do their work in different ways. We can lay out basic elements of a narrative speech model as follows:

[Rhetoric]

Narrator   Story   Audience

[Setting — Character(s) — Plot]

A story includes, first of all, a narrator.[4] The narrator may be named or unnamed, may be presented in some way or simply assumed. In Genesis, for example, we have an anonymous narrator. We do not know if the narrator is one or many; there is simply a voice. Because that voice never speaks in the first person, we are scarcely aware that it is a voice, one with a perspective and one that makes narrative decisions. The anonymity of the voice focuses all of our attention on the subject matter of the story, making the teller of the story invisible. But when we consider the narrator, we become aware that this telling does have a point of view, an angle on the characters and events that unfold. Moreover, the narrator, named or anonymous, projects some kind of authority claim for the narrator, the story, or both.

The narrator expresses the story through a certain voice, vocabulary, feeling, and tone, as well as by various devices — such as suspense, foreshadowing, commentary, repetition, and so forth. In short, the narrator uses *rhetoric* to convey the story. Rhetoric is always social: it relies on a set of shared assumptions and expectations and involves a relationship between the speaker and the audience in which the communication to the audience is not just what is said (content) but who says it and the way it is said.

---

4. Here we are slightly adapting the work of Seymour Chatman in his highly influential work *Story and Discourse: Narrative Structure in Fiction and Film* (Ithaca, NY: Cornell University Press, 1978). Chatman's work was used by David Rhoads and Donald Michie in their book *Mark as Story: An Introduction to the Narrative of a Gospel* (Philadelphia: Fortress Press, 1982), and subsequently by many others. For a very helpful overview of narrative criticism in postmodern biblical studies, see George Aichele et al., *The Postmodern Bible* (New Haven, CT: Yale University Press, 1995), pp. 70-118.

Narratives also include elements of setting, character, and plot through which problems or conflicts are presented and actions are undertaken by various agents, which leads to some kind of outcome — whether resolution, further complication, or both. The narrative may imply or name an audience, sometimes within the narrative text (such as a story about Moses addressing the Israelites), sometimes outside the text (such as Israel or the community of the Beloved Disciple or a more general reader). The narrative *implies an audience,* treating that audience in a way that attributes explicit or implicit attitudes to the audience (such as hostility, receptivity, seeking, questioning, etc.) and attributes a sociocultural identity to the audience (e.g., Mediterranean, Greek-speaking, or Hebrew-speaking). Sometimes historical reconstruction can help us pinpoint the actual audience more specifically: Antiochene Christians as the audience of Matthew, for example, or Jewish exiles in Babylon or recently repatriated to Jerusalem as the audience of Deuteronomy. But the implied audience is usually more general, permitting a story to make sense to both its intended audience and also other audiences from the same cultural context with little or no need for special explanation or commentary.

The elements of narrator, setting, characters, plot, implied audience, and the particular rhetorical devices used in the construction of the story all combine to create what David Rhoads and others have called the "story-world" of the text.[5] In the same way that one can get lost in a novel and feel that one is inside a closed world that exists unto itself, so biblical narratives — all narratives — create story-worlds.

Story-worlds vary not only in subject matter but also in the particular shape, use, relative balance, and importance of the different elements of narrator, character, plot, audience, and rhetoric. One story may be dominated by the voice of the narrator (Jeremiah's autobiographical speeches); in another the narrator may be all but invisible and the characters and plot may be in the foreground (Exodus, the Gospels). In one narrative, the audience may be treated as "in the know" (the Gospels of Mark and John); in another the audience may be treated as sincere seekers (the Gospel of Luke); in yet another as moral failures or their descendants (Deuteronomy). Moreover, tone and feeling, conveyed in language that may be dra-

---

5. David Rhoads, "Narrative Criticism and the Gospel of Mark," *Journal of the American Academy of Religion* 50 (1982): 413.

matic, ironic, satirical, playful, and so on, also vary from narrative to narrative and within narratives.

In what follows we examine several of the different kinds of stories found in the Bible. We do not aim for an exhaustive treatment of biblical narrative; rather, we have made an illustrative selection, analyzing the nature of different story forms and showing how they might be retold in incarnational translation.

The Priestly Account of Creation (Genesis 1:1-2:4) and the Story of Gideon (Judges 7): A Comparison

Incarnational translation requires some understanding of how the ancient biblical stories are put together, so that we can consider functionally equivalent ways of translating the stories into our own settings. It may be helpful to illustrate how the elements of the basic narrative model — rhetoric, narrator, plot, characters, and implied audience — are used in two different kinds of story: the creation story of Genesis 1:1–2:4 and the story of Gideon in Judges 7.

The Priestly Creation Story

Genesis 1:1–2:4 is commonly regarded as a Priestly writing, having its original home in liturgy,[6] connecting narrative to ritual, as André LaCocque observes.[7] It is *myth* in the sense of a broad genre, not as something "untrue" but as a story that gets at the truth not literally but symbolically and metaphorically. As such, Genesis 1 is less a storyteller's tale than a mythic hymn, something to be recited or sung in a liturgical setting.[8] The architecture of

6. See, for example, Claus Westermann, *Genesis 1–11*, John J. Scullion, trans. (Minneapolis: Augsburg Publishing House, 1984), pp. 1-19.

7. André LaCocque and Paul Ricoeur, *Thinking Biblically: Exegetical and Hermeneutical Studies* (Chicago: University of Chicago Press, 1998), p. 11.

8. Gerhard von Rad rejected the presence of hymnic language in this text and saw it as doctrinal and didactic. See von Rad, *Genesis: A Commentary* (Philadelphia: Westminster Press, 1974), p. 46. But Walter Brueggemann has also strongly affirmed the liturgical nature of the passage; see Brueggemann, *Genesis: A Bible Commentary for Teaching and Preaching* (Atlanta: John Knox Press, 1982), pp. 22ff.

the passage moves dramatically from the heaving chaos of the beginnings of creation ("The earth was a formless void and darkness covered the face of the deep"), through intricate ordering and elaboration, to climax and culmination in the creation of humankind and the Sabbath rest. Rhythmic patterns, dramatic recitative formulas ("And God said . . ."), and rich word play evoke and mirror the architecture, complexity, and founding of the world.[9] The mythic form is especially good at conveying the grandeur of the subject, and this genre also suits ritual performance.

Certain aspects of the narrative strategy deserve notice. We are hardly aware of the narrator, who is implied, not named. As an anonymous voice, the narrator is not tied to any particular person, time, or place. The narrative voice is not God, since God is spoken of in the third person. But the narrative voice is sovereign and invisible, speaking from a universal perspective, perhaps even all-knowing, and yet not intruding itself as a character in the story, much less explaining how it came by its knowledge of the origins of the cosmos. Like the omniscient narrator of some novels, the narrator of Genesis 1 speaks from no identifiable point of view. The story has no introductory prologue, makes no reference to its source, offers no apologia or defense of itself. It simply declares, "In the beginning. . . ." By making no claim to authority in terms of specifics that might suggest qualification or limited credibility, it makes an absolute claim. Moreover, as we meet this voice in the text of the Bible — not in the mouth of the one or ones who first said these things — it is almost as if the narration (not a narrator as a person) speaks. Through its absolute declaration, the narration makes a powerful theological statement about the content of the story.

Consider the difference a slightly altered first verse would make: "Moses said, 'In the beginning. . . .'" Indeed, much later tradition attributes Genesis to the authorship of Moses, and some commentators have treated Moses as author of the Pentateuch. But the text itself makes no such claims about its authorship.[10] The actual inauguration of the book of Genesis acknowledges no human mediation. It declines to take up the role of being a

9. For a splendid translation and commentary that brings these dimensions of the passage forward, see Everett Fox, trans., *The Five Books of Moses: Genesis, Exodus, Leviticus, Numbers, Deuteronomy* (New York: Schocken Books, 1995).

10. See, for example, how Luther's commentary on Genesis actively positions Moses as narrator-author and reflects on his authorial intentions; see *Luther's Works*, vol. 1: *Lectures on Genesis, Chapters 1-5* (St. Louis: Concordia Publishing House, 1958).

tradition, or a teaching, or anything that might make it one story among other stories. In its own terms it is not even a witness or testimony. Genesis 1 presents "unwitnessable events," to recall Meir Sternberg's phrase.[11] By its sovereignty and invisibility the narrating voice claims epistemological privilege. "The narrator stands to the world of his tale as God to the world represented by that tale, each reigning supreme in his own sphere of activity."[12]

Another feature of the first creation story is the absence of a prologue about setting or plot. Likewise, the "events" it describes do not so much take place as make place. The story is not in a setting but establishes a setting — setting *as such* — where before there was chaos, which makes both setting and plot impossible.[13] Similarly, there is no account of God's motivation, no "plot before the plot." There is nothing to tell about "before" (not even Luther's jesting speculation that God was "making hell ready for those who pried into meddlesome questions"),[14] because there is no "before," no prior order of time.

Against this backdrop of chaos and the "unnarratability" of what comes before, God is the character by whose action there are a world and history and the possibility of story itself. God is both the source and the limit. As Dietrich Bonhoeffer, with great insight, observed: "No question can penetrate behind God creating, because it is impossible to go behind the beginning."[15] There are setting and plot, time and narration at all because of God. In all of this a profound theological statement is made; and it is expressed *narratologically*. It is not established by argument; rather, it is announced by means of a story about the creation of the conditions that make story possible.

The audience for this story is also not named, but it is positioned in a

---

11. Meir Sternberg, *The Poetics of Biblical Narrative: Ideological Literature and the Drama of Reading* (Bloomington, IN: Indiana University Press, 1985), p. 41.

12. Sternberg, p. 83.

13. The Hebrew admits an alternate possible sense for its opening statement: "When God began to create. . . ." This translation could imply a pre-existing chaos (formless and empty, watery earth) existing in some "time" before creation. Its origins would be unknown. The more traditional translation suggests that God first created the earth without form before giving it order.

14. *Lectures on Genesis, Chapters 1-5*, p. 10.

15. Dietrich Bonhoeffer, *Creation and Fall: A Theological Interpretation of Genesis 1–3* (published in one volume with *Temptation*) (New York: Macmillan, 1974), p. 17.

particular way. As a mythic and ritual text, Genesis 1 places readers in the realm of liturgical performance, where their role is to witness and celebrate. Any hearer can be in this place before this text. By contrast, Psalm 136, a thanksgiving hymn that also belongs to a worship context, projects a more specific audience. By linking God's acts of creation with God's redemptive work on Israel's behalf, Psalm 136 implies an audience of Israelites who celebrate God's creative-redemptive activity in a world that had become hostile to Israel. A non-Israelite reader who wants to pray this psalm in the assembly must find a point of connection, a way of identifying with Israel of old. Not so for the readers of Genesis 1. At the literary level at least, it speaks from nowhere and anonymously (i.e., not from any "social location"); it addresses its audience in universal terms, and, in its only reference to human beings, portrays them in their universal origins.

Of course, one qualification must be made on this characterization of the literary level: the voice of the anonymous narrator is in the Hebrew language. And that is a sign that the anonymous and universal voice of Genesis 1 does have a social location, belongs to a tradition, and may be telling this story in competition with others who tell stories about founding events. The posture of anonymity and universality should not be naively accepted as a bar to historical investigation of the origins and place of this Hebrew narrative in the history of Israel and the wider Mediterranean world of antiquity. Nevertheless, understanding how this story works in making its theological statement requires that we consider its anonymity and claims to a universal perspective as essential parts of its message.

If Genesis 1 is about the conditions that make story possible, it is also about what makes liturgy possible and implies something important about the nature of liturgy. Genesis 1 is about the beginning of worship in a primordial theological sense. In this way it establishes conditions for worship. The text nowhere describes what the response of the audience to its story should be. It calls for no action, issues no commands or directives, offers no examples to be imitated. Yet its mythopoeic form and the signs of priestly theology offer a clue: that the right response is celebration, a celebration that includes the recitation of the story. The form of response to the beginning of the world is *celebratory recitation*. The recitation is not about the beginning of worship. It makes no historical claims about how human beings began to worship, how the Hebrew people learned to call upon the name of God, or how temple worship arose in ancient Israel.

What contemporary form of speech can re-enact through incarnational translation the union of narrative voice, mythopoeic form, positioning of the audience, and the specific content of this story? Imitating the third-person narration can cast narrator and audience in the same anonymous and universal forms. A more difficult question is this: How, in the modern world, in cultures shaped by modern scientific knowledge, can one start at the absolute beginning without giving an introduction or implying a past? A related question is how to narrate the story of creation in ways that do not simply repeat ancient cosmological ideas but at the same time do not sacrifice the mythopoeic form to scientific language. Can one use quasi-poetic language in a way that breathes the cosmological air of our time just as the ancient text breathed the cosmological air of its time? And here one must make some judgment about whether the ancient Hebrews who created and recited this story understood it literally, figuratively, or (as seems more likely to us) as a kind of *qualified literal speech,* participating in the literal and metaphoric with no sharp line between the two.[16]

The story poses other problems for those shaped by a scientific worldview and a distinction between the discourses of science and religion. How should we render the episodic structure of days of creation, the divine pronouncement of the goodness of creation at the close of each day, the seventh-day rest, the hierarchy of creation, and so forth? The narrative of how the world came into being implies moral and spiritual values reflected in the order of events, their purposes, and the resultant structure of the world. Can one retell the story in a narrative shaped by modern science and still attach moral and spiritual meaning to the process and structure (as the original does)? Or would that imply scientific justifications or evidence for such moral and spiritual meaning, judgments that lie outside science? There are those today who advocate a kind of technical mixing of science and religion in descriptions of cosmological and biological evolution, maintaining that a scientific theory can legitimately include religious elements of explanation and interpretation.

There are a number of problems with this. One is that it tends to make

16. Claus Westermann speaks of a unique "fusion of poetry and prose" in Genesis 1; see Claus Westermann, *Genesis 1–11: A Continental Commentary* (Minneapolis: Fortress Press, 1994), p. 90. Westermann also understands the scheme of the seven-day creation as serving in the Priestly writer's own purpose not as a literal succession of twenty-four-hour days (the Priestly writer knew that there could be no literal twenty-four-hour day before the earth and sun were created!) but as a kind of parable.

God an observable actor in the process about which one can theorize, as if God could be part of a scientific theory. We think questions about God lie outside the domain of science and its methods. A second problem is the implication that theology can speak about science in ways that make sense in scientific terms. It is true that theology has a legitimate calling to speak about any subject — but from a theological point of view. Theology does not dictate the rules of interpretation and judgment for non-theological disciplines, whether science, literature, music, or history. Christian theology can speak of the significance of these things for Christian faith and practice and in so doing bring its own interpretations and judgments to bear. But as theology, it cannot establish historical facts, define the nature of tropes, account for physical relationships between bodies carrying mass, interpret the development from polyphony to homophony, and so on. So the challenge is to avoid a scientific description that locates God in the gaps of human knowledge (gaps today that are likely to be filled by science tomorrow) and at the same time not to fall into two-sphere thinking that relegates faith to only "religious" parts of life in an otherwise secular society dominated by scientific and technological ways of thinking.[17]

How, then, can we retell the story of Genesis 1 without mixing scientific and theological description in confusing and misleading ways? One possibility, which many modern Christians have already embraced, is to recite the original version of Genesis 1 but treat it as figurative speech, as a kind of nonliteral poetry. As we have said, the original may have already been understood in antiquity by at least some readers as quasi-literal. In any case, to take the entire account as nonliteral speech is a kind of retranslation. By treating Genesis 1 as figurative rather than historical description, we have in effect performed in our minds an incarnational translation through transgenrelization.

We can also recast the story in a nonliteral retelling of our own making. In one setting, that retelling may turn knowledge gained from science into figurative language and poetry, so as to contemporize the story without implying that the story's engagement with modern cosmology is meant as a scientific statement. In another setting, scientific knowledge

---

17. Astute readers will note our indebtedness to Bonhoeffer here with respect to the "God of the gaps" and the problem of relegating religion to a separate sphere of life; see Bonhoeffer, *Letters and Papers from Prison,* enlarged edition, Eberhard Bethge, ed. (New York: Macmillan, 1972), pp. 281-82, 311-12, 325-29.

may be left aside and the text may be imagined in a different kind of poetic idiom for the community to which it is addressed. We have a famous example of this in the first poem of James Weldon Johnson's *God's Trombones*, which draws on traditional African-American preaching of the nineteenth century to craft a poetic narrative of creation. It is doubtful that the preachers who created this tradition understood everything they said literally. Johnson himself surely did not. And certainly modern readers who treasure this poem also do not take it literally. Here are the opening stanzas of "The Creation":

> And God stepped out on space,
> And he looked around and said:
> I'm lonely —
> I'll make me a world.
>
> And as far as the eye of God could see
> darkness covered everything,
> Blacker than a hundred midnights
> Down in a cypress swamp.[18]

This is a beautiful example of recontextualizing the form and content of Genesis 1:1-2.

Returning to the possibility of retelling Genesis 1 in a way that makes poetic use of scientific knowledge, we suggest the following as one example of how the opening lines might be recast:

> When God created the universe, the universe was a tiny speck of infinite mass bearing in its dark core the code of God's design and packed with God's energy. And the speck, in which everything to come was hidden, exploded into billions upon billions of pieces, infinitesimal particles and unimaginably huge orbs, as well as every shape and size in between, all hurtling into the void. And the void was filled with light from the flaming orbs, light to measure the universe and link its countless parts. And God smiled on the light and the burning orbs and the lonely cooling masses, and the intricate, hidden, ceaseless transformations, and called it a good beginning.

18. James Weldon Johnson, *God's Trombones: Seven Negro Sermons in Verse* (New York: The Viking Press, 1969), p. 17.

This incarnational translation exploits one of two possibilities for interpreting the opening words of Genesis 1. We can interpret "in the beginning God created the heavens and the earth" as one sentence. Or we can take these opening words adverbially: "When God began to create the heavens and the earth, the earth was without form and void." This suggests a relative beginning, a creation out of previously existing material, perhaps an earlier history of God creating that is left un-narrated. In that case, Genesis 1:1 is about the creation of the world as we know it. Our incarnational translation follows this interpretation, allowing for "something before" that the text does not describe.

To say "universe" instead of "the heavens and the earth" is to shift away from the ancient conception of the earth as a flat disk with heaven literally above as a kind of dome or canopy. We conceive the earth as a small part of a planetary system that revolves around the sun, our solar system is part of the Milky Way galaxy, and so forth. The word "universe" is our term for all these systems.

Our incarnational translation uses quasi-poetic language to describe something like a "Big Bang," and also seeks to accommodate, without lapsing into technical language, the idea of the universe evolving through unspecified time under divine direction, which gives order and beauty to the universe. We imply that the "wind of God" that moves over the face of the waters in the original account represents a divine energy. This energy brings about the creation, giving it order and infusing it with life. Some English translations have "Spirit of God" here (KJV, RSV). The NRSV has "wind of God" ("spirit of God" in a note). It is difficult to know how best to render this in an incarnational translation once we have substituted the image of a black hole for a primal sea. Finally, we have not rendered God in scientific terms (or have tried not to) but have used unabashedly anthropomorphic language. Of course, one could mistake our intention and imagine that our narrative is an effort to present a kind of "creation science," a theologically informed scientific account of the beginnings of the universe. But a close look should reveal that it is really not a scientific account, even in its physical descriptions, but poetic prose that draws on modern notions of the world and its beginnings.

Gideon and the Midianites

The story of Gideon and his small army attacking the Midianites (Judges 7) contains some narrative features that are similar to those of the Priestly account of creation, but other features that are quite different. Here we also find an anonymous and omniscient narrator, but this narrator speaks with a different voice, that of the storyteller skilled in setting forth a plot with suspenseful action. The episode of the attack on the Midianite camp stands at the high point of the whole story of Gideon (Judg. 6:1–8:35), which chronicles Gideon's rise to leadership and his overthrow of the Midianite oppressors. That story is linked explicitly to the larger narrative of the Exodus: God heard Israel's cry in Egypt and freed them from their bondage so that they might worship God alone, but Israel turned away (6:6-10). Now God calls up Gideon to deliver Israel again. God directs him into a provocative destruction of the altar of Baal, which lures a great Midianite army (plus Amalekites and people of the east) to cross the Jordan and camp in the valley of Jezreel.

The plot then tracks God's winnowing away of Gideon's army from 22,000 to 10,000 to 300, so that the victory to come will be clearly credited to God, not to Israel. In the middle of the night an anxious Gideon goes down into the valley of Jezreel, where the Midianites are "thick as locusts," outfitted with vast numbers of camels, and "countless as the sand on the seashore" (7:12). There he overhears a Midianite storyteller recounting a dream and his comrade interpreting it as foretelling that Gideon will be victorious in the coming battle. Fortified by this disclosure, Gideon unfolds a crafty plan: he divides his small army into even smaller units and launches a surprise attack that causes panic among the Midianites, who begin to flee. Gideon's army pursues and destroys the confused Midianite army.

After this the story tells of Gideon's revenge against the cities that refused to come to his aid; Israel's invitation to him to establish a dynasty and Gideon's refusal; the gathering of tribute; the strange erection of an ephod that proved "a snare to Gideon and to his family" (8:27); and forty years of peace until Gideon's death. Yet, as soon as Gideon died, the story says, the Israelites forgot the God who delivered them and went back to worshiping Baal-berith.

Thus we have a larger narrative framework in which the principal characters are God and Israel. The setting is the land given to Israel by

God, who drove out their enemies. The overarching plot is oppression, cry, deliverance, and forgetfulness, which is presented as a *pattern*. The particular plot of the Gideon cycle of stories is one instance of this pattern within the larger plotted action of the Hexateuch.

Analysis of how this Yahwistic narrative is stitched into Deuteronomistic cloth goes beyond our scope here, but it is important to point out that the function of such narratives can be seen as didactic. The story of Gideon has its peculiar delights and horrors, achieves its particular effects by noteworthy means (foreshadowing, suspense, surprise, violent action, comedy, irony, etc.) and offers multiple possibilities for commentary on the ways of God and humankind. Yet what seems to matter most is not that it is distinctive but that it is *typical*. It is a dramatic pattern (a tragic pattern, we could say) presented in the service of a larger interpretive goal of instruction: the people of Israel do what is evil in God's sight; God gives them over to oppressors; Israel serves the oppressor for a period of years and finally cries out to God; God sends a deliverer empowered by "the spirit of the Lord"; the deliverer defeats the oppressor; the land has rest. A central lesson of this pattern is that God threatens destruction to those who worship strange gods; therefore, be faithful to God, who has been forgiving and faithful to Israel. The story within the Story is thus presented as a pattern to be recognized as governing history outside the narrative, so that the proper response by the audience is to see their place in relationship to this pattern. Are they like Israel of old? Can they be any different? If Genesis 1 prompts celebratory recitation, the Gideon cycle calls for communal self-examination. If Genesis 1 disallows inquiry into the story behind the story, Judges 6–8 positively encourages it. If Genesis 1 invites the audience to sing before the mighty power of God, Judges 6–8 calls members of the community to repent of their own worship of strange gods and to return to the One who has the power to deliver them. To the extent that there is exemplary behavior in the narrative, a natural inference is that later Israelites or Christians should imitate that good behavior in the expectation that God will be faithful in the same ways.

But we need to be cautious. As a story, Judges 6–8 is not prescriptive speech — like the Law or the Proverbs. Moreover, if later Israelites have grounds for reading themselves into the story, Christian readers must first negotiate the question whether they are like Israel. And even if later Israelites and later Christians are justified in reading themselves analogically into the story of Gideon, taking its typical patterns as a word for themselves, later readers cannot assume that the plot of the Gideon story will always be the plot of their own lives in service to God. Sometimes when we yearn for signs, God refuses to give signs. Sometimes when we are too weak for the battle, God does not give victory.

One challenge for recontextualizing the Gideon cycle — or part of it — is how to translate the "Israel = the audience" connection that is essential to the rhetoric of the cycle. If our incarnational translation is for the church, is the church, then, the audience that is like Israel of old? Or must one think in national terms? Is one's own nation the contemporary analogue for Israel? Certainly there are tendencies in the religio-political rhetoric of some groups in the United States to think of the United States as a kind of Israel, a chosen people (and Christian nation) with a divine mission in the world. Sometimes this involves an uncritical patriotism, sometimes a prophetic call for national repentance so that America can be God's servant in the world. Can any such analogizing be justified theologically? And if it can, how far does it extend? And what qualifications are necessary?

In preaching as commentary on the text, it is easy to elide the most challenging questions about how the "Israel = the audience" connection is to be conceived in contemporary terms. One can choose this or that aspect of the text and draw lessons from it. Or one can simply recite the text and let the audience make its own connections — wholesale or piecemeal. But incarnational translation of form and content forces us to wrestle with the story's meaning for us *as a whole*. Wrestling with how to translate that whole may lead us to conclude that the story in its integrity is no longer a pattern in which we can find ourselves, that we can appropriate a word for ourselves from the story only by breaking it up and choosing among the pieces. If that is the conclusion we draw, the effort at incarnational translation will have helped us see more honestly how we are using the text and to confront the hermeneutical questions that it raises.

For example, we may discover that we have a habit of turning literal war in the Hebrew Bible into analogues in which "war" is a metaphor for moral or spiritual struggles or "wars" against impersonal enemies such as disease, poverty, social disintegration, and so forth. The use of analogical reasoning in incarnational translation forces us to ask how analogizing differs (if it does) from allegorizing. As we contemplate this question, it may be helpful to lay out a set of hermeneutical frames by which modern preachers typically appropriate holy-war stories such as those in the conquest traditions in the books of Joshua and Judges.

One hermeneutical frame is the individualistic approach. The people of Israel or its army become the Christian engaged in a moral/spiritual struggle with the powers of temptation and sin. Another frame is the ecclesial, which equates Israel or its army to the church struggling with spiritual and social forces that impede its mission. In both the individualistic and the ecclesial approaches today, the means of battle with the "enemy" are typically not military but spiritual or political (prayer, spiritual discipline, engaging in struggles of power through nonviolent means, etc.). The individualistic and ecclesial hermeneutical frames are the most common, but a third frame deserves mention as well: the nationalist frame. In the nationalist approach, biblical Israel is equated with a particular modern people or nation. In Jewish and Christian Zionism, that nation is the modern state of Israel. In other nationalist hermeneutics, biblical Israel equates to a modern nation such as the United States when it is conceived as bearer of a God-given role or destiny in history. In the nationalist approach, the correlations between the basic elements of the biblical story and the incarnational translation are much more literal: a people (nation or state) engaged in conflict with other peoples (nations, states) or other geopolitical forces (including cultural and economic forces). The conflict at times involves military battles, and, in any case, the threat of military force often lies in the background.

The justification for any one of these three frames is the conviction that God works in the life of the individual, in the mission of the church, and in the life of nations in ways that are similar to how God worked with Israel of old. But the crucial questions for incarnational translation are: "What counts as *similar* ways?" "Who will play the role of the enemies?" and "Who gets to be Israel?" We can also press questions arising from a consideration of the larger context of the Pentateuch. For example, does the application of the Exodus and conquest stories to a new time and place require that the beneficiaries of divine help stand in a covenantal relationship to God — as Israel of old did? If so, does God have a covenant with humanity? With each individual human being? With the oppressed, whoever they may be? With the church? With the modern state of Israel? With the modern Palestinians? With the United States?

Analogizing from battle stories to other kinds of narrative is already seen in the Hebrew Bible itself. Joshua Berman has shown that the tendency to present narrative doubling in a given context, often with a battle story and a non-battle story, is widespread.[19] An example is the second battle of Ai in Joshua 8:1-29 and the trial of Achan in Joshua 7:10-26. The parallel phrases and other clues shared by these and other narratives suggest that they are to be read in the light of each other. Hence, the battle of Ai is about the external enemy, and the story of Achan is about the enemy within. In the stories that Berman analyzes, the analogical movement is not strictly from battle narratives to non-battle narratives and has nothing to do with a battle narrative being reinterpreted as a non-battle narrative. The texts simply present us with analogical patterns and associations suggesting that the two stories shed light on each other.

From a theological point of view, Berman's analysis invites the inference that, for the biblical writers, plot patterns in life (and in God's providence) repeat themselves in a variety of settings, so that war plots imitate other plots and vice versa. And we also have the examples of biblical typology in which one narrative is treated as paradigmatic for a very different kind of event, such as the typological allusions to the Exodus and conquest stories in Isaiah and in the Gospels. In the Gospels, the appropriations of the Exodus/conquest paradigm to describe the advent of God's redemptive work through John the Baptist and Jesus assume that the original paradigm can also be applied to nonviolent forms of deliverance. A similar interpretive assumption seems to be operative in the book of Isaiah as well, depending on how one interprets the use of the Exodus motif in relation to various conceptions of redemption in different parts of the book of Exodus, whose long and complex composition history makes for considerable variety of vision.

With the preceding considerations in mind, let us return to Gideon, focusing on the following passage from Judges 7, which describes events the night before the battle with the Midianites:

> That same night the LORD said to him, "Get up, attack the camp; for
> I have given it into your hand. But if you fear to attack, go down to
> the camp with your servant Purah; and you shall hear what they say,
> and afterward your hands shall be strengthened to attack the camp."
> Then he went down with his servant Purah to the outposts of the

---

19. Joshua A. Berman, *Narrative Analogy in the Hebrew Bible: Battle Stories and Their Equivalent Non-battle Narratives* (Leiden: E. J. Brill, 2004).

armed men that were in the camp. The Midianites and the Amalekites and all the people of the east lay along the valley as thick as locusts; and their camels were without number, countless as the sands
on the seashore. When Gideon arrived, there was a man telling a
dream to his comrade; and he said, "I had a dream, and in it a cake
of barley bread tumbled into the camp of Midian, and came to the
tent, and struck it so that it fell; it turned upside down and the tent
collapsed." And his comrade answered, "This is no other than the
sword of Gideon son of Joash, a man of Israel; into his hand has
God given Midian and all his army." When Gideon heard the telling
of the dream and its interpretation, he worshiped; and he returned
to the camp of Israel, and said, "Get up; for the LORD has given the
army of Midian into your hand" (Judg. 7:9-15).

Christian preachers usually do not connect the story of Gideon with
war in our time. The most common approach is to see Gideon as an example of how God chooses someone who is humble and lacks adequate resources and uses that person to do great things. Those great things are usually translated into some aspect of the church's mission in the world. In
this kind of analogy, the "Midianites" are obstacles — sometimes personified — to the church's mission. In traditional expository preaching, the analogical connections are usually made verse by verse. The preacher offers
three or four points, stated in declarative or prescriptive form as life appli-
cations. Each point may be given its own illustration. Rarely does the expository preacher weave all the contemporary connections into a larger
narrative pattern, a single unified illustration that shows the possible inter-
connections in the life of the hearers. In the case of Judges 7:9-15, can we allow the form and structure of the Gideon story (or one of its units) to
guide the way we redescribe in narrative form a meaning of the text for us?

A first step in this direction is to ask a question that preachers often
pose with such a story: Who is Gideon (or Gideon and Israel) and who are
the Midianites for us? In personal or ecclesial readings of the Gideon cycle,
we (as individual believers or as the church) are usually associated with
Gideon (and Israel), and the Midianites, typically, are personal and impersonal forces opposed to God, however these may be identified.

But why do we assume that we are Gideon or Israel — rather than the
Midianites? The answer is that a set of theological assumptions guides the
church's reading of the Scripture of Israel. We assume that we have a cove-

nant with God that is *like* Israel's covenant with God or that our covenant with God is an *extension of* God's covenant with Israel. This assumption justifies our identification of ourselves with Gideon and the Israelites. There may be grounds for questioning this assumption or at least for doubting that it always applies. But for the moment we will accept it and consider the possibilities it presents for incarnational translation.

If we translate the story of Gideon into terms of the church's mission, then the military struggle with the Midianites becomes a metaphor for the struggles and challenges of the church's mission. There are many possibilities for concretely imagining a new Gideon story in some corner of the church's mission today. Here is one possibility, based on Judges 7:9-15:

> Jackson Gideon was invited to be the new director of Passageway, an urban shelter and assistance center for children. He did not feel up to the job. He had far less experience than the board of directors seemed to think. Yes, he'd been a pastor for five years in a downtown church and had served in a three-month intensive internship in an urban mission back when he was in seminary. These experiences were not an adequate preparation to run Passageway. But the board was desperate.
>
> Jackson spent a month deciding whether to accept the board's invitation. He prayed. He worried. He analyzed the job from every angle he could think of. He asked God for signs. Three days into this time of searching, he was descending a short stairway from the living room to the front door of his suburban home. At the bottom of the stairs was a mirror. As he looked into the mirror he heard a voice, which seemed almost audible, telling him to accept the call to Passageway. This is God's voice, he thought. But he could not bring himself to say yes. Two weeks later, he was in his backyard trimming bushes. It was early evening. A rabbit appeared at the edge of the yard; time seemed to stand still. Jackson stood transfixed, staring at the rabbit. He was suffused with a love for the animal, the grass, the trees, the world. He felt as if the borders of his being were melting away and flowing into the things around him. Then, after a passage of time he could not calculate, he came back to himself and he heard the voice again. He had no doubt that it was God's call. The next morning, he accepted the invitation to be the new director of Passageway.
>
> His third night living at the shelter, around 11:30, he heard

some noise outside and looked out to see a group of young men hanging out in the parking lot. One of them was holding a baseball bat and thumping it against the side door. He went back to bed, hoping they would go away. Then he heard the sound of broken glass. He couldn't decide whether to call the police or go downstairs and confront them. He was afraid to go down. After a few minutes he peeked through the curtains. The young men were gone. In the morning, he found gang signs spray-painted on the side of the house near the side door, which now had a broken window. *I thought we were off limits,* he wondered to himself.

He still wasn't sure whether he should call the police. He felt that maybe he should see if they came back the next night and should go down and talk to them. But he desperately wanted a sign from God that this would do some good and that the center would be safe.

He decided to fix the window himself, which made him feel fatherly and protective, and he asked Charmaine, a seasoned fifteen-year-old resident who liked to help out, to find some paint in the basement and cover over the gang signs. She appeared with a brush and a bucket while he was measuring for the pane of glass. He asked her if she knew what the gang signs said.

"Help," she offered, "Help us. What do you think they mean?"

For a fleeting moment Jackson could not speak because, when Charmaine said the word "help," he saw the rabbit again and the grass and the trees and he felt the gentle evening light and the loss of the borders of his being. When he came to himself after a period of time he could not calculate, Charmaine was looking at him quizzically.

"I think you're right," he said. "You know what the Bible says?"

Charmaine waited.

"It says," he laughed, "there is no one like Jackson Gideon, a servant of God, and into his hand God has given all the gangs of Detroit."

Charmaine smiled. "I don't think that's in the Bible, Mr. Gideon. Anyway, we don't have room for all the gangs of Detroit."

That evening after supper, Jackson walked down to Grace Tabernacle Church, two blocks away, and prayed alone for some time in the great sanctuary. Then he went back to Passageway and attended to his duties. At 11:15, after lights out, he got a chair from the kitchen and went outside. He placed the chair in front of the gate to the parking lot and sat down, with his hands on his knees, thinking of the gangs of Detroit, thick as locusts in the shadows beyond the circle of light from the street lamp at the edge of the parking lot.

This incarnational translation combines into a unified contemporary narrative the following elements of the original: the weakness of Gideon and his army, the overwhelming force of the Midianites, Gideon's fear and desire for assurance from God, God's gift of signs, including a sign from the enemy, and Gideon's decision to stand up to the enemy. To show the logic of the incarnational transformation of the passage, we can lay out these basic elements with their contemporary correlations:

the weakness of Gideon and his army

This idea is conveyed by the description of Jackson Gideon's unpreparedness for his new job and by the obvious fact that a center like Passageway is no match, by itself, for the destructive forces of the city.

the overwhelming force of the Midianites

The Midianites are equated to the gangs of Detroit, who threaten the children of the city by recruiting them for a violent, dehumanizing way of life. The gangs are people with agency and also products of social forces in the urban environment. Implicit is the idea that centers like Passageway are efforts to take back the city from the gangs, just as God told Israel to take the land of Canaan from its inhabitants, whom the book of Judges describes as idolaters and oppressors. But an important difference between Judges 7 and our incarnational translation is that the gangs are not just enemies. They include the children Passageway seeks to serve. Or one might say that the social forces that create the dehumanizing and violent sides of urban life in poor neighborhoods are the enemies from which the people of the city must be rescued. Moreover, from the standpoint of the Hebrew Bible as a whole — and also the gospel of Jesus Christ — it is appropriate to any translation of Judges 7 in which *people* figure in the role of "Midianites" that they also be regarded as subjects of God's love and concern.

Gideon's fear

Jackson expresses his fear throughout the narrative. A contemporary listener, urban or suburban, can readily understand his anxiety. Jackson and Passageway have received some kind of threat or challenge, which is symbolized by the broken window and the gang graffiti. Jackson is not a former gang member who knows the streets and has connections; he has difficulty understanding the nature and magnitude of the threat.

Gideon's desire for reassurance from God

Gideon's desire for signs to reassure him about his call is a prominent theme in Judges. A famous example is the story of the fleeces at the end of Judges 6. Even after he knows what God wants him to do, he seeks signs. In our translation, we have given Jackson two experiences of what he understands to be direct communications from God. But he needs a third sign before he is willing to act.

God's gift of a sign from the enemy

In Judges 7, it is an enemy who has a dream that gives Gideon the sign he seeks. In our incarnational translation, the "enemy" writes graffiti that is interpreted as a sign that the enemy wants help. This is consistent with the double-reading of the gang imagery: they are enemies because of their threatening gestures, but they are also subjects of divine mercy whom God seeks to reach, deliver, and protect through the agency of Jackson and Passageway.

Gideon's decision to stand up to the enemy

The sign given through the dream revelation in Judges 7 gives Gideon the courage to stand up to the enemy. Charmaine's one-word interpretation of the graffiti and Jackson's mystical experience upon hearing that word give him the courage to sit outside the next night and wait for the young men to return.

As the preceding shows, our incarnational translation re-creates the narrative pattern of the original passage of Scripture, but we have made some important interpretive decisions. First, we have decided not to literally take over the sanctioned violence of holy war on the part of Gideon and his troops. Second, we have reinterpreted the Midianite enemies as social forces in which human beings figure as both victims and agents. These transformations can be justified only theologically. We have been guided by the following theological convictions: that God does not command the church to violent conquest of enemies or territory, and that human beings who threaten the church and its mission are not simply enemies but brothers and sisters to whom the church owes love and service. Moreover, the church, too, in its moral frailty and sin, is both friend and enemy of God at the same time.

The Healing at the Pool and Modern Storytelling

We immediately recognize stories in our English Bibles as stories. But are biblical stories in translation really the same kinds of stories they once were? Do we hear them the same way they were heard in ancient Israel and the early church? Do they have the same or similar rhetorical functions for us that they had in antiquity? Does transgenrelization require more than imitation with updating of characters, places, and setting if incarnational translation is going to re-create that unity of sense and form that achieves something like the rhetorical impact of the original? We think the answer is often — perhaps usually — yes. At least some reflection on how the biblical narrative works in its cultural context is necessary for us to discover what contemporary narrative form might be the same kind of communication.

For example, Richard Pervo has argued that Acts stands within the novelistic style of ancient history-writing.[20] But Acts does not "read" like a novel in modern English translations. One reason is that biblical stories are highly economical by our standards. Modern novels and short stories tend to be rich in detail of setting, action, and the inner life of the characters. If we retell biblical stories by adding such detail, does this count as "translation"? It depends on what we mean by translation. Josephus claimed that his retellings of Israel's story in his *Antiquities* were *translations* of the Jewish scriptures (*Ant.* 1.5). In fact, Josephus's translations are also rather free transgenrelizations. In addition to incorporating many extrabiblical traditions, Josephus retells the biblical stories in popular Greek historiographic style, including the invention of speeches for char-

---

20. Richard I. Pervo, *Profit with Delight: The Literary Genre of the Acts of the Apostles* (Philadelphia: Fortress Press, 1987).

acters as well as inventive novelistic description of their thoughts, feelings, and actions. In effect, Josephus updates and rhetorically refashions the biblical history for a Greco-Roman audience.

Ancient storytelling in its popular oral form was "garrulous," full of detail.[21]By contrast, the stories about Jesus in the Gospels and many of the stories in the Hebrew Bible seem very short and devoid of detail. Is this because they were originally meant merely as performance notes, springboards for oral performance that would expand the story? This is surely an over-generalization, but probably it contains some truth. Antony Campbell has argued that the short narrative units of the Hebrew Bible, stories encompassed within ten to forty verses, are not records of how these stories were actually told but summaries that the storyteller was expected to develop in oral performance.[22] On the other hand, one of the differences between the first five books of the New Testament and the apocryphal Acts is that the latter are much closer in genre to ancient novels than the New Testament narratives are. This contrast may offer a kind of canonical caution against over-novelizing the retelling of biblical stories. The contrast between the New Testament narratives and the apocryphal Acts consists primarily, however, in the fabulous elements that appear in the apocryphal Acts, not in the fact of greater narrative detail.

Was the Hebrew practice of using the reported story as a basis for a much longer oral performance continued in the synagogue, in Hellenistic and Roman times, as a form of sermonic rendition of the recited text? Suggestive of this possibility are examples of rewriting and embellishing biblical stories in *Jubilees*, Josephus's *Antiquities*, *The Genesis Apocryphon*, Pseudo-Philo's *Liber Antiquitatum Biblicarum*, and Philo's *Life of Moses*.[23] It may be that creative retelling of this kind took place in synagogue sermons following the recitation of the Torah. We know that the reading of Scripture, in at least some Palestinian synagogues, was followed by an Aramaic translation *(targum)*,[24] and some of these were rather free expan-

21. See Alex Scobie, "Storytellers, Storytelling, and the Novel in Graeco-Roman Antiquity," *Rheinisches Museum für Philologie* 122 (1979): 234.

22. See Antony F. Campbell, S.J., "The Storyteller's Role: Reported Story and Biblical Text," *Catholic Biblical Quarterly* 64 (2002): 427-441.

23. The *Testaments of the Twelve Patriarchs* might be mentioned as well, since they put long speeches (as "last words") into the mouths of the patriarchs of Israel as each lay dying.

24. We know that such *targumim* existed as early as the first century because fragments have been found at Qumran.

sions of the biblical text, suggesting a kind of embellished retelling. These targums and the other instances of embellished biblical narrative from ancient Judaism are ancient examples of incarnational translation.

Our incarnational translation of Judges 7:9-15, presented above, follows a style of embellished retelling. Let us now look at an embellished rendering of another story, the first part of the account of the healing of the lame man by the pool in John 5.

Peter and Thomas thought Jesus was taking them straight to lunch at *Giorgio's,* but Jesus turned at Fourth Street and entered Parkside Hospital, a gleaming skyscraper made of graceful concrete, steel, and glass. In the carpeted foyer, he stopped at a reception desk and requested passes to go to the ninth floor. Parkside was a new hospital, right in the center of downtown, and the elevator was on the exterior of the building with glass windows showing a view of the city. Peter smiled at the receptionist and complimented her on the hospital decor. Thomas observed to himself that it was almost like being in a hotel, as if sickness and death had nothing to do with this place.

Room 907 was a haze from a steady stream of warm mist generated, one guessed, by a vaporizer located somewhere in the room — it wasn't clear exactly where. Peter's glasses immediately fogged up, and he had to take them off repeatedly and wipe them on his shirt in order to see. The room was occupied by only one patient, a pale, wasted man with bright blue eyes that seemed unnervingly alive in an otherwise ghostly and expressionless face. Thomas thought of the colored marbles he used to play with as a child, some of them cobalt blue like this man's eyes. He was grateful he was not in charge, not expected to speak or act. He could turn the man's eyes into marbles from his childhood and wait for Jesus to take over.

Jesus said to the man, "Do you want to be healed?"

In this incarnational translation, the man needing healing is in a modern place of healing. The pool by the Sheep Gate is equated with a modern hospital. The small details that paint the scene and the action draw the reader into the story and help foster reader identification with the minor characters (Peter and Thomas). This adds realism and also gives the reader different perspectives within the story from which to observe Jesus. But since the original story does not mention any disciples, only portrays Jesus and the sick man, it is fair to ask whether the narrative device of depicting the scene and the action partly through the eyes of minor characters is sufficiently faithful to the original. Using such a device in an incarnational translation of the Priestly story of creation would probably ruin the perspective, which is universal and anonymous. But here, in this story of the man by the pool in John 5, creating multiple perspectives seems permissible. The Gospels give such perspectival views from characters: they describe what Jesus and those around him say and think.

We have been focusing largely on the genre of John 5. Attending more carefully to its content might lead us in a direction different from using a modern hospital setting for retelling the story. In John 5 the narrative continues with an act of healing by Jesus, a description of an ensuing controversy about breaking the Sabbath (the healed man by carrying his mat and Jesus by healing on the Sabbath), and a charge that Jesus makes himself "equal with God." One thing to consider is that the healing itself may be less about bodily restoration in a biomedical sense and more about the restoration of social relationships.[25] The paralyzed man is apparently without connection to friends or family because he has no one to put him into the water, and his condition makes him a beggar. The pool near the Sheep Gate was a place not only for seeking the curative properties of the waters but also for begging.

The reference to the man's sin (v. 14) also points to a social dimension in the story. In the ancient Mediterranean world it was commonly assumed that sin causes illness and hence that an illness is a sign of sin. The Gospel writer does not tell us that the man had sinned in some egregious way that brought so serious an illness upon him. Perhaps that is implied by Jesus' admonition to the man not to sin again — so that nothing worse will happen to him. This connection between the man's sin and his condition is significant not only as an explanation of the man's illness. It also points to the common assumption that the sick are sinners undeserving of the same social accommodation and deference that healthy people enjoy. When Jesus heals the man, he restores him both bodily and socially.

The preceding take on the story argues for an incarnational translation in which a socially marginalized and vulnerable person in our society

---

25. See Bruce J. Malina and Richard L. Rohrbaugh, *Social Science Commentary on the Gospel of John* (Minneapolis: Fortress Press, 1998), pp. 108-115.

is the recipient of Jesus' kindness. We might think of someone with a physical illness that causes him social ostracization and poverty. But if the dominant idea is that the man's sin produced his condition and if that condition was not conceived by ancient people in what we think of as biomedical terms, then functional equivalent analogizing does not necessarily require that his condition be a physical ailment in our contemporary rendering of the story. Pursuing this line of analogizing promises to bring us up short before a pervasive tendency in our culture to have sympathy toward the poor, the marginalized, and the ostracized only if we perceive them as innocent — as victims of the wrongful actions of others or of circumstances outside their control. But when we know (or think we can assume) that someone's bad condition is the result of his own bad acts, we tend to be less willing to extend help. Hence, the temptation in reading the story of John 5 from a modern perspective is to gloss over the reference to the man's sin and to focus our moral disapproval only on the Pharisees — so that we can feel good about the man Jesus has healed. This easily leads us to a contemporary rendering in which the recipient of Jesus' help is not morally stigmatized in our eyes. But faithful incarnational translation might call for a story of grace toward someone who is not morally deserving of help and is estranged from friends, family, and society.

The Gospel Controversy Story

Another familiar narrative form in the Gospels is the controversy story, which often includes a pronouncement. We find a series of controversy stories in Mark 2:1–3:5. This series ends with an ominous statement foreshadowing the crucifixion: "The Pharisees went out and immediately conspired with the Herodians against him, how to destroy him." As a group, these stories introduce the tenor of Jesus' mission and explain the opposition to him by portraying religious leaders in opposition to his teaching and practice. One of these stories tells how Jesus' disciples provoked criticism from certain Pharisees when they plucked grain on the Sabbath.

> One Sabbath he was going through the grainfields; and as they made their way his disciples began to pluck heads of grain. The Pharisees said to them, "Look, why are you doing what is not lawful on the Sabbath?" And he said to them, "Have you never read what

David did when he and his companions were hungry and in need of food? He entered the house of God, when Abiathar was high priest, and ate the bread of the Presence, which is not lawful for any but the priests to eat, and he gave some to his companions." Then he said to them, "The Sabbath was made for humankind, and not humankind for the Sabbath; so the Son of Man is lord even of the Sabbath" (Mark 2:23-28).

This story includes an argument from Scripture in which Jesus adduces a precedent for the action of his disciples. The precedent supplies a warrant for the principle enunciated in verse 27: "The Sabbath was made for humankind. . . ." And with his final pronouncement in verse 28 ("The Son of Man is lord even of the Sabbath"), he claims authority to interpret the Sabbath command. With that authority he has reduced the fourth commandment to its fundamental purpose.

One way to understand Jesus' judicial temperament in this story is to see him integrating the two great principles of the Law that he and a scribe affirm in Mark 12 — love for God and neighbor. This goes against the tendency to sharply distinguish laws governing proper relations with God, such as the Sabbath law, from laws having to do with social relations. In this way of conceiving the Law, it is possible for one set of commandments to compete with the other. Those operating with a bifurcated understanding of the Law might reasonably maintain that, in cases of a conflict of laws, loyalty to God supersedes obligations to neighbors. In the case of the Sabbath commandment, observing the Sabbath supersedes human need; therefore, supplying that need would be improper if it would entail violation of the Sabbath. We do not know how many people in Jesus' day took this unyielding approach to Sabbath regulations. There is no reason to think that all Jewish teachers did — or even that a majority of them did. In any case, Jesus interprets the Sabbath commandment as having concern for humanity at its heart. As an obligation to God, it is an obligation to one's neighbor. The two obligations are in unity at the level of the Sabbath law's fundamental purpose. Therefore, one should not keep the Sabbath in ways that are harmful to one's neighbor, whether the harm comes through acts of commission or omission.

The precedent from 1 Samuel 21 (David procuring the bread of the Presence, the shewbread, as food for himself and his companions) appears to operate, in Jesus' understanding, by this logic. The shewbread is dedicated to God and is not available for ordinary human consumption. Only the priests are permitted to eat it, and they must do so in a holy place (Lev. 24:5-9). But in circumstances of human need, the shewbread can be used as an ordinary food for non-priests. The customary regulations regarding its consumption can be lifted. Jesus implies that the high priest in 1 Samuel 21 understood this when he gave that sanctified bread to David and his men. We take the overall aim of the controversy story in Mark 2:23-28 as both legal (hermeneutical) and Christological. As God's anointed, Jesus authorizes a particular interpretation of the Sabbath law for a particular situation (case); but in so doing he also authorizes an approach to the Law that his disciples should imitate.

Here is a contemporary incarnational translation of the story in Mark 2:

> Very early one chilly Sunday morning in November, a homeless mother and her hungry children found themselves in an alleyway behind a large stone church. A thunderstorm had just descended on the city, and the rain was coming down hard. Seeking shelter, the mother tried a door at the back of the church and discovered it unlocked. Once inside, she and her children groped their way through the darkness up some stairs and found themselves in the sanctuary. The morning light filtering through the stained glass windows dimly revealed an altar fully prepared for communion. Thinking just to take enough to calm the ache in their stomachs, they began to eat. Suddenly, lights went on in the sanctuary, exposing them to the eyes of two deacons who had come to make sure that everything was ready for the service. When the deacons saw what the mother and her children were doing, they were horrified and began to scream at them, raising their complaints to high heaven. They chased the intruders from the building and reported the incident to the pastor, confident that they would be praised for protecting the sanctuary and the communion table from any further desecration. To their surprise, the pastor was not happy with them. The pastor asked, "Why didn't you try to find out how we could help the mother and her children instead of chasing them away? Jesus told us to feed the hungry and clothe the naked. And don't you remember how his disciples plucked grain on the Sabbath, breaking the Sabbath law, but Jesus permitted it because they were hungry — just like this mother and her children? Jesus said that the Sabbath is

made for humanity, not humanity for the Sabbath. So it is with the communion table and the altar. We were not created to serve the altar. We are not here to protect the communion bread from hungry children. The altar and the table were created for the sake of all of us. We were not created to serve the altar but to serve God and to serve the people of God by loving our neighbor as ourselves."[26]

Parables

We conclude our illustrative survey of incarnational translation of biblical narrative by looking at a story form that does not lend itself to "novelizing" but is inherently spare in detail: the parable. Parables are a remarkable form of narrative: they are the shortest of short stories. A familiar example is the Parable of the Lost Sheep in Luke 15:4-7:

> Which of you, having a hundred sheep and losing one of them, does not leave the ninety-nine in the wilderness and go after the one that is lost until he finds it? When he has found it, he lays it on his shoulders and rejoices. . . .

This parable appears in Luke 15, along with another "lost and found" parable, that of the woman who has lost a coin. Both sound ordinary, but they contain hidden surprises. We are lured by the form of the rhetorical question ("Which one of you. . .") and by the ordinariness of the examples (looking for a sheep or a coin) into anticipating that the answer must be along the order, "Of course we would do what the shepherd does or the woman does." On closer inspection, however, the shepherd and woman behave in surprising, even extraordinary ways. Leave ninety-nine sheep in the wilderness to go after one! It seems economically imprudent. Unless it was a special sheep. Call your neighbors together to celebrate with you because you found a lost coin! It seems excessive. Unless it was a special coin. Commentators throughout history have attempted to explain the shepherd's and the woman's behavior by suggesting that the lost sheep and the lost coin were not ordinary but unique, carrying superlative worth.[27] But

26. We owe this incarnational translation to Melbalenia D. Evans; used here by permission.

27. The Gospel of Thomas contains the Parable of the Lost Sheep and says that this

perhaps the point of these parables is not that the lost objects are extraordinary compared to other sheep and coins but that the shepherd and the woman are extraordinary. Most shepherds would cut their losses, figuring it better to keep the herd safe rather than go after the one sheep and risk the other ninety-nine. Most women would be happy to find their lost coin, but would they call their friends and neighbors to celebrate with them? The shepherd seems to overvalue the one sheep, the woman to overvalue the single coin. In just this way the shepherd and the woman display something of God's character and the way life ought to operate in the kingdom of God.

Here is a moving incarnational translation of the Parable of the Lost Sheep by John Witkop:

> Which of you, having all the blessings of this world and hearing a cry for help, does not immediately leave all that you have at the risk of violence, fire, injury and even death in order to care for one in need or to give a family peace that their loved one has been found, and when you find someone in the rubble, rejoice that you have been blessed to serve regardless of the cost?[28]

The occasion of this incarnational translation was a worship service in the aftermath of the terrorist attacks of September 11, 2001. The incarnational translation, which takes its cue from the original, poses a question with an assumed affirmative answer: "Which of you . . . does not . . . ?" In other words, "Wouldn't all of you, if you . . . ?" Wouldn't any New Yorker? Any American? Yet, if we respond honestly, we would probably have to answer: "Some but not many of us . . . some, but maybe not me." We all recognize in the self-giving and courage displayed by the New York firefighters something of how the world ought to be . . . but generally isn't.

This incarnational translation succeeds at springing a surprise on us through the form of its question. But some may judge that it differs from the original in that the element of noncalculation in the incarnational translation is directed toward the rescuer (the firefighter who does not calculate the risk to himself or herself), whereas the noncalculation in the

---

sheep was the *biggest*. A popular modern interpretation of the Parable of the Lost Coin is that the ten coins were not ordinary silver coins, each worth a day's pay for a laborer, but parts of her dowry that she may have worn around her neck.

28. Used by permission.

original is focused on the value of the sheep (not weighing the economic value of the single lost sheep against the value of the ninety-nine who may wander off or fall prey to wolves in the wilderness). In short, the incarnational translation does not appear to contain a functional equivalent for "leave the ninety-nine in the wilderness." In defense of the creator of this incarnational translation, we can point out that he chose not to imitate in a strict way the form of the parable but to design a functional equivalent with its own *logic of surprise*.

Another question we may pose about this incarnational translation is whether it remains true to the parable genre. The Parable of the Lost Sheep is a metaphor in story form, that is, it is not about literal sheep or a literal shepherd. Does the incarnational translation exchange metaphor for realistic narrative in describing the actions of firefighters and others on behalf of people on 9/11? Not necessarily. It depends on how the incarnational translation is used in the sermon. The sermon could suggest that the way of the firefighters is a metaphor for the way of the kingdom of God or of God's love for the lost. If it is offered as a metaphor for the way of the kingdom, it approaches realistic example. If it is a metaphor of God's commitment to the lost, it is a nonliteral analogy.

It is important to emphasize that our analysis of the Parable of the Lost Sheep is not a substitute for the parable or its incarnational translation. As provocative stories, parables cannot be reduced to theological assertions, which are a different genre of speech. Analysis can help us understand parables, but it cannot replace them.

So what are parables? Are they straightforward object lessons, moral tales drawn from everyday experience, allegories to be deciphered, paradoxical puzzles, veiled (or not so veiled) sociopolitical critiques of the status quo, poetic word feasts? Commentators have found all of these and more in the parables of Jesus.[29] As a genre of biblical literature, parables may well be the most complex and difficult to characterize. The history of parable interpretation testifies to the challenge of even coming to a common definition — much less common interpretation — of individual texts.

---

29. See W. Dow Edgerton, *Speak to Me That I May Speak: A Spirituality of Preaching* (Cleveland: Pilgrim Press, 2006), ch. 4. For a helpful recent overview of the history of parable interpretation and current discussion, see David B. Gowler, *What Are They Saying about the Parables?* (New York/Mahwah, N.J.: Paulist Press, 2000).

In the New Testament the parables of Jesus are both typical of his ministry ("without a parable he told them nothing" — Matt. 13:34) and as elusive as their speaker himself. We could argue that one of the most characteristic features of the parables of Jesus is their resistance to some final interpretation. (In saying this we readily add a question mark to the interpretations we have given above to the lost-and-found parables in Luke 15.) It is instructive to muse over parable interpretations and notice how often our response to the parable's resistance to being interpretively pinned down is to transform it into some other genre—for example, teaching, wisdom, law, moral tale, or prophecy. So the Good Samaritan becomes a lesson about helping the neighbor, the Parable of the Talents becomes a recommendation of the virtue of prudence, the Widow's Mite becomes an example of sacrificial giving, the Wicked Tenants becomes a foreshadowing of Judgment Day. Go and do likewise — or don't do likewise — but repent.

In some ways parables invite such interpretations. According to Mark 4, Jesus himself gave interpretations of parables. Nevertheless, the interpretation is not the parable; otherwise there would be no need for parables. Moreover, the parable is not simply an illustration — as example or analogy — of some truth that can be stated in other terms, as if the purpose of parables were to translate such truths into more accessible forms. In fact, it's exactly the other way around: the interpretations are "illustrations" designed to make the parables more accessible. Parables have yielded rich insights to a welter of methods and approaches and yet have been subdued by none. This resistance to neat and final interpretations is an essential feature of the ways of knowing that parables represent. They show *and* they hide; they are ordinary *and* strange; they are commonsensical *and* subversive.

This paradoxical way of regarding parables seems to be implied by Mark's Gospel. In Mark 4, Jesus, quoting Isaiah, says that everything is in parables so that the "outsiders" will not understand (4:11-12), making parables obtuse riddles. Jesus also says that the "secret" ("mystery") of the parables has been given to the disciples, which makes the disciples "insiders" who do understand or at least have privileged information to guide them toward understanding. But the disciples do not understand Jesus' first parable for them (4:10, 12), so he begins to explain his parables to them. Mark 4:14-20 is an example of this kind of explanation: Jesus tells the disciples what the different kinds of "ground" stand for in the Parable of the Soils. Mark ends the scene by commenting that Jesus always spoke in parables, "but he explained everything to his disciples privately" (4:34). All of this seems pretty straightforward. But as the story progresses, the disciples turn out to be uncomprehending despite the "secret" they have been given and despite all the explanations of the parables that Jesus has been giving them privately. In fact, we are told (in Mark 6:52) that the disciples' astonishment at seeing Jesus walking on the sea was because "they did not understand about the loaves, but their hearts were hardened." This echoes the words from Isaiah that Jesus applied to "outsiders" (in Mark 4); then in Mark 8:21, again with reference to the multiplication of the loaves, Jesus asks, "Do you not yet understand?"

Several things are worth noting about what we have seen thus far. First, the disciples have a "key" (the secret or mystery of the parables) that they don't know how to use, and they receive explanations of the parables that do not lead them to understand what Jesus is doing or who he is, which shows that they are not really understanding the explanations of the parables he has been giving them. Second, in view of the disciples' repeated failures to understand (a special emphasis of Mark), the whole ministry of Jesus begins to look like a mysterious parable. Third, the uncomprehending disciples, for all their privileged location and information, begin to look more and more like outsiders, people who have ears but do not hear and eyes but do not perceive. A final irony is that in the story in Mark 12, a quintessential outsider, a scribe, receives an unqualified commendation for his understanding. Jesus tells him that he is "not far from the kingdom of God" (Mark 12:34). No other people in the Gospel of Mark — certainly no disciples — receive such an approving judgment from Jesus about their understanding. So who are the insiders and who are the outsiders?

One response to the portrait of the disciples in Mark is to say that they are spiritual dullards who do not understand what readers of Mark are quite capable of understanding. Thus the problem of how to interpret the parables lies in the hearers, not in the nature of the parables. This is certainly part of it: the parables remain opaque unless readers/hearers bring something to them, operate with certain keys that unlock them. But what are the keys? How do Mark's readers know that *they* have the keys? And if Jesus' explanations of the parables do not lead the disciples to understanding, how can we be sure that *we* understand the parables? Not only that, we have to ask this obvious question: Why does Jesus speak to the crowds of outsiders at all if he aims only to conceal his message? Surely, teaching through parables is an effort at communication. Mark implies quite emphatically that Jesus came to communicate a public message and gain a public response: "Repent and believe in the good news" (Mark 1:14-15). Not only that, he also taught the disciples in parables and explained his parables to them only because they were unable to use the "secret" that was supposed to guide them to understanding, implying that the explanations are a second-best expedient, a last resort. Otherwise, Jesus could have taught his disciples (the insiders) without parables.

So the parables must be viewed as efforts to communicate, not to obscure, and we are encouraged to see them as a form of communication that cannot easily be replaced by other forms of communication. This conclusion is consistent with the fact that, except for the Parable of the Soils, the other parables in the Gospel of Mark are presented without explanation. As such, they stand on their own as communications to the reader. So we are back to the impression that parables both show and hide: this is their *mode of communication.*

We suggest, then, that parables do what they do because of and by way of their paradoxical qualities — showing and hiding, being ordinary and strange, being commonsensical and subversive. We also believe that these qualities are inherent to the form of the parable (or at least the form of many of the parables). Therefore, whatever interpretations we give in another form (analyzing, commenting, explaining, etc.) are likely to miss something essential. They are a last resort or perhaps a detour that can lead us eventually to an interpretation that answers parable with parable. Analysis and commentary have their place as a way of talking about parables and testing whether our parabolic incarnational translations do justice to the original; but they are not a substitute for the parables themselves.

The parables' resistance to neat explanation and the indispensability of the form of the parable mean that parabolic disclosure takes place within the interpretive process itself.[30] The product is not by itself the "point"; the point includes the process. The point or aim of the parable is to lead us into a process of reflection. The way of knowing that is peculiar to parables is via the hearer's engagement with the parable. The struggle to see into and through the parable is an essential part of this way of knowing, part of what one learns from parables.

The authority of the parable is also shared with the reader. The author

---

30. Paul Ricoeur and Mark I. Wallace, *Figuring the Sacred: Religion, Narrative, and Imagination* (Minneapolis: Fortress Press, 1995), p. 149.

of the parable does not give it a single, straightforward meaning—as though the parable were simply a container. The parable is a story open to multiple meanings. Whatever meaning a parable may have depends heavily on context, yet most of the parables come to us without specific contexts or are underdetermined by their contexts. Furthermore, we know that the contexts in which they are found in the Gospels are not original to them. The parables of Jesus circulated independently and were put to different uses by different teachers, made to speak about different subject matters. Therefore, modern interpreters must supply or complete contexts for the parables. Of course, some may insist that the ministry of Jesus or the preaching of the "kingdom of God" is the appropriate macro-context for interpreting parables. That makes eminent sense to us. But if we take this view, we are only saying that a context that poses its own extraordinary challenges to interpretation — the ministry of Jesus as a whole! the mysterious "kingdom of God"! — must serve as the guide to the individual parable. A context of that kind creates a thicket of interpretive possibilities; it does not eliminate parabolic polyvalence. Thanks to the underdetermination of context, the openness of the parable to different senses, and the puzzles and surprises that parables often contain, readers are cast willy-nilly into highly creative roles as coauthors of the meaning of the parables. The parables authorize this role of the reader. At the same time, the parables challenge every interpretation they provoke (lest we become too wise in our own conceits).

With the preceding in mind, let us consider an incarnational translation of the Parable of the Good Samaritan (Luke 10:25-37) prepared as a bibliodrama by a group of students in a doctor of ministry class. In the incarnational translation the lawyer is a doctor of ministry student who asks Jesus what he must do to inherit eternal life. The opening lines of their dialogue are a verbatim recital from the NRSV version of Luke 10:25-29. Then Jesus gives his parable in the following incarnational translation:

> A student was returning from the Loop to Hyde Park, but at the transfer point from the Red Line to the 55 bus on Garfield, he found himself in the wrong place at the wrong time. While he was standing at the bus stop, he was yanked into a car, robbed, stripped, and left for dead in Washington Park. Now it just so happened that a seminary professor was jogging down Cottage Grove Avenue, next to the park. When she saw the man lying in the grass, she ran to the

other side of the street because she was afraid the guy would hit her up for a buck. Then a group of UCC preachers on study leave walked by and saw him, but they were late for their D.Min. class on how to present concrete contemporary appropriations of Scripture in preaching. Besides, each thought silently, "I deal with enough of this sort of thing in my daily work." So they kept on going. Then a member of the Christian Coalition came by—on his way to the Republican National Convention in his BMW. When he saw the man sprawled naked in the park, he stopped his car and went over to him. He pulled out his cell phone and called 911, and he stayed with the man until the paramedics arrived. He followed the ambulance to the University of Chicago Hospital, where he put down his credit card to ensure that the man would be treated without proof of insurance. After the man was released from the hospital, he took him to the Weston Hotel on Michigan Avenue, charged a room for him to his credit card, and said he'd be back in three days to settle the bill. Then he went on to the Republican National Convention.[31]

The bibliodrama ends with a recital of the closing words of the story: "'Which of these three, do you think, was a neighbor to the man who fell into the hands of the robbers?' He said, 'The one who showed him mercy.' Jesus said, 'Go and do likewise'" (Luke 10:36-37).

In order to obey Jesus' "Go and do likewise," we have to "get" the parable. When it was originally presented, the incarnational translation prevented its audience from romanticizing the parable and domesticating it morally because it was difficult for those of us who witnessed its live performance in Chicago's Hyde Park to imagine ourselves imitating the man who stopped and helped. The concreteness of the incarnational translation made the idea of "being Good Samaritans" seem impractical, foolish, and frightening. It is easier to avoid these responses when one reads the parable in its original, distant cultural form, especially with the help of explanations that tend to be generalizing rather than concrete. But the incarnational translation did something else. It forced us into debate about its meaning: What did it show us — about ourselves and about our world? In the end, we were not all agreed that "Go and do likewise" meant simply to imitate what the representative of the Christian Coalition did,

---

31. Incarnational translation by Roland Lindeman, Darrell Griffin, Emmanuel Osei, Sandy Chrosowski, and Joseph Clifford; used by permission.

and we were also not agreed about the meaning of "neighbor" in the parable, given the shift in the story from "identifying my neighbor" to "acting as a neighbor."

Not only that, the parable in its incarnational translation seemed to be bigger than its ostensive context (providing an answer to the lawyer's/student's question), because it was also possible to see it as being about who has the correct interpretation of the Bible. No one in the class seemed to mind that a Samaritan might be a better interpreter of the law than an ancient Jewish lawyer (quite a barb to Jesus' hearers of it), because none of us were ancient Jewish lawyers. But when the incarnational translation implicated current political lines of division and conflict in America, it became obvious that it was not just about helping those in need but had something to say about religious fights in America over how God wants us to live. Whether such an incarnational translation is implicitly addressed to liberal Christians with a member of the Christian Coalition playing the Samaritan or is told to fundamentalists with a liberal Christian playing the Samaritan, it is about our willingness to believe that a member of a group of whom we are not fond and with whom we have grave disagreements about the true meaning of Christian faith might understand something important about "the Law" (Scripture) better than we do.

There is another way in which the incarnational translation did its work. We found ourselves analyzing it and asking questions, just as the lawyer in the original did. Confronted with God's moral imperative to love his neighbor as himself, the lawyer asked a question that prolonged the conversation and placed part of that imperative under a question mark. And that is what the incarnational translation had us doing: even though we, like the lawyer, could give the right answer — "The one who showed him mercy" — like the lawyer, we were still not sure what that answer meant for us. Perhaps the correct interpretation of the parable, in the end, is not simply a good answer to Jesus' question but good actions in response to the final command of the story: *Go and do likewise.* Yet, instead of giving straightforward instruction in the form of specific moral laws and principles, Jesus tells a parable, a rhetorical form that both hides and reveals. The telling of the parable gives us no choice but to be like the lawyer and ask questions, weigh possibilities; the final word of the story gives us no choice but to be like the Samaritan and act.

CHAPTER FIVE

Law and Wisdom

The two broad biblical genres of Law and Wisdom overlap. They are linked historically and theologically. We presume that in time immemorial, both Law and Wisdom were closely connected as forms of familial and tribal ethos. Eventually, Law became separated from tribal wisdom and was developed in its own institutional settings. But even after the institutional separation between Wisdom and Law, sages in Israel continued to consider their relation. A famous example is the identification of heavenly wisdom with the Law of Moses in Ben-Sira (Sirach). Referring to the teaching of Wisdom, who speaks in Sirach 24, the sage comments: "All this is the book of the covenant of the Most High God, the law that Moses commanded as an inheritance for the congregations of Jacob" (24:23).

Like other genres of Scripture, Law and Wisdom are also diverse. As macro-categories, they contain a variety of forms developed over many centuries. They also display elements of other genres. For example, narrative and poetry can be found in Wisdom texts, and Law is sometimes issued in oracular, prophetic form. Although they often present a face of timelessness and universality, Law and Wisdom teachings arose in specific sociohistorical circumstances and have been shaped by sociohistorical forces. Sometimes it is possible to recover the original life setting of a Law or Wisdom teaching. But as they were passed down through time, they were developed and adapted for new circumstances until they finally reached a stable form in Scripture. Often the particulars of life setting, which shaped the traditions of law and wisdom at various points and places in time, have been effaced by the traditioning and canonical process. Incarnational translation of Law and Wisdom texts seeks to find contemporizing forms that do justice to the varying degrees of cultural specificity and generality found in these scriptural voices.

Law

There are varieties of prescriptive instruction in Scripture: the diverse kinds of commandments found in the Mosaic Law (e.g., in the Ten Commandments, the Covenant Code, and the Levitical legislation); the ethical teachings of Jesus (in the Sermon on the Mount and in Gospel controversy stories); the *paraenesis* we meet in New Testament Epistles (particularly in the Pauline corpus and in James); prophetic sentences of holy law in early Christianity;[1] the admonitions of Wisdom literature (Proverbs); the exhortations of Prophetic and Apocalyptic literature — all such speech is prescriptive in the broad sense of that term. Perhaps a better word is the Hebrew term *halakah,* which means instruction in the way of life to be lived out before God and neighbor. Likewise, *torah,* the Hebrew word for law, means instruction. Biblical law in the broad sense of *torah* and *halakah* means prescriptive instruction in how to live.

As practical instruction, law is meant to be repeated and handed down but, even more importantly, to be embodied. As a mode of revelation or knowing, law completes disclosure in obedient hearing. Knowing the law is incomplete apart from doing the law. Of course, one can be held accountable for knowing but not doing. Yet, in order to know the good that the law offers and to know the One who gives good laws, one must be a doer.

We can picture the basic components of the halakic speech model as follows:

God / Teacher → Teaching → Hearer → Practice

completion of
revelatory disclosure

This connection between knowing and doing appears in a number of forms in the Bible. One is the idea that knowledge of the law should be in-

---

1. See Ernst Käsemann, "Sentences of Holy Law in the New Testament," in *New Testament Questions of Today,* trans. W. J. Montague (Philadelphia: Fortress Press, 1969), pp. 66-81.

ternal, integral to Israel or the church, so that doing it happens as a kind of second nature. In practicing the law, we are doing what we *are*, and in this way we discover a unity of self in the good that God discloses in the law: "Keep these words that I am commanding you today in your heart. Recite them to your children and talk about them when you are away, when you lie down and when you rise. Bind them as a sign on your hand, fix them as an emblem on your forehead, and write them on the doorposts of your house and on your gates" (Deut. 6:7-9). Jeremiah looks forward to a day when God will write the law "on their hearts." Then "I will be their God, and they shall be my people" (Jer. 31:33). We learn both what the law is and who we are by doing it: "For if any are hearers of the word and not doers, they are like those who look at themselves in a mirror; for they look at themselves and, going away, immediately forget what they were like" (Jas. 1:23-24).[2] And 1 John teaches that love "in truth and action," not mere "word or speech," is the precondition for knowing "that we are of the truth" (1 John 3:18-19). Likewise, in the Gospel of John, Jesus describes keeping his commandments as the form in which his followers will "know the Father" and be united with Jesus and the Father through the Paraclete (John 14:15-24).[3] Knowing means doing, and by doing one knows what can be known in no other way.

In Exodus and Deuteronomy, instruction is bound to a larger narrative of creation, election-love, liberation, presence, promise, and relationship (or covenant). *Halakah* is part of the story of God's actions on behalf of Israel and humanity. Law is not simply a moral code but a relational code. Human beings are called to obey because God created the world and made it good. Israel is summoned to walk in God's ways because God delivered Israel from the land of Egypt and made promises to Israel's ancestors (Gen. 2:2-3 and Ex. 20:8-11; Ex. 20:2 and Deut. 5:15; Deut. 7:7-9 and 8:1-2). Observance of the teaching is also the means by which the story of blessing and deliverance becomes a promise about the future as well, and recitation of the story establishes the link between past, present, and future (Deut. 6:20-25). Recitation binds doing to its foundation and goal.

2. It is possible to take "self in the mirror" as a metaphor for the law and not the self. But we understand the metaphor in a more complex way: the mirror is the law in which both the law and the self are disclosed, but the one who merely hears without doing immediately forgets what the law reveals about itself and the hearer.

3. In the Gospel of John, believing is the prerequisite for seeing (knowing [John 14:21]), which is the prerequisite for believing (John 20:8; 20:31). Doing and knowing the truth form an unbroken circle.

In the New Testament we find similar dynamics, a configuration of law, presence, and promise within the redemptive story. Matthew connects the command to teach what Jesus has taught to the ongoing presence of the risen Christ (Matt. 28:20). In John's Gospel, Jesus' farewell discourse links discipleship, keeping his commandments, and abiding in love (John 15:10). The story of Jesus in Acts, culminating with his resurrection, evokes repentance, and those who repent respond by embracing a new way of life in community devoted to the apostles' teaching, the *koinonia*, the breaking of bread, and prayers (Acts 2:22-42). The name of the group established by these events is the Way (Acts 9:2), which refers to the story of Jesus' way — his teaching and practice, which his followers have taken up in the strength of the Spirit. The same connection between command and story is found in Paul. For example, in the book of Philippians, Paul offers the story of Jesus' self-emptying, death, and resurrection as the motivation and model for community practice (Phil. 2:1-13). The "law of Christ" in Galatians can be interpreted as a way of love embodied in Jesus' own story.[4]

All of this shows that the kind of instructive discourse we call "law," "commandment," *paraenesis,* and so forth is more than naked prescription backed up by divine authority. We find powerful elements of narration, recitation, and performance that serve to authorize practice, connect practice with divine presence and salvation, which actualizes the redemptive story in the present and projects it into the future as promise. Biblical *halakah* belongs to biblical *haggadah,* the narrative of God's redemptive purposes and actions. With this in mind, we could diagram the speech model of Law as follows:

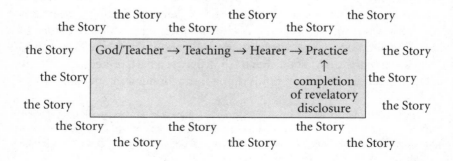

4. See Richard B. Hays, "Christology and Ethics in Galatians: The Law of Christ," *Catholic Biblical Quarterly* 49 (1987): 268-290.

Specificity, Force, and Scope of Regulative Speech

We have emphasized knowing in doing and the link between *halakah* and *haggadah* because these important features of prescriptive instruction are easy to overlook. But Law also requires interpretation. As a form of regulative speech or "rule," Law calls for interpretation that pays attention to three aspects of all rules: specificity, force, and scope.[5]

Generally speaking, rules lie on a continuum, with concept-specificity at one end and action-specificity at the other. We often call a concept-specific rule a *principle*. A principle is a ruling concept. For example, when we think of "love" as a moral idea, then it is a principle (as opposed to an emotion). "Love your neighbor" expresses the moral concept of love in rule form; this command does not specify any particular action. This means that in concrete life situations we have to figure out what love requires, based on our understanding of the concept of love. An action-specific rule defines required and prohibited behavior. For example, we know the conventional meaning of this familiar rule, "Keep off the grass." Because it is action-focused and not concept-focused, we don't have to work out the meaning of any concept or principle to understand its application.

Rules also have different kinds of force: they can be absolute or, in varying degrees, presumptive or relative. An absolute rule admits no exceptions; a presumptive rule holds unless a sufficient showing can be made that an exception is warranted; a relative rule is simply one rule among others, enjoying no greater weight than any other rule and less weight than any other presumptive rules. Relative rules might be better described as maxims. Here are some pedestrian examples of each type:

- *Absolute rule:* A pawn is not permitted to move backwards in chess.
- *Presumptive rule:* Always drive on the right of the solid yellow stripe on U.S. highways (admitting exceptions in emergency situations).
- *Relative rule,* or maxim: Brush your teeth after every meal.

Degree and kind of force are almost never expressed in the rule itself; they are implied by the context of the rule. Game rules are inherently absolute.

---

5. For a more detailed discussion of the nature of rules and appeal to biblical moral rules, see Charles H. Cosgrove, *Appealing to Scripture in Moral Debate: Five Hermeneutical Rules* (Grand Rapids: Eerdmans, 2002), pp. 12-50.

Traffic laws are robustly presumptive (nearly absolute). What about the biblical rules — the Mosaic Law, the moral instructions of Paul, the commands of the Sermon on the Mount?

The question of force bears on incarnational translation of biblical Law when we want to signal, in or around our translation, the force we think a given law carries. The Bible sends such signals primarily by genre. For example, we recognize prescriptions in Proverbs as relative rules, not absolute ones, because we take it to be the nature of "proverbs" as a genre to offer maxims, not absolute rules. The question of rule force is less immediately apparent from genre when it comes to other forms of prescription in Scripture, for example, rules in the Sermon on the Mount and in the Mosaic Law.

A third aspect of rules is scope. What situations, domains, persons, and so on, does the rule purport to cover? Is the rule limited by time, place, or culture? Questions of scope have long been part of Christian debate about biblical law. Answers to questions of scope are built into some of those codes of analogy that guide our appropriation of Scripture. In the case of biblical law, this may involve the judgment that the church is obliged to keep some or all of the Mosaic Law (that the Christian life lies within the scope of the Mosaic Law), or that the church has no obligation to keep the Mosaic Law (the Christian life lies outside the scope of the Mosaic Law), or some mediating position between these two.

Since scope is not a question of genre, we will not treat it here in any further detail, except to point out its relevance for the practice of incarnational translation. When we create an incarnational translation for a particular audience, we are assuming that Scripture addresses that audience or can be appropriately directed toward that audience. That is, we are assuming that our audience lies within the scope of the text. Incarnational translations of biblical law require prior theological judgments about the scope of the law in question.

Incarnational Translation of Specific Kinds of Law

There are many forms of *halakah* in Scripture. We cannot begin to treat them all. Instead, we offer some basic analysis and illustration of incarnational translation from two forms of biblical *halakah*, selected from the Mosaic Law and from the teachings of Jesus.

The Ten Commandments

The Ten Commandments are called "apodictic" law because they command without specifying circumstances. In this respect, they differ from case law. Case law, such as we find in the Covenant Code, gives rules for specific circumstances (using an "If . . . then . . ." formulation or its equivalent). Apodictic law simply pronounces in universal terms.

What kind of specificity do the apodictic prescriptions of the Ten Commandments display as rules? At least some of the Ten Commandments more closely resemble *principles* in rule form, that is, concept-specific rules as opposed to action-specific rules. For example, the Fifth Commandment, "Honor your father and mother," does not prescribe specific behaviors. Likewise, the Eighth Commandment, "You shall not steal," does not specify particular prohibited actions, although original hearers probably had a good idea of what specific actions counted as stealing. We place this commandment in the middle of our continuum, since the term "stealing" is rather specific, but not so specific as to make clear what we are to do in borderline or ambiguous cases. The First Commandment, "You shall have no other gods before me" (Exod. 20:3), is a principial rule if it is taken as a separate commandment (the traditional way of enumerating the Ten Commandments). The Second Commandment (against idolatry) and the Seventh Commandment (against adultery) lie on the action-oriented end of the spectrum. Nevertheless, each uses terminology that invites moral conceptualization. Hence, the idolatry prohibited by the Second Commandment need not be only the making of literal idols, and the command against adultery may have implications that are broader than the sexual act. The Sixth Commandment is an action-specific rule if it refers to killing; it is closer to a principial rule if the verb means "murder," which calls for distinctions between lawful and unlawful killing. We place the Ninth Commandment, "You shall not bear false witness," in the middle of the spectrum for the same reasons that we put the Eighth Commandment there: to a large extent, "bearing false witness" refers to well-known behaviors, but the full extent of its meaning requires interpretation of false witness as a concept. The Tenth Commandment is an action-specific rule, treating desire as an action. But this commandment may also imply that one should not engage in any schemes, including lawful ones, to acquire the possessions of one's neighbor or spend one's life trying to attain the standard of living of one's neighbor. If so, the Tenth Commandment may be a bit fuzzier about its action prohibition, requiring that we interpret "covet" as a complex concept involving both passion and external behavior.

What is the quality or force of the Ten Commandments? It is not our aim to give a definitive answer to this question. Readers need to make their own judgments. We will offer just two general observations. First, the more we move toward action-specific orientation, the more problematic it becomes to ascribe absolute force to a rule. The converse is also true. The more abstract the rule, the easier it is to attribute absolute force to it. The conceptually abstract "Love your neighbor as yourself" can be treated as an absolute rule; the more action-specific "You shall not steal" is best treated as a presumptive rule. The reason is that, the more specific the action, the more likely it is that reasonable exceptions exist for which the rule should be suspended, such as an emergency situation in the case of stealing.

Second, rules of any kind can conflict with each other. When rules collide, at least one of them must be treated as less than absolute. Consider, for example, whether situations might arise where the Fifth Commandment ("Honor your father and mother") conflicts with the First Commandment ("You shall have no other gods before me"). Consider also whether there are cases in which one of the Ten Commandments might conflict with the command in Leviticus 19:18 to love one's neighbor as oneself. Close analysis may indicate that at least some of the Ten Commandments are best treated as robustly presumptive rather than as absolute.

How might we reformulate the Second Commandment in contemporary form? If our audience does not include people who have a propensity toward literal idol worship but who do succumb to the temptation to assign ultimate value to what is finite, then we might recontextualize the Second Commandment as follows:

> You shall not love or trust anything but God as ultimate or divine, whether another person you are in love with, a child who means everything to you, an art form (music, poetry, painting, sculpture) that satisfies you deeply, a vocation that gives you the sense of self-worth or power you crave, or the pursuit of some pleasure or way of forgetting (through sensuality or drugs) to which you are ready to sell your soul.

Where the original version uses the architecture of the three-story universe to state the all-encompassing scope of the commandment, our incarnational translation uses a list of types of passions or pursuits. Implicit in this sort of list is an unstated "and so on."

The following are two different incarnational translations of the Tenth Commandment:

> You shall not desire your neighbor's house; you shall not desire your neighbor's spouse, or hired help, or car, or riding lawn mower, or stock portfolio, or summer home, or anything else belonging to your neighbor.

or

> Don't spend your life competing with the Joneses, letting the sight of their possessions entice you into acquisitiveness and materialism.

The first of these translations treats the Tenth Commandment as a specific prohibition of the internal attitude of desiring what someone else has. The second treats the Tenth Commandment as implying a more complex principle involving both desire and external behavior.

The Sermon on the Mount

There is more than one plausible way to interpret what Jesus is up to in the Sermon on the Mount. What follows is one account, which we find especially compelling as a moral vision and strategy for authentic discipleship.

The teachings of the Sermon on the Mount are new torah that develops a dialectical approach to the Mosaic Torah. We recall that torah means prescriptive instruction about how to live rightly with God and neighbor, instruction that can take a variety of rhetorical forms. As we see it, Jesus affirms the Mosaic Law, relativizes the Law, goes beyond the Law, and presses the concern for justice and humanity inherent to the Law in radical directions. The torah of Jesus interprets the Torah of Moses and places it in a new light.

We will focus on Jesus' torah in the so-called "antitheses" (Matt. 5:21-48). Each antithesis consists of a recital of a sentence from the Law or a traditional saying, introduced by the formula "You have heard that it was said," and followed by a contrasting instruction introduced by the formula "but I say to you." The contrasting instructions can be called "law" because the subject of Jesus' teaching is the Law of Moses, and the form of his teaching is prescriptive. But we must be cautious here. There are different forms of Law. Jesus is not promulgating a legal code. And most of the rules he gives are probably best understood as examples embodying concept-specific principles, not action-specific prescriptions. This judgment is extremely significant for incarnational translation.

In Matthew 5:21-26, Jesus teaches about murder and anger, then gives two concrete examples of how to live out some of the implications of his teaching. The first example goes like this: "So when you are offering your gift at the altar, if you remember that your brother or sister has something against you, leave your gift there before the altar and go; first be reconciled to your brother or sister, and then come and offer your gift" (Matt. 5:23-24). In order to produce an incarnational translation, we have to identify the basic rhetorical elements that give this sentence its sense and its punch. The scene is an individual Israelite going up to the temple in Jerusalem to offer a sacrifice. Let's call him Jacob. Jacob is standing at the low wall that separates the public area from the sacrificial precinct. At this low wall, Jacob is about to hand over his sacrificial animal to one of the priests, who will offer it on the altar. At just this moment, Jacob remembers that his brother or sister "has something against him," that is, has a reason to be angry with him. So, says Jesus, Jacob should leave his sacrifice there at the altar and go be reconciled to his brother, then come back and finish his sacrifice. From the standpoint of practicality, this directive is almost unthinkable because there is no institutional mechanism to accommodate it. Is Jacob supposed to put his sacrifice down on the stone courtyard floor and leave it there while he goes and makes peace with his brother or sister? What if that person lives in another town? Is the priest supposed to keep the sacrifice in a safe place? For how long? What priest would be willing to alter the ritual of sacrificial offering in this way? The effect of Jesus' impractical suggestion is to make reconciliation stand out as urgent, as important above all else — as if being reconciled is an emergency requiring the suspension of conventional behavior. Here is one effort at an incarnational translation of Matthew 5:23-24 that seeks to recontextualize the key elements of Jesus' directive, including its provocative qualities:

> If you are about to place your offering envelope in the collection
> plate and remember that your sister in Christ, who is sitting four

pews away, has something against you, ask the usher to hold the plate while you find your sister in Christ and ask her to forgive you; then return and place your offering in the plate.

In this contemporary translation, the sequence of actions — requesting that the usher hold the plate, getting up and going to another pew to ask someone for forgiveness, returning to make the offering — give the act a more public character and make it an act of witness to others in the congregation about what is most urgent, what counts the most, in the life of the church. This aspect of public witness in the incarnational translation has no counterpart in Jesus' example in Matthew 5:23-24 (unless we are to imagine the worshiper explaining to the priest why he must interrupt his offering); thus the incarnational translation adds an additional dimension to Jesus' instruction. This often happens in incarnational translation because it is usually impossible to find exact functional equivalents from one culture to another, equivalents that say no more and no less than the original. For this reason, we must always examine the additional meanings and effects that our chosen functional equivalents bring in, to determine whether they are appropriate. In the case at hand, the idea of a public witness seems to fit Jesus' teaching in general, unless it is done in a manner of religious self-display like what is condemned in Mattew 6:1-6. That is not a problem here because religious self-display takes the form of acts of piety that are conventional and self-exalting ("sounding a trumpet before you," "standing and praying in synagogues and on street corners"), whereas interrupting one's offering to publicly ask for forgiveness is a self-abasing act.

Here is another incarnational translation of Matthew 5:23-24:

When you are about to get out of your car to walk down to the Vietnam Veterans Memorial in Washington, D.C., to lay a bouquet of flowers at the base of the wall in honor of your soldier son, and you remember that you haven't spoken to your living son back in Davenport for almost a year because you got into an argument last Christmas about pacifism, leave your bouquet on the front seat of your rental car and fly back to Davenport and be reconciled to your son. Then make your offering at the wall.

This incarnational translation is a bit more descriptive, which has the effect of drawing us in emotionally. This is a technique of modern storytelling, which seems appropriate for a modern restatement of a moral teaching that comes to us from Jesus in the form of an example containing a story designed to awaken our moral imaginations. How faithful is this incarnational translation? The offering of flowers at a war memorial to a dead son is not a close functional equivalent for offering a gift in the temple. The temple offering honors God, while the flowers are offered to the memory of a human being. On the other hand, laying flowers at a war memorial is a religious act for many, often accompanied by prayer. Moreover, when family members of dead soldiers travel to a war memorial, their journey and acts of honoring their dead often have a ritual quality and the whole event can be a kind of pilgrimage. This incarnational translation also conforms to the original by describing a private act, not a public witness. And like the original, it includes a preposterous directive. Where our first-century Jacob in Jesus' instruction is to leave his gift at the altar, go make peace with his brother or sister, then return to offer the gift, our twenty-first-century father is to leave the flowers in the rental car, fly back to Davenport, reconcile with his son, and then go back!

Later in the Sermon on the Mount, Jesus teaches about the ancient rule "an eye for an eye and a tooth for a tooth." In words that have become very familiar to us, Jesus gives the following instruction:

> You have heard that it was said, "An eye for an eye and a tooth for a tooth." But I say to you, Do not resist the evildoer. But if anyone strikes you on the right cheek, turn the other also, and if anyone wants to sue you and take your coat, give your cloak as well; and if anyone forces you to go one mile, go also the second mile. Give to everyone who begs from you, and do not refuse anyone who wants to borrow from you. (Matt. 5:38-42)

These are examples of the kinds of responses one should give to an enemy or opponent. They may assume that the parties in conflict know one another. Moreover, they are *disarming* responses, not conventional ones.

One way to interpret Jesus' instructions is to see them as suggestions for creative responses designed to disrupt the typical patterns of interaction between the parties in order to break the cycle of animosity or violence and open up possibilities for a new relationship. In that case, to treat these teachings as action-specific rules misses the point. They are not rules but illustrations of possible responses. If cheek-turning isn't working, try something else. Notice as well that Jesus treats the legal sentence "[You shall give] an eye for an eye" as a principle and not as an action-specific rule. This is evident from the fact that his counterexamples deal with matters well beyond the kinds of cases in which the Mosaic Law introduces the law of retaliation. Jesus treats "an eye for an eye" as standing for a concept of negative reciprocity in all relations, not only legally actionable ones. We might render Jesus' instructions into an incarnational translation as follows:

> You know the saying "an eye for an eye, and a tooth for a tooth." Here's what I say: Don't fight back. If someone publicly insults you, ask him if he has anything more to say. If your neighbor sues you for damage your child allegedly did to his garage, pay for the repairs and send him a gift certificate to a nice restaurant. If your boss gives you extra work because she doesn't like your race, do more than she asks. Give to anyone who asks something of you. Don't refuse anyone who wants to borrow from you.

Another interpretation of the Sermon on the Mount sees Jesus' instructions not as strategies for challenging the principle of violence with a constructive response but sees them as calls to holiness, regardless of its effectiveness in the world. According to this interpretation, Jesus' admonitions are simply the right way to live, whether they work to foster peacemaking or not. Of course, the first interpretation does not exclude seeing Jesus' instructions as a call to holiness. But, unlike the second interpretation, it appropriates these instructions as strategy and thus as invitations to creative peacemaking. The second interpretation suggests that the instructions are to be taken more strictly as behavioral rules.

Both interpretations are viable, along with construals that mediate between the two. Jesus' instructions can as easily be seen as a demand for generosity toward others and refusal of violence as a call for disarming behaviors to provoke a constructive change of relationship. The final step toward understanding comes with trying to put one or the other interpretation into practice. Incarnational translation offers a way to imagine the possibilities for practice.

Wisdom Literature

The Bible contains three primary Wisdom books: Proverbs, Ecclesiastes, and Job. But there are also Wisdom Psalms (e.g., Pss. 1, 49, and 112). Moreover, among the so-called Old Testament Apocrypha are other Wisdom books — Ecclesiasticus (Sirach) and the Wisdom of Solomon — both of which were part of the early church's Greek Bible. Wisdom literature takes a variety of forms, from the pithy sayings of Proverbs to the reflections on the nature of life in Ecclesiastes. Moreover, the borders of the Wisdom genres are fluid, shading into Apocalyptic and Law and Poetry. Wisdom can be understood as a kind of instructive discourse, but with distinctive features. If biblical Law and Prophecy present themselves as the voice of God in the mouth of a Moses or an Isaiah, Wisdom presents itself as the voice of experience. The wise are those who have learned wisdom through experience; they are also those who have collected and interpreted the experiential and practical knowledge of sages before them.

In its proverbial forms this experiential knowledge takes the form of mnemonically patterned sayings designed to accompany the hearer through life as a fund of practical knowledge lodged in ready memory. Proverbial wisdom is a distillation from experience of truth that will apply again and again. The Wisdom teacher offers that truth to a student and sends the student into the world to affirm its validity in the test of life. The basic model can be represented as follows:

Experience → Sage → Saying → Student of Wisdom → Experience

If we can speak properly of a locus of revelation, it is in experience at both ends. Moreover, these are not two different kinds of experience. Experience as the locus of the discovery of truth is always the place where one is testing the received tradition. The student thus becomes in time a sage, and the sage is always also a student, a pursuer of wisdom.

In Proverbs the pursuit of wisdom is the path of such virtues as prudence, honesty, humility, righteousness, generosity, moderation, harmony, good counsel (given and received), industriousness, foresight, integrity, and piety. Following this path leads to such rewards as prosperity, respect, security, honor, peace, contentment, and good standing before God and community. Fools choose violence, thoughtlessness, disrespect, insolence, intemperance, gluttony, selfishness, contentiousness, laziness, and immoderation.

We find an interesting variation of this model when the book of Proverbs personifies wisdom. The eighth and ninth chapters of Proverbs present Wisdom as a woman of divine origin, the first of God's works of creation, who has become a master worker in partnership with God and in this role is God's delight. Her activity in the creation of the world gives her intimate knowledge of how the world works. She knows (and has seen to it) that reward and punishment, judgment and justification are woven into the fabric of life as surely as are seedtime and harvest. She offers happiness to those who keep her ways and death to those who turn away from her instruction. The trial of life issuing in one or the other verdict requires no judge or adjudication; it is part of the natural order of things.

If prophetic speech is driven by disclosure or making manifest something that is hidden in God, in Proverbs wisdom depends on the recognition and acknowledgment of what has been, is, and will be. Proverbial wisdom presumes a world that is fundamentally ordered, continuous, dependable in its moral and natural laws, which reflect God's trustworthy providence structured into the created order. If you want to test the validity of the sayings, you need only choose wisdom or folly and see for yourself what happens.

The book of Job, by contrast, presents a powerful confrontation between the claims of wisdom and the experience of suffering. Job's comforters and counselors present various defenses of God's justice, and Job defends his own questioning and impatience. At the end of these debates, God at last addresses Job directly from out of the whirlwind. God becomes the questioner who challenges Job to explain the mystery and complexity of creation in which Job's own life is so small a part. In the end, the book depicts Job's acknowledgment of the hiddenness and unsearchability of God's ways, as well as his repentance for going on about what he did not understand. God rebukes the comforters and counselors (though without specifying precisely where they went wrong), affirms the speech of Job (also without specifying where or how he spoke rightly), and restores to Job family and property even greater than what he lost.

Different readers will form their own opinions about the ending of the book of Job as an answer to Job's suffering. Is it an adequate conclusion of the matter, or does it invite more discussion such as is found in the dialogues? In any case, the question of knowing and its relationship to experience becomes much more complex with the book of Job. The premise that the natural order of things is translucent to the discerning eye, which can then trace out the path from action to prosperity, falls under a question mark. Wisdom is not manifest but hidden; God alone knows the way to wisdom (Job 28:1-28). There are, indeed, order, architecture, and justice, but on a scale of intricacy, complexity, and time that humankind can never comprehend. Our experience gives access to only a fragment of the whole. Thus the fear of the Lord (who knows all) is the beginning and farthest reach of the wisdom that a human being can attain. Our diagram looks like this:

Mystery [Experience → Sage → Saying → Student of wisdom → Experience] Mystery

Mystery besets experience from behind and before, and stands as a limit to human wisdom and any articulation of divine wisdom. The mystery at the limit puts in doubt everything within the brackets, bringing experience, sagacity, saying, reading, and validation all into question. Nevertheless, wisdom and justice are affirmed, but as transcendent values guaranteed by God, who alone is great enough to understand them.

Ecclesiastes pushes the questioning of Job even further and without the tidying up we find at the end of Job. Ecclesiastes can be read as an example of what wisdom sounds like when the wise come to terms with the disappointment of wisdom's promises, the chastening of hope for a confirmation of justice and virtue in the real world. How does one live wisely when wisdom and virtue meet with punishment as often as with reward, and folly and vice are as likely to be accompanied by worldly success as by failure?

As a genre, then, biblical Wisdom presents many faces and brings forward the question of the authority of experience in competing and paradoxical ways. On one hand, the Wisdom tradition in Scripture affirms the role of ordinary experience as a realm in which the workings of God's design and intention for creation can be encountered and confirmed. It affirms a kind of moral intelligibility at work in experience, which, if it is often more subtle and difficult to discern than the regular patterns of created life (planetary motion, seasonal change, biological growth and development, etc.), is nonetheless ultimately dependable. On the other hand, biblical Wisdom literature brings forward the question that experience puts to the notion of wisdom itself. As we find in Job, the experience of undeserved suffering challenges every claim to moral intelligibility in the order of things, turning the light by which we thought we could live into darkness. By challenging the assumption of order and justice in the realm of experience, a challenge met only by recourse to mystery, the book of Job brings the very meaning and authority of wisdom into question.

The Wisdom genre negotiates its authority, we could say, through the dynamics of a mutual exchange between local experience and universal cosmos, the ordinary and the ultimate, the seeming and the real, the seen and the unseen. In the tension between the confident practical wisdom of Proverbs and the reverent skepticism of Ecclesiastes, Wisdom shares common borders with the genres of argument, lament, and praise. Wisdom invites reflection and thus responses of agreement, disagreement and restatement according to ordinary canons of logic and evidence. But Wisdom also confronts the reality of contradiction and suffering, and thus it invites the response of lament, the prayer of desperation. Wisdom also affirms a greater wisdom surpassing our own and thus invites responses of awe and praise. We sing what is too wonderful for us in words that are symbols, not facts or formulas.

Incarnational Translations of Wisdom Texts

Incarnational Translations of Proverbs

There is a generality about many of the teachings of Proverbs that makes incarnational translation relatively easy. In fact, at many points there is little difference between a historical translation and a contemporizing one. For example, the NRSV rendering of Proverbs 15:1-2 needs no contemporizing to communicate directly across time and culture.

> A soft answer turns away wrath, but a harsh word stirs up anger. The tongue of the wise dispenses knowledge, but the mouths of fools pour out folly.

Of course, even when a historical translation works well enough in direct application to a contemporary setting, some reworking of its language might give it a more modern sound. In the case of Proverbs 15:1-2, we might choose a word other than "wrath," which is not part of our everyday speech. In place of "tongue" of the wise (a Hebrew idiom), we might say simply "voice." Similarly, the NRSV rendering of Proverbs 6:6-11 ("Go to the ant. . . .") does not need any substantial updating to make it communicate directly to twenty-first-century Westerners, but changes in language, metaphor, and example can give it a new ring and a closer-to-home feel. In the following translation we might have retained the exemplary ant, but the squirrel offered a fresh alternative as a familiar animal of the city and suburb whose industry and foresight are proverbial for most of us.

> Learn from the squirrel, you couch potato;
> consider its ways, and be wise.
> Without having a pension fund or financial adviser,
> > it gathers food all summer and stores it away
> > > in preparation for winter.
> How long will you sit there in front of the TV,
> > couch potato?
> When will you get up?
> A little sleep, a little unfolding of the Lazyboy to rest,
> and poverty will break into your house and rob you;
> > destitution will hold you up at gunpoint.

Incarnational Translations of Ecclesiastes

The Book of Ecclesiastes opens with the following familiar lines:

> The words of the Teacher, the son of David, king of Jerusalem.
> > Empty air, empty air! says the Teacher,
> > Everything is empty air!
> What do people gain from all the toil
> > at which they toil under the sun?
> A generation goes, and a generation comes,
> > but the earth remains forever.
> The sun rises and the sun goes down,
> > and hurries to the place where it rises.
> The wind blows to the south,
> > and goes around to the north;
> round and round goes the wind,
> > and on its circuits the wind returns.
> All streams run to the sea,
> > but the sea is not full;

To the place where the streams flow,
    there they continue to flow.
All things are wearisome;
    more than one can express;
the eye is not satisfied with seeing,
    or the ear filled with hearing.
What has been is what will be,
    and what has been done is what will be done;
there is nothing new under the sun.
Is there a thing of which it is said,
    "See, this is new"?
It has already been,
    in the ages before us.
The people of long ago are not remembered;
    nor will there be any remembrance
of people yet to come
by those who come after them.

                                          Ecclesiastes 1:1-11

In some ways this passage is easy to transform into an incarnational translation. It speaks with a level of generality to which anyone in any time and place can relate to one degree or other. On closer inspection, however, it poses special challenges. The proofs that "all is vanity" rest on cosmological claims that may hold at the experiential level for many moderns but are no longer tenets of the modern scientific worldview. Consequently, we are faced with two different avenues for incarnational translation. We can imitate Ecclesiastes at the experiential level by looking for contemporary forms of existential experience of the sameness of all of life, or we can ask whether any modern cosmological assumptions produce grounds for the inference that "all is vanity" — even if they are different grounds from those in Ecclesiastes. Here is an incarnational translation that follows the first approach:

The words of the Teacher, son of a Baptist preacher and
    Franz Bibfeldt Chair of
    Philosophical Theology, Washington School of Theology:
Empty and pointless, says the Teacher,
    empty and pointless! Everything is empty and pointless.

What do people gain from work,
    from being cogs in the machine of labor?
A generation goes, and a generation comes,
    but the universe goes on interminably.
The city never sleeps,
    night and day, day and night it is awake, repeating itself.
Today the wind is blowing south down Third Street.
    Tomorrow it will blow north.
    The day after it will blow south again. It is boring just
        to mention this, much less experience it.
Traffic pours down the streets,
    endlessly.
It is exhausting just to watch
    — and tedious.
Everything is tedious,
    beyond words.
The eye yearns for something new,
    but the newest art work bores, the TV bores.
The ear longs for a beautiful sound that satisfies
    rather than the old song that bores or only awakens new longings.
Who can stand the monotonous music on the radio?
    Who can stand the boring silence when the radio is off?
Today is no different from yesterday;
    tomorrow will be the same.
Try moving to a different corner of the globe.
    Rest assured that it will have its own endless repetitions.
    Ennui, not entropy, rules the universe.
Is there a thing of which it is said,
    "See, this is new"?
Well, people may say it, but look beneath the surface.
    Behind the patina of fresh paint, the latest fad,
        the cutting-edge technology, the newest jargon,
    is something old, weary, and familiar,
        masquerading as something bright and new.
    It has already been,
    in the ages before us.
No one remembers the dead;
    the future dead — you and I — will not be remembered either.

This incarnational translation is a modestly modernizing paraphrase of the text that converts cosmological assertions into impressions of experience. We know that the universe is not literally a series of endless repetitions without change and that human history brings innovations of social form and material culture. Yet human experience in the voice of the Teacher discovers behind it all a sameness that is empty and pointless.

Our second approach is to consider whether a modern cosmology that sees constant and endless change, chaos, accident, capriciousness, chance pattern, non-teleological evolution in all things provides grounds for the conclusion that all is vanity.

The words of the Teacher, student of Russell, Oppenheimer, and
       Heisenberg Professor of Physics, lapsed Episcopalian:
Black hole, says the Teacher,
    black hole upon black hole!
  Everything begins and ends in a black hole.
What is the point of human activity
    in the vast schemelessness of things?
A generation goes, and a generation comes,
    each one absurdly different from the next.
The universe expands interminably, then contracts,
    then expands again.
Every infinitesimal moment in the pulse of ever-writhing matter
      is unique and meaningless,
   unreapeatable and unrecoverable.
A solar wind sifts the cosmic dust.
    Each particle of that dust is a speck among millions and billions
      and trillions of specks driven aimlessly and unobserved.
The whole universe comes from a black whole where everything
      is the same,
    explodes into an unimaginable array of difference,
   and returns to a knot of sameness only to become different again.
The universe does not weary of this endless change.
    Nietzsche dreamed of a spider and an eternal return.
     There is no return.
   The eye and ear long to discern a pattern.
   Patterns are only illusions of return.
No one can go home again.

There is no home.
The hearth of the universe changes minute by minute.
    The door to the place you once were is no longer there.
    Only a simulacrum remains. Turn the key and enter. No one you
        know is there.
You are not there. "You" are simply a series of molecules
    changing their relations from one instant to the next,
        an illusion of a whole,
    in truth a random coming together and falling apart.
The universe has no trouble forgetting you
    since you are only an accidental clump of atoms
loosely connected in constantly shifting ways for a cosmic blink
        — and then you are gone.

We have given two examples of incarnational translations of Ecclesiastes 1:1-11 by focusing on internal questions of form and content. We have not inquired into the sociology of this kind of Wisdom literature. An important source and setting of the Wisdom teachings of the Hebrew Bible was the royal court, and many of the Wisdom sayings presume a prosperous male audience. In Ecclesiastes we have the voice of the leisured elite, personified in King Solomon, who has the luxury of experiencing everything and investigating everything, unencumbered by the distraction of making sure he and his family have enough to eat. It is fair to ask to what extent Ecclesiastes deals with a rich person's problem. At the very least that question argues for viewing Ecclesiastes within a larger canonical perspective in which the answer to Solomon does not always take the form he seeks. One answer from other parts of the canon is that the meaning and purpose he wants cannot be found in the pursuit of pleasure, knowledge, and beauty. Another answer is that his whole intellectual project is tainted by the inherent injustice of the economics that make it possible. What gives him and his social class the right to idle pursuits while the poor struggle and starve? What gives any of us such a right? Perhaps the message of Ecclesiastes is not simply its ostensible teaching but the question, When I get bored, who pays the price? That a question like this one may be at stake in our encounter with the text is perhaps easier to see in an incarnational translation. The words "the wind blows to the south, and goes around to the north . . . and on its circuits the wind returns" sound quaint and venerable. Our incarnational translation has a different ring: "Today the wind is blowing south down

Third Street. Tomorrow it will blow north. The day after it will blow south again." Suddenly the voice is not archaic but near, acquiring a concreteness that invites new questions. Is this the voice of someone who is clinically depressed? Or is it the voice of a clearheaded realist, perhaps of an existentialist, a follower of Sartre? Or is it the voice of someone who is simply self-absorbed and bored? What possibilities for being are offered here? What is the appropriate response to the text? A final redactor has given us some guidance: "Fear God and keep his commandments; for that is the whole duty of everyone" (12:13). We are left to discover what kind of answer this is.

Another familiar text from Ecclesiastes is found in 3:1-8. It resembles in certain ways the kind of wisdom we find in Proverbs, which assumes that things have a right way, time, and place. Here is an incarnational translation of the passage:

> For everything there is a season, and a time for every matter in
>   the universe:
>   a time to be born and a time to die;
> a time for meetings and consultations and a time
>   to let what we have planned unfold and produce its results;
> a time to fight and a time
>   for conflict resolution;
> a time to dismantle present operations and a time
>   to start something new;
> a time to cry and a time
>   to laugh;
> a time to mourn and a time
>   to celebrate;
> a time to clear off the desk and a time
>   to pile up papers;
> a time for lovemaking and
>   a time for abstinence;
> a time to reach for the stars and a time
>   to let go;
> a time to hang on to things and a time
>   to clean out the basement;
> a time for taking things apart and a time
>   for putting things back together;
> a time to keep quiet and
>   a time to speak up;

a time to love and a time
   to hate;
a time for war and a time
   for peace.

Incarnational Translations of Job

The book of Job, which contains some of the most ancient poetry in the Bible, deals famously with the problem of theodicy. If God is all-good and all-powerful, why do the weak and the innocent so often suffer and find no protection from the divine hand? Job himself is an instance of this question, but he also speaks on behalf of other sufferers. In the poem of chapter 24, Job asks why God is absent while the wicked oppress the vulnerable. The opening lines of Job's questioning are as follows:

"Why are times not kept by the Almighty,
   and why do those who know him never see his days?
The wicked remove landmarks;
   they seize flocks and pasture them.
They drive away the donkey of the orphan;
   they take the widow's ox for a pledge.
They thrust the needy off the road;
   the poor of the earth all hide themselves.
Like wild asses in the desert
   they go out to their toil,
scavenging in the wasteland
   food for their young.
They reap in a field not their own
   and they glean in the vineyard of the wicked.
They lie all night naked, without clothing,
   and have no covering in the cold.
They are wet with the rain of the mountains,
   and cling to the rock for want of shelter."

Job 24:1-8

The expression "the wicked" in verse 2 renders an anonymous "they" in the Hebrew text. The NRSV translators specify this subject as "the wicked" in view of the fact that they do things typically deemed as works of the wicked in other biblical texts. The appearance of the expression "the wicked" in verse 6 confirms this translation decision. The opening question of our passage seems to ask why God does not keep appointed times for judgment. A time for judgment probably means both punishment of the wicked and vindication of the rights of the poor and the weak. When the wicked oppress the vulnerable, why doesn't God intervene? We might translate verses 1-8 into contemporary terms this way:

> "Why doesn't God keep appointments with justice?
>   The day for divine help against oppression comes and goes.
> Why doesn't God put in an appearance?
>   They alter documents on-line
>   and steal the property of honest people.
> They turn the teenager into a junkie.
>   They finagle widows out of their life savings.
> They ban begging in the streets,
>   cut funding to public institutions for the mentally disabled,
> slash the budgets for homeless shelters,
>   eliminating publicly funded childcare programs.
> The poor live in run-down highrises in dangerous neighborhoods;
>   the homeless hide beneath the viaducts
>   and in the alleys.
> Like the sleek rats and ghostly possums that prowl the city in secret,
> they go about their daily work;
>   they scavenge in the dumpsters for food.
> They collect cans from the gutters.
>   They sleep in filthy clothes.
> When it is cold, they cover themselves with newspapers
>   to keep warm.
> The snow and rain soak the newspapers.
>   They huddle in entryways to escape the weather."

This incarnational translation adopts the ancient version's use of an anonymous subject for the actions that harm the poor. That subject is probably to be taken as different kinds of people who act wickedly. But the focus is more on the plight of the oppressed than on the wicked. This anonymous "they" includes conventional larcenists and thieves as well as those who oppress under cover of the law. Producing an incarnational translation of this passage compels one to cast certain people in contemporary society in the roles of these lawless and law-abiding oppressors. In the example above, one can guess that it is cyber-thieves, drug dealers, and governmental bodies (backed by popular sentiment?) who mistreat the poor. Some may object that it oversimplifies a complex urban problem to depict governmental bodies as wicked for public policy stances expressed in ordinances and funding decisions that have the effects described in this incarnational translation. Incarnational translators may disagree about how best to depict the agents and mechanisms of injustice in the plight of the poor and the homeless in a modern city. But the translation cannot be faithful to the original if it attributes the various harms solely to dishonest and illegal activity. In the ancient version, the wicked do some things legally. Verse 3 says, "They take the widow's ox for a pledge" (cf. v. 9); verse 6 describes the poor laboring in fields and vineyards that belong to the wicked, who are rich and powerful. An ancient audience would have assumed that the rich and powerful acquired these lands through means both legal (e.g., foreclosure) and illegal (e.g., moving land markers). Moreover, in verses 10-11, the plight of the poor seems to be that they are not given a living wage: "Though hungry, they carry the sheaves; . . . they tread the wine presses, but suffer thirst." One benefit of creating an incarnational translation of this passage is that it alerts us to the probability that the author of Job was taking a contested political position in his day in his description of the plight of the poor. Not everyone would have agreed with him. In fact, the answer of Bildad the Shuhite in chapter 25 implies that the poor are not innocent and thus are not victims of unjust suffering.

God's speech in Job 38–41 is the climax of the book. In two long sequences (chapters 38–39 and 40–41) the speech poses a series of cosmological challenges in answer to Job's questions. The effect is to render Job humble and virtually speechless. Readers, too, may feel the sting of God's sarcastic questions, finding themselves in Job's shoes. They may also chuckle at Job — and at themselves — appreciating the wit of the divine barbs, or they may begin questioning God's questions, entering into dialogue with the wisdom teachers who crafted the book of Job.

The divine speeches of Job 38–41 pose special challenges for incarnational translation. We will concentrate on some examples from Job 38. The divine speech in 38:4-11 rehearses some of the events of creation in ways similar to Genesis 1: God commands and it is so. Elsewhere in Job 38, the text assumes that the ongoing processes of the created order are sustained by a similar ongoing divine activity. Just as God commanded in the beginning and the sea obeyed its boundaries (38:8-11), so now God commands the dawn each day (38:12), leads the stars in their courses (38:32), and tells the clouds when to give rain (38:34). A contemporary theology of creation may assume that God has designed the universe so that processes of nature operate on their own without direct iterative divine actions to keep them going. Or it may assume that God sustains the universe not only by virtue of an "initial" design but also by an ongoing providence that works through the "laws of nature." Admittedly, these are crude ways of putting two of the popular theological options. In any case, a modern Christian who is not in revolt against modern science is not likely to think of God's relationship to the created order the way ancients did: that storms are of God's direct intervention or that the stars are quasi-supernatural powers that move as they do at God's direct command.

An incarnational translation might convert the language of iterative fiat into natural processes designed by God and structured into creation, or it might imitate the archaic language via metaphor. Here we should also keep in mind that Job is quite capable of using figurative language for natural occurrences. For example, Job 38:12-13 has God commanding the dawn to grab the skirts of the earth each morning and shake the earth like a garment until the wicked tumble out. If the grabbing and shaking are metaphorical, is the divine commanding also metaphorical? Certainly the begetting and birthing language for God's control of weather in Job 38:28-29 is figurative.

A related question is when to substitute a more contemporary metaphor, one informed by scientific understanding, for an ancient metaphor based on Wisdom cosmology. For example, many ancient Mediterraneans imagined that things such as rain, snow, and hail were kept in unseen storehouses in the heavens. The gods — or at least certain gods — had control of these storehouses and opened them to produce rain or snow or hail on earth. The ancient Israelites of Job's time thought that the Lord God had charge of these storehouses. Now maybe they thought of these holding places in only quasi-literal terms; on the other hand, later Apocalyptic literature contains descriptions of heavenly journeys where a seer or heavenly traveler, such as Enoch, *sees* the places where the various forms of weather are kept. The basic cosmological assumption in Job 38:37 that rain is stored in heaven informs a figurative depiction of how God sends rain on the earth: "Who can tilt the waterskins of the heavens . . . ?" Modern science has a different conception of where rain comes from: a cloud is a rising bubble of moist air (evaporated water and air); in this bubble the water condenses on tiny particles (aerosols) to form droplets that collide with each other to form larger clusters until they are heavier than air, so that they fall to the ground. What sort of *figurative* expression might reflect this scientific conception? Perhaps, as a substitute for a tilted skin of heavenly rainwater, we might imagine water molecules "huddling together" in droplets.

Another challenge for incarnational translation of the divine speeches in Job concerns human power over the natural order. Ancient people felt generally impotent before natural forces, which they believed either were gods or were entirely in the hands of the gods. One might pray to, propitiate, or magically bind a deity in order to control (what we would call) a natural process; but one did not think to understand it in terms of physical laws that human beings might discover and engage technologically. Of course, there was technology in the ancient world. But many things were assumed to lie completely outside human power. In particular, anything lying in the domain above the earth (the firmament, heavens, etc.) or having its source there was treated as entirely outside ordinary human power — except through religion or magic. And anything having to do with the processes of life (plant and animal) was regarded as fundamentally mysterious, open in only modest ways to technological influence (through medicine, agricultural practice, etc.). Various statements in Job 38–41 assume that, when it comes to the physical world, there are some things that only God can know, some things that only God can do, some places that only God can go. Moderns can agree — but only from a very different perspective and set of assumptions. For modern people, the boundaries of human knowledge of, power over, and presence in the physical universe are continually being expanded by modern science and technology. This creates a clash between ancient and modern presuppositions over what Job 38:16, for example, asserts through its rhetorical question:

> Have you entered into the springs
>> of the sea
> or walked the recesses of the deep?

The obvious answer for an ancient is no; the obvious answer for a modern is yes. Or consider Job 38:33:

Do you know the ordinances
   of the heavens?
Can you establish their rule
   on the earth?

In ways and degrees inconceivable to ancient people, modern astronomy and astrophysics give us knowledge of "the ordinances of the heavens." Modern science rejects the notion that these "ordinances" "rule" the earth, an idea in Job that appears to be astrological — that the stars, by divine design, control human destiny.

One may ask whether the question is what modern science and technology know and can do versus what ancient wisdom and technology knew and could do, or what an ordinary modern individual can know and do versus what Job knew and could do. Job did not know the "ordinances of heaven," and neither does Charlie Cosgrove or Dow Edgerton. We are neither astronomers nor astrophysicists. But in Job, the point is not what Job the individual knows or is able to do but what human beings know and are able to do. God's questioning of Job loses much of its force unless Job's knowledge and power are humanity's knowledge and power. The contrast is divine power and knowledge versus human power and human wisdom. Hence, an incarnational translation must assume modern science and modern technology as contemporary forms of human wisdom and power.

The preceding raises a further question, which we can illustrate by using Job 38:31-32 and 34-38. It is difficult to imagine that human technology will ever advance to the point where human beings can control constellations of stars ("bind the chains of Pleiades, or loose the cords of Orion"). But causing clouds to produce rain is technologically possible under certain conditions: they must contain supercooled water, that is, liquid water colder than zero degrees Celsius. It is also likely that human technology will afford increasingly greater control of weather in the future. Thus the modern answer to the question "Can you lift up your voice to the clouds, so that a flood of water may cover you?" is yes — under certain conditions, given the present state of technology — and probably yes on a grander scale in the future. Let's assume that somewhere between seeding clouds and moving around stars lies an unknown future limit to human technology. Is that limit the boundary between the divine and the human? Or does such thinking fall into something like what Dietrich Bonhoeffer called the "God of the gaps," the tendency to "locate" God — and the need for God — just beyond the ever-receding limits of human knowledge and technology?[6]

From an ancient perspective, modern science looks like an expansion of the boundaries of human knowledge and power into what was assumed to be an exclusively divine domain. On ancient assumptions, this kind of expansion looks like encroachment, a human transgression into the divine domain, the kind of thing that God seeks to thwart. The story of Adam and Eve eating the forbidden fruit of knowledge and the story of the tower of Babel come to mind. But the question of transgressing boundaries of knowledge set by God does not arise in the book of Job. Instead, Job assumes that certain boundaries between divine and human knowledge of the cosmos cannot be crossed: they lie fundamentally beyond human reach. Much modern theology has followed in Bonhoeffer's footsteps on this question, resisting the temptation to define the boundary between God and humanity in terms of wisdom about natural processes, and has instead distinguished scientific knowledge and theology as different kinds of knowledge — different "spheres of discourse," different "language games." Science can expand the boundaries of knowledge about physical laws and processes, but it cannot answer ultimate questions like these: Why something and not nothing? Does the universe have a purpose?

In the preceding we have focused on philosophical issues in recontextualizing the message of Job 38–41 for a contemporary audience. But considerations of genre and rhetorical form are equally important. One feature of the poetic genre of God's speeches is their length. This is a matter of rhetorical strategy. What the speech "does" is in part an effect of God's sheer volubility in response to Job. The content might easily be boiled down to something short and simple like: You are a mere human being with extremely limited knowledge, and you certainly do not comprehend the beginning and end of all things, so your challenges to the ways of God, who created all things and knows all things, are not to be taken seriously. *Be quiet!* But it's not just what God says but the piling up of divine questions, the unrelenting torrent of divine challenges to Job, that leaves the latter speechless and shapes how listeners experience the text. The following incarnational translation renders the whole of chapter 38 in order

---

6. Dietrich Bonhoeffer, *Letters and Papers from Prison*, enlarged edition, Eberhard Bethge, ed. (New York: Macmillan, 1972), pp. 311-12.

to convey something of God's volubility, and also to illustrate ways of dealing with some of the challenges discussed above. We have supplied verse numbers to help the reader correlate the incarnational translation with the original.

1 Then God answered Job out of the whirlwind:
  2 "Who is this who pontificates out of ignorance?
3 Stand up and show me what you know!
  I will question you and you will answer me.

  4 "Where were you when I created the universe?
    Tell me, if you're so smart.
5 Who decided how big the universe would be —
  surely you know!
6 Who invented curved space?
  What is the physiological principle
by which everything holds together,
  and who conceived it,
7 in the beginning of everything
  when the angels sang for joy?

8-11 "Who saw to it that dry land would emerge
  from the primal sea of the infant earth,
that continents would form and endure for millions of years,
  safe from the great dark oceans?

12 "Was it you, perhaps when you were just a child,
  who first determined that the earth
should rotate every twenty-four hours,
  bringing dawn each morning,
13 so that dawn and the imitators of dawn —
  electric lights and security cameras —
might bring all the dark corners of the earth into view
  until the wicked come into focus, exposed in their deeds?
14 The earth changes under light,
  like a lens turning into focus,
like a color photograph developing in its chemical bath.
15 Light is withheld from the wicked,
  and their trigger finger is paralyzed.

16 "When *National Geographic Magazine*
    or the science channel on cable TV
takes you to the bottom of oceans
    or the remote trails of underwater caves,
are you able to figure out the meaning of life
    from the things you see there?
17 Do you know the meaning of death?
18 Are you confident that when science has taken you
    to every corner of the universe
you will then know everything about the universe?
    Speak up!

19-20 "Where do light and darkness come from,
    and how we can we find out?
Show us the scientific path to their absolute origin,
    the answer to the question *Why something and not nothing?*
21 Surely you know,
    for you are older than the universe,
and you were there
    when God was drawing up blueprints for creation.

22 "You watch the weather channel.
    It's on twenty-four hours a day.
It tells you where dangerous weather comes from.
    23 Does it tell you when divine judgment will come?
Does it tell you whether I am behind the flood, the tsunami, or the
earthquake,
    whether they are my instruments of battle?
24 When the meteorologists tell you
    the precise moment of dawn
        in each time zone
    and the speed and direction of the wind
        in each region of the earth,
do you thereby assume that you understand light and wind?

25 "Who designed the world so that the rain falls
    and the lightning flashes
26 in places where no one lives
    in the desert, which is devoid of human life,

27 to nourish barren and desolate lands
   and to water the ground so grass will grow?

28 "Does the rain have a father,
   or whose children are the drops of dew?
29 From whose womb does ice come,
   and who has given birth to the frozen dew?
30 The waters become hard like a stone,
   and the lakes and seas freeze over.

31 "Can you change the movements of the stars
   or give the planets new orbits?
32 Do you have any influence over the appearance of the Big Dipper
   or the position of Alpha Centauri?
33 If you understand the basic laws of astrophysics,
   does this mean that you can move stars around at will?

34 "I follow your meteorology and your science fiction.
Do you imagine that because you can
      create storms in a movie
         or even rain in a biosphere,
you can control clouds and floods and lightning
      around the globe?
35 Can you push a button and make snow fall in Ossining, New York,
   or rain in Cairo, Egypt?
Or do you have a voice-activated system,
   so that you can call for, say, bolts of lightning
and they will instantly appear overhead
   and say, 'Here we are'?
36 Who has given the human brain the capacity to think,
   to understand, to produce scientific knowledge?
37-38 Who has the scientific knowledge
         to add up all the molecules of water
      in all the clouds?
Or who can make those molecules
   huddle together in droplets
and produce rain wherever the ground is dry?
39-41 You protect endangered species in zoos
   and manage ecosystems.

Does this give you the idea that you are
    the benefactor of creation,
the gracious protector of all the living creatures,
    the dolphins and the sea lions,
the beetles and the owls?
Are you the answer to every danger that threatens them?"

The last question of this incarnational translation points up an irony in the difference between the theological argument of Job and our own engagement with Job. Job confronts God with the question of his own suffering as an innocent, a righteous man undeserving of his trouble. God's answer points out to Job how weak in knowledge and power the human being is who asks such a question as if to put God on trial. But the modern person who belongs to the industrialized world and approaches God with the question of the suffering of the innocent also bears a burden of responsibility that Job did not have. The scientific knowledge and technology that might, in Job's terms, give the modern person greater standing to question God, also makes the modern human being guilty in a way that an ancient person could not be. We may say that we *have* been to the bottoms of oceans and *do* know the laws that govern the stars and the weather and many other things completely beyond the ken of the ancient person. But by this knowledge we have become not only the benefactors of humanity but also a danger to life on this planet — to innocent human beings and innocent creatures. Hence, when God puts us in the dock in an incarnational translation of Job 38, the question is not only whether we have enough knowledge to ask our questions of God intelligently as the well-informed innocents who have a right to find fault with God, but also whether our wisdom and its technological products are not already an embarrassment to us when we claim to know even better than did Job what is wrong with God or belief in God in a world where the innocent suffer.

CHAPTER SIX

Text and Meaning

Incarnational translation is a hermeneutical method, and books on hermeneutics often begin with a theoretical discussion. We have postponed sustained discussion of hermeneutical theory to the end, along with a number of questions about criteria for devising and judging incarnational translations. We have two reasons for placing this theoretical chapter last. First, not everyone exposed to this approach requires an introduction to theoretical hermeneutics, either because they possess a theoretical habit of mind and a range of hermeneutical knowledge that lets them fit incarnational translation into their own framework without assistance from us or, alternatively, because they find theory uninteresting or even annoying. Whatever the case, we have not wanted to make any readers impatient or irritated by front-loading this book with theory! A second reason for bringing up hermeneutical theory in a formal and more systematic way at the end is that we think theoretical discussions can be best engaged once concrete examples and questions of interpretation are on the table. The preceding chapters evoke general hermeneutical questions, as well as sharpen concerns about methodological criteria. What follows is a general introduction to hermeneutics that considers incarnational translation in its relationship to a number of hermeneutical models. This leads to a description of a model that we find especially helpful, which is based largely on the work of Paul Ricoeur. We conclude by examining some frequently asked questions about criteria and controls in incarnational translation.

Faith and History

A fundamental assumption of incarnational translation is that when contemporary readers take up Scripture, they read from a different place and age than that of Scripture and its writers. Vast distances of time, history, understanding, language, and culture stand between the origins of our Scripture and our own reading. The fact that the biblical writings come from the past is part of their identity and authority as Scripture. Israel and the church, though composed of many different inner histories, point to Scripture to indicate their foundations. The testimonies of Israel and the church come as witness to a history. Confessions of faith and professions of practice are responses to that history. Christian proclamation is inherently bound to the testimonies of the ancestors as these witnesses point to the deep fountains of faith and life.

Scripture itself also has a history: its composition, transmission, combination, canonization, and interpretation (within Scripture itself, as well as in tradition). Beyond this, it has even *made* history: that is, it has led to events, institutions, movements, cultures, and practices from the ordinary to the epic that have shaped the ways it is perceived and understood. When the scriptures are read, it is in an astonishing range of contexts, with their own particular histories, institutions, languages, cultures, and practices, their own various testimonies, confessions, and professions. They are also read by particular flesh-and-blood readers, each of whom has a special configuration of history, location, identity, and stake in reading.

All of this seems self-evident. Nevertheless, while the fact of distance and difference can be readily seen and understood, it is all too easy (even for trained readers) to read forgetfully — forgetful of the challenges that distance and difference present. These challenges, however, and the difficulties they pose, are at the very heart of the problem of interpretation. In some ways, this problem touches any reader reading any text of history or myth, philosophy or poetry, literature or law. Yet for communities whose faith and life include accountability to their scriptures and traditions (however their authority may be understood), the problem has a special urgency. For such communities there is a necessary joining of the issues of historical understanding and contemporary life, making their life, indeed their identity, inherently hermeneutical. They *must* read texts from and for another time and place, they *must* interpret in and for their own time and place, and they *must* find ways to shape their faith and practice through this hermeneutical life.

What Does a Text Mean? How Do We Know?

These are fundamental questions that come down to us from ancient times. They are also fundamental contemporary questions — though perhaps for different reasons. In his classic work *The Mirror and the Lamp*, M. H. Abrams describes four basic orientations in the history of Western criticism: mimetic, pragmatic, expressivist, and objectivist.[1] Each orientation represents a different approach to the question of meaning in a text and where it is to be found. Although they are drawn from traditions of criticism of art and literature, they all have their counterparts in the way Scripture has been read; indeed, the reading of Scripture in the West has corresponded strongly to other cultural practices of reading. Augustine noted this long ago. In the reading of Scripture, he pointed out, meaning may be revealed by God, but the alphabet has been learned humanly. If one is to demonstrate the validity of interpretation and communicate with others, it will have to be through the conventions of human language, not divine. Although the content is holy, reading is reading.[2] Augustine would have appreciated Abrams's concerns and observations.

All of the orientations Abrams describes may be found not only in tradition but in the ordinary work of interpretation preachers undertake each week. As we seek to characterize certain twentieth-century developments, we will need some additional categories, but these four offer a good starting point. The following diagram presents the primary focus for each orientation. The text, or "work," is put at the center, and the arrows indicate different locations toward which interpretation seeks to move.

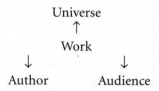

"Mimetic" theories approach a work as being in some way imitative of aspects of the world or reality (universe). The *reference* of a work is the

1. M. H. Abrams, *The Mirror and the Lamp: Romantic Theory and the Critical Tradition* (London: Oxford University Press, 1953).
2. Augustine, *On Christian Doctrine*, trans. D. W. Robertson, Jr. (Indianapolis: Bobbs-Merrill, 1958), p. 4.

subject matter it imitates, and to understand a work in this mode is to grasp its relationship to the appearances of reality or reality itself.[3] In naive mimetic notions of text and meaning, one treats the text as a kind of mirror of its referent. Questions of interpretation scarcely arise. One knows about self, God, and world simply by repeating the words of the text, unaware of the hidden hermeneutical transformations that inevitably take place in such repetition. In the modern period, various forms of fundamentalism exhibit naive forms of the mimetic notion of text and meaning.

Where mimetic approaches involve awareness that the text is not a polished and luminous mirror but a dark glass requiring interpretation, a more sophisticated notion of mimesis develops. This approach has its roots in Platonic understanding. Plato distinguished three categories: the eternal and unchanging Ideas (including the Forms); the world of sense and appearance (including things natural and artificial); and the realm of shadows, images, reflections, and the arts.[4] For example, the form of the flower becomes manifest in an actual flower, which is imitated in a representation of a flower. The form of a virtue may be manifest in a virtuous action, which is imitated in a representation (a drama, let's say) of an action. Forms are intelligible but not visible. They can be known to reason but not literally seen except in manifestations (flowers, mountains, chairs, chariots). Manifestations are visible but not intelligible; they cannot be understood by themselves but only through reference to the forms. In *The Republic,* Plato has Socrates affirm that knowledge pertains to the realm of the Ideas (or Forms) and that the philosopher is the person who can grasp both the eternal Idea and the manifestations, not confusing the likeness with the form.[5] Representations are at two removes from the reality of the forms, which are imitations of imitations and therefore inferior. The philosopher seeks to move from the lesser to the greater.

Both Hellenistic Jewish and Christian interpreters were profoundly influenced by this understanding, especially those who wished to appeal to the cultural elite of the Greco-Roman world by demonstrating the "sophistication" that lay behind the seeming "crudeness" of Scripture. Interpreters took up practices of reading Scripture that sought to go from texts to moral principles or doctrine or revelation. Allegorical interpretation, a

---

3. Abrams, *The Mirror and the Lamp,* p. 10.
4. Abrams, *The Mirror and the Lamp,* p. 8.
5. § 476a, 507b.

method previously applied to rescue literary and religious texts (such as Homer) from various scandals of crudity or offense, sought the higher truth behind the letter. The Christian theologian Origen proposed a three-fold distinction of body, soul, and spirit that roughly corresponded to literal/historical, moral, and spiritual.[6] Augustine presented a highly developed theory of signs by which all things finally refer to God. Medieval interpretation distinguished literal, moral, mystical, and anagogical (the world to come) levels of meaning in Scripture. Pico della Mirandola affirmed seven different levels, with seven sublevels within each *(Heptapla)*.[7] Even more literal (plain sense) approaches, such as those advocated by the school of Antioch, sought to move to higher levels of meaning behind a text.

Mimetic theories may also appear as historical approaches. In such cases the text is seen as a manifestation of some antecedent history or culture, and one reads to discover what the historical or cultural referent is. We read the story of the Exodus, let us say, to grasp God's action in history. We read a certain Psalm to discover clues to how worship was conducted at the Temple in Jerusalem. From a collection of laws and instructions, we try to reconstruct the forms and dynamics of how a religious system was practiced. From a group of letters and sermons we try to discern the shape of the early Christian community. One branch of the Biblical Theology movement in the twentieth century was devoted to this conception of the Bible and history. Its advocates located revelation in the historical event and saw the Bible as a window to those events.

Although mimetic approaches come in different forms and may ask very different questions, they share a concern to go through the text to find connection to some prior or transcendent world, universe, or reality — whether it is historical, doctrinal, metaphysical, or philosophical. What is the stance of incarnational translation to mimetic models of the text? Incarnational translation, as a way of rendering Scripture in the homiletical here and now, assumes that the text does point beyond itself, that it speaks transcendently, that it witnesses to God. Moreover, incarnational translation also assumes that, in speaking to us about God,

6. Origen, *On First Principles*, trans. G. W. Butterworth (Gloucester, MA: Peter Smith, 1973), IV.II.4.

7. Pico della Mirandola, *Heptaplus*, trans. Paul J. W. Miller and Douglas Carmichael, Library of Liberal Arts (New York: Macmillan, 1985).

the text reveals something about us as human beings in all the variegated forms in which we embody a human condition addressed by the gospel. But with respect to one end of the spectrum of mimetic models of text and meaning, it does not assume that the text is a mirror of the subject or reality it describes. And with respect to the other end of the spectrum, it also does not treat the text as a cryptic, crude, or inferior mode of expressing its referent, which can be better known and described through a different kind of language, whether philosophical or theological. Whatever the value and possibilities for knowing through a different linguistic mode than the genres of the text, incarnational translation is a wager that we can encounter the subject of the text by hearing a mimetic rendition of the text. That rendition is not simple repetition but a transformation that attends to the unity of content with form. It does not reject but makes use of philosophical and historical modes of understanding, but it does not convert the text into historical reconstruction or philosophical restatement.

"Pragmatic" theories of text and meaning approach a work through its effects on its audience. Aristotle studied how art and rhetoric effect change in the beholder, including teaching, delighting, and moving the audience, persuading them to action. Augustine's *On Christian Doctrine* is the classic example of pragmatic theory applied to preaching. Augustine used rhetorical criticism to analyze passages from both Old and New Testaments, noting their eloquence (although praising and commending even more their wisdom).[8] Rhetorical criticism focuses on the *means* used within a text to communicate to and affect an audience, not the status of the text's relationship to some reality or truth beyond it. It seeks to identify the strategies by which the text moves and persuades the reader intellectually, aesthetically, emotionally, or morally.

The work of Athanasius provides an ancient Christian example of the pragmatic-rhetorical model of text and meaning. In his *Letter to Marcellinus,* Athanasius relies on classical understandings of literary genre when he describes the various kinds of excellence peculiar to different kinds of writing in the Bible — history, wisdom, law, prophecy, and so on. He then describes the book of Psalms as a kind of "super-genre" that includes all the other kinds but offers a marvel all its own — "namely, that it contains even the emotions of each soul, and it has the changes and rectifications of these delineated and regulated in itself . . . [there] one also com-

---

8. *On Christian Doctrine*, IV.vii.11-21.

prehends and is taught in the emotions of the soul . . . and is enabled by this book to possess the image deriving from the words."[9] The history, wisdom, law, and prophecy are the same content as may be found elsewhere in Scripture, but in the Psalter they work to a different effect by the poetic form's operation on the soul. Athanasius then goes on to discuss a wide range of Psalms in relationship to various human situations and their emotions, and how their words effect emotional transformation in those who hear them and recite them.

When an interpreter asks how a text would have been heard by some original audience and how they would have likely responded, that is a historical form of pragmatic or rhetorical criticism. Whether the audience is identified as the actual interpreter, some general, universal, or ideal reader, or some particular community of reference (original audience), pragmatic approaches focus on a kind of psychology of response or reception. Pragmatic theories carried the greatest influence in criticism up through the eighteenth century and have been called the "principal aesthetic attitude of the Western world."[10] One could argue that twentieth-century approaches to "reception theory" or "reader-response theory" are later versions of pragmatic criticism. Some approaches to cultural or political criticism that focus on how a text's rhetoric functions to persuade or form the reader may also be seen in this category.[11]

The conception of incarnational translation for preaching that we have been advocating is indebted to the pragmatic-rhetorical tradition of meaning in texts. When we insist that not only the "content" but also the "genre" of the text must be translated, we are aligning ourselves with those who say that meaning includes the effects of the text and that those effects are functions of rhetoric, which is at least in part a matter of form or genre. Incarnational translation seeks to *say and do* what the text once said and did. That aim is pragmatic-rhetorical.

"Expressive" theories of criticism focus on the author behind the work

---

9. Athanasius, *The Life of Anthony and the Letter to Marcellinus,* trans. Robert C. Gregg (New York: Paulist Press, 1980), p. 108 (§ 10).

10. Abrams, *The Mirror and the Lamp,* p. 21.

11. See, for example, Terry Eagleton's self-description of his own practice of political criticism as a pragmatic, rhetorically focused approach: *Literary Theory: An Introduction* (Minneapolis: University of Minnesota Press, 1983), p. 206. Wayne Booth has recouped the traditional idea that classic texts shape readers morally; see Booth, *The Company We Keep: An Ethics of Fiction* (Berkeley, CA: University of California Press, 1988).

and view the work essentially as "the internal made external."[12] A text is a representation of the mind of the author, disclosing the author's perceptions, thoughts, and feelings. In the Romantic version of the expressive model, the external world is transformed by the author (or artist) as creative genius. The work leads us not to the world but to the mind and genius of the author and perhaps to a transcendent reality beyond this world that we cannot see without the author's help.[13] Following the expressivist theory of text and meaning, the interpreter may pursue the mind of the author in a mode of aesthetic appreciation, conceptual reconstruction, or psychological analysis; but it is the author — not the world, not the audience, and not even the voice of the text — that one seeks.

It should be evident that an expressivist theory can assume features of the mimetic idea of text and meaning. Both involve a dynamic of reconstruction: discovering a meaning that lies behind the text. For example, one can think of the text as window to the mind of the author-genius who offers understanding of eternal truth beyond the external world of temporality and appearances. In Christian hermeneutics, one model of the Bible sees it as a text composed by authors who are in effect "geniuses" by virtue of their divine inspiration. One looks through the text into the mind of the author to find knowledge of the mind of God. Modern Christians who embrace this model of Scripture have often assumed that it is the original and traditional view. But whatever its antecedents in antiquity and in the medieval period, it owes much in its modern form to Romanticist hermeneutics. Augustine, for example, did not understand the inspiration of the Bible as solely a matter of the inspiration of its authors. He held that Scripture may contain some things by divine inspiration of which its authors were not aware, truths they had not intended.[14] In other words, the *text* is inspired.

Some modern Christians who do not affirm a robust theory of the divine inspiration of the authors of Scripture, or who confess the inspiration of Scripture without adopting a particular view of inspiration, assume at least the expressivist idea of biblical text and meaning and hold that, whatever meaning the Bible contains, it contains that meaning as an expression of the mind or intentions of its authors. One reads Romans, let us say, to

12. Abrams, *The Mirror and the Lamp*, p. 22.
13. Abrams, *The Mirror and the Lamp*, pp. 22-23.
14. *On Christian Doctrine*, 3.85 (XXVII).

discover the mind of Paul, perhaps to discover Paul's doctrine and reconstruct it as a theological system. How can one commune with the thoughts of Paul? Or the author of the Fourth Gospel? Why does he see and tell things so differently from the others? How can one understand the character of David through reading the Psalms that bear his name? Or how can we discover the thoughts of the anonymous poets and wisdom teachers of ancient Israel who, over generations, crafted and shaped ("edited") the Psalms, Job, Ecclesiastes?

As we have noted, expressive theories are especially associated with Romanticism, and they had great impact on modern hermeneutics, particularly through the work of Schleiermacher and Dilthey. Schleiermacher sought to combine methods of philology (or "grammatical" interpretation, to use his term) with what he termed "technical," or psychological, interpretation. This focused on the particular, individual, expressive, and artistic means by which the author externalizes thought in language. Grammatical interpretation was necessary because it showed the connections of vocabulary, syntax, composition, and style; however, all these point to the mind of the author.

In the grammatical work, interpretation is scientific; in the psychological, it is "divinatory,"[15] that is, it requires establishing a kind of intuitive relationship or imaginative connection. David Klemm summarizes this approach: "In the end, the meaning of the expression can only be approximated in the understanding by feeling, since what is most important about the expression as an aesthetic construct is the original experience behind the thought that is expressed."[16] Although the history of the discussion is very complex and has many variations, we could say that there has endured a strong current of argument that affirms the role of connection, empathy, participation, relationship, and "fusion of horizons" in the work of interpretation, all of which can be related to expressivist criticism.

The Romantic notion of the author in expressivist hermeneutics led in two directions. In one conception, the author is a kind of master teacher who, through his or her text, communicates something to ordinary readers who cannot arrive at the same knowledge on their own. In another conception, the readers — or certain readers outfitted with special methods —

15. *On Christian Doctrine*, p. 15.

16. David E. Klemm, *The Hermeneutical Theory of Paul Ricoeur: A Constructive Analysis* (New Brunswick, NJ: Associated University Presses, 1983), p. 21.

go behind the text to the creative, productive moment so as to understand authors better than they understood themselves (Dilthey[17]). These two conceptions of the author are often combined, existing side by side in perhaps uneasy tension. Hence, one is not often sure whether an interpretation purports to be simply a representation of the mind of the author or something more — a better, more sophisticated, more profound understanding of something that the author only dimly glimpsed.

It is important to recall that the expressivist theory is an approach belonging to *general hermeneutics.* Its advocates in the domain of biblical studies claim no special method for reading the Bible apart from whatever specific demands any text makes (linguistic, grammatical, etc.). Particularly through the later work of Dilthey, expressivist approaches became a foundation for hermeneutical understandings of the *Geisteswissenschaften,* or human sciences.[18] Within the range of expressivist approaches, the way in which the relationship with the author is conceived can vary significantly. On one hand, we have the more empathetic and affective relationship (which nevertheless depends on a close reading of the text); on the other hand, we have a more restrained conception of the intent of the author. In the latter case the interpreter is seeking not so much a relationship with the mind of the author as a re-creation of the author's intention in producing the work. In this view, the author's intention is the normative meaning of a text, and that intention is objectively present in the verbal meaning of a text, which can be determined objectively through philological analysis (E. D. Hirsch[19]). This theory of interpretation concerns itself with appropriately objective methods and seeks a demonstrably valid rendering of verbal meaning. This brings it closer to the objectivist approach (see below), and in some ways to the mimetic. Nevertheless, because the intentionalist approach locates the normative meaning in the author's intention, it can still be viewed as expressivist.

Incarnational translation can certainly be carried out on expressivist assumptions. One can make an exegetical search for the intention of the author a prerequisite of incarnational translation. In that case, to speak in Hirsch's terms, an incarnational translation is an expression of what the

---

17. See Josef Bleicher, *Contemporary Hermeneutics: Hermeneutics as Method, Philosophy, and Critique* (London: Routledge & Kegan Paul, 1980), p. 15.

18. See Richard Palmer, *Hermeneutics: Interpretation Theory in Schleiermacher, Dilthey, Heidegger, and Gadamer* (Evanston, IL: Northwestern University Press, 1969), pp. 98-123.

19. Palmer, *Hermeneutics,* p. 60.

translator sees as the significance of the author's verbal meaning for another time and place. And the audience of an incarnational translation has the task of discovering the intended significance that the translator has sought to express through the incarnational translation. But there is nothing in the nature of incarnational translation that requires an expressivist theory of text and meaning. Moreover, the model of incarnational translation that we have proposed assumes that the text as communication is more than a "significance" to be grasped intellectually. The text is a union of form and content that produces rhetorical effects. Following the intentionalist-expressivist model, incarnational translation presupposes a discovery of the author's rhetorical aims and strategies in the text and seeks to reproduce these in a contemporary restatement of the text. Although we ourselves do not think that authorial intention is the sole locus of textual meaning (see below), we do not insist that incarnational translation must be carried out on the basis of a non-intentionalist or non-expressivist theory of text and meaning.

"Objectivist" approaches direct themselves to the internal design of the text. In their strictest forms they seek to establish no correspondence of the text to the universe; they do not inquire into the effects of the work on an audience; and they seek to re-create no person, intention, or experience behind the text. Instead, they aim to discern and elaborate the internal structure and dynamics of the work as a closed system.

One of the most influential objectivist approaches is formalism. Formalism, as a method of literary criticism that developed in the twentieth century, strongly asserts the semantic autonomy of a text (the independence of language from the author's sole control of meaning) and resists the re-creation of any personal, historical, or cultural archaeology as the key to its understanding. A text is to be read strictly on its own terms (and the terms of its literary tradition), and the ideal reader is one who is "disinterested" (that is, impartial) and appropriately "scientific" (that is, seeking to have the method correspond to the nature of the object under investigation).[20] The locus of meaning is *in* the text, not outside it in the biography of the author or in some other place to which the text points or bears witness. The text is its own world, and its meaning arises from intratextual relations, a kind of self-referentiality.

20. Lynn Poland, *Literary Criticism and Biblical Hermeneutics: A Critique of Formalist Approaches* (Chico, CA: Scholars Press, 1985), pp. 74-78.

Whether or not formalism can withstand the hermeneutical criticisms that have been directed against it, it has spawned (and recovered) an interpretive attitude or orientation that has considerable merit as a way of attending to texts. In biblical studies it has been especially fruitful as a way of reading narrative, and it has natural affinities for the close readings and the attention to interconnection that many schools of exegesis have always prized. It encourages a kind of literary criticism of biblical stories that brackets questions of historical reference and authorial intent and asks how the text is put together, including questions of character portrayal and development, plot, tensions and ambiguities — all the questions that arise in keen minds who enter the world of the story and pay close attention to its architecture. Obviously, this sort of careful exploration of the internal world of a text is valuable to any kind of preaching based on Scripture. For incarnational translation, perhaps the greatest value of formalist literary criticism is the way it can teach the interpreter how to make a good text. Incarnational translation as creative mimesis of Scripture can benefit from training in attentive examination of texts as unities of form and content.[21]

Abrams's typology remains very useful as a way of distinguishing broad families of criticism and reading practice that are still quite actively in play. Indeed, most preachers will likely recognize their own interpretive work, and that of the commentators they consult, as aligned with one or more of these basic orientations. As we have already suggested, biblical studies, though it has different nomenclature, has used all of these methods — and in various combinations. We can summarize these relationships by considering three broad types of biblical criticism: historical, literary, and cultural.

Historical criticism approaches the text as a *means* of getting at a world/history or an author's mind that the text represents.[22] Interpretation

---

21. Structural linguistics in the twentieth century also contributed to objectivist hermeneutics. Structuralism focuses attention on the *system* of language itself, its structure and dynamics, as a pattern of differences and similarities. While not the same as formalist literary criticism (which focused on the structure of the work), structuralism's focus on a closed system rather than anything beyond the system (world, author, audience) shares an affinity with formalism. In structuralism, to analyze a text is to discern the way the surface structure of the text actualizes the system behind and beneath it.

22. Our discussion of method in biblical interpretation follows the scheme of Fernando F. Segovia's chapter, "'And They Began to Speak in Other Tongues': Competing Modes of Discourse in Contemporary Biblical Criticism," in Fernando F. Segovia and Mary Ann Tolbert, eds., *Reading from This Place: Social Location and Biblical Interpretation in the United States* (Minneapolis: Fortress Press, 1995), pp. 1-32.

seeks to get "behind" the text to this world of the author's mind because that is where meaning lies: the referent is behind the text, and the function of the text is to direct the reader there.

Literary criticism approaches the text as a *medium* that encodes a message.[23] Without any necessary reference to a historical world or a particular author, the task of interpretation is to discern and unfold the code or structure the text presents. Literary approaches focus their attention on the immanent patterns of the work. The world, people, and events depicted are interpreted as literary features (setting, characters, plot, etc.) that may or may not have reference to any actual history.

Cultural criticism approaches the text both as means *and* medium.[24] As means, it does indeed have a referent behind the text, which is the social, economic, and cultural system (or world) from which the text emerges. As medium, the text is a manifestation of that deeper system that can be found inscribed in the codes present in the text. The surface message and the deeper structures (whether within or behind the text) may be significantly different or even contradictory. Interpretation seeks to read not only the explicit message but also the message implicit in the coded social world within and behind the text. Take, for example, a parable in which the realm of God is compared to a wealthy absentee landowner who sends a messenger to collect his money from the tenants. What are the social relationships presented in the parable, and what is implied about them? What are the messages that the parable sends, and to whom? Do they help us understand anything about the social, economic, and cultural forces at work in the situation that produced the parable?[25]

In historical, literary, and cultural approaches to the Bible, the approach of the interpreter has often been positioned as detached, objective, and analytical. Whether as historian or critic, the interpreter is presented as concerned with establishing "the facts" or "what the text says" or "how the text works" or "the codes of the text" — as if from behind a one-way mirror. That is, the interpreter perceives but does not affect the world or meaning of the text; nor is the actual interpreter necessarily addressed or affected by

23. Segovia, "'And They Began to Speak,'" p. 15.

24. Segovia, "'And They Began to Speak,'" p. 21. "Cultural criticism" is Segovia's term for a range of sociological foci.

25. See, for example, the provocative sociopolitical analyses of the parables in William R. Herzog, *The Parables as Subversive Speech: Jesus as Pedagogue of the Oppressed* (Louisville: Westminster/John Knox Press, 1994).

the text and its world. The history, meanings, or codes can be retrieved and reconstructed analytically, and the task of the interpreter once again is to find what is "there." The question of the cultural codes within and behind the text, however, inevitably leads to the question of the cultural codes within and behind the interpreter. Indeed, Western literary theory since the nineteenth century can be seen as moving from a focus on the author to a focus on the text to a focus on the reader.[26] This came about through the convergence of two quite different streams of argument.

One of the strongest themes of the twentieth-century hermeneutical discussion was the relationship between *explanation* and *understanding*. We saw the beginnings of the discussion in the approaches of Schleiermacher and Dilthey in which they made a distinction between the task of objective, scientific explanation and the task of understanding the experience behind the text (or, as in Dilthey, understanding expressions of human life).[27] The task of explanation brings to the foreground such values as method, objectivity, distance, and validation. The task of understanding brings to the foreground the values of empathy, participation, relationship, and response. If the goal of explanation is some form of reconstruction or analysis, the goal of understanding is some form of intersubjectivity or "fusion of horizons," and application to the world and life of the interpreter. Objectivity sought to be free from the projected world and subjectivity of the interpreter; subjectivity sought ways to overcome the alienation of objectivity.

If classical hermeneutics focused on methods for correctly interpreting meaning in texts, through the influence of Heidegger — and later Gadamer — interpretive attention came to be focused more and more on understanding as a way of being in the world and on the process of understanding, whether of texts, things, the world, or ourselves.[28] In this project of understanding there is no standpoint outside of concrete existence from which to interpret objectively, and interpretation is shaped by the pre-understandings that flow from that existence. We are always already immersed in tradition and a world of experience. Both "subject" and "object" are encompassed by a larger reality within which we live. The reality of that

26. Terry Eagleton, *Literary Theory,* p. 74.

27. Palmer, *Hermeneutics,* p. 105.

28. Gary B. Madison, "Beyond Seriousness and Frivolity: A Gadamerian Response to Deconstruction," in Hugh J. Silverman, ed., *Gadamer and Hermeneutics* (New York and London: Routledge, 1991), p. 125.

life addresses itself to us, particularly in art and language, in which we can hear the "speaking of Being." The project of understanding, therefore, takes on the dynamics of dialogue, conversation, call and response. The two poles of the discussion (explanation and understanding) became increasingly alienated (along the classic lines of subject-object split) so that they came to be viewed as alternatives, perhaps even antitheses.[29]

The powerful influence of Marx, Nietzsche, and Freud was also developing from the nineteenth century onward. In their analyses of economics, power, religion, culture, and the human psyche, they developed a hermeneutics of suspicion that sought to uncover how the surfaces of these systems constituted a false consciousness or ideology that masked an underlying dynamic (class struggle, will to power, desire, etc.). The hermeneutics of suspicion called into question both the so-called objective and subjective poles by examining the hidden social interests (or powers of the unconscious) that they mask—and are *intended* to mask. Increasingly, the analysis took the form of critical theories seeking to disclose the substructure of various forms of politics, culture, social organization, racism, sexism, the construction of gender, and the very concepts of objectivity and subjectivity themselves.[30] In a related development, the approach known as *deconstruction* (most commonly identified with Jacques Derrida) began to explore how texts manifest — even in their own surface structures — the gaps, reversals, contradictions, and ambiguities that undermine ideological fictions of fixed meaning, break open the seemingly self-evident "way things are," and disclose radical new possibilities.

The concluding decades of the twentieth century, then, saw the question of interpretation turn the spotlight on the position of the interpreter. The one-way glass behind which the interpreter sat was taken away. It was no longer tenable to assume that the interpreter is an ideal, expert, neutral, objective reader who searches out only what is within or behind the text. This new theory of interpretation views the text as a *construction* (built on and reinforcing underlying interests), and it sees interpretation as the work of a particular flesh-and-blood reader, who is also situated in concrete locations of race, class, gender, ethnicity, ideology, and interest. The

29. See, for example, the discussion of the disagreements between Betti and Gadamer in Palmer, *Hermeneutics*, pp. 46-65.

30. Two focal examples of this are found in *The Hermeneutics Reader*, ed. Kurt Mueller-Vollmer (New York: Continuum, 1988). See the selections for Hans-Georg Gadamer and Jürgen Habermas.

interpreter inevitably — and sometimes intentionally — reads through the lens of his or her location (which can be quite complex and polyphonic). The cultural criticism directed at the text is expanded and turned upon interpreters, whose interpretation discloses the prejudgments and frames of reference they bring. In this approach, rather than producing a single, universally valid reading, we seek to recognize and take responsibility for our own particular interpretations in dialogue with other interpreters situated in other locations.[31] This does not rule out working as historians or literary critics or social anthropologists, but it powerfully affects the claims made about the text, its referents, and the authority of the interpreter. We may see a further implication of this turn toward the reader: if interest can be viewed as a matter for suspicion, it can also be viewed as something that is *productive,* in a positive sense. By making the reader's frame of reference more and more manifest and consciously bringing it to bear, we bring forward the interests of heretofore excluded perspectives, both to interpret and to be interpreted by the text. In biblical interpretation this has been seen most clearly in liberation hermeneutics, which brings to the foreground the historical experience, culture, and political situation of particular communities interpreting biblical texts. The work of interpretation is conceived as part of a larger responsibility or advocacy: that is, hermeneutics is an *ethical* task.

Therefore, to Abrams's categories of World, Audience, Author, and Work we could add Interpreter; and to the historical, rhetorical, psychological, and literary approaches we could add cultural, ideological and ethical criticism.

This brief sketch suggests key features of the landscape over which interpretation has traveled, and the challenges to be found on that landscape. In the next section we will indicate a possible path that is oriented to the hermeneutical task that confronts communities whose existence is shaped by reading between their texts and their lives.

Approaching the Hermeneutical Challenge

Ever since the time of ancient Greek philosophy, Western tradition has wrestled with the problematical relationships between reality, perception,

---

31. Segovia, "'And They Began to Speak,'" p. 31.

reason, intention, language, speaking, writing, and reading. Each step of the process of perception, representation, and communication entails a transformation, not simply a complete and faithful reproduction; each step of the process entails loss; each step adds something new; each step creates yet another undecidability, or indeterminacy, of meaning. It is rather like the old game of "telephone," where a message is passed from person to person and becomes increasingly garbled or changed, except that in this case the message moves through more complex transformations of perception, thought, language, and context. We could express the problem in this way:

God (or the Really Real) ≠ World ≠ Mind of Author ≠ Speech ≠ Writing ≠ Interpretation

The burden of the model is that at each step there is a gap, which is symbolized in our diagram by a cancelled "equal" sign. The gap problematizes the passage from one term to the next, and each passage entails transformation, loss, and addition. This dynamic applies in both directions, that is, in the production of a text and in the interpretation of a text. There is no sure transfer of meaning going forward and no sure recovery of meaning going backward.

As a distinctly theological issue, these problems take center stage in such influential works as Augustine's *Confessions* and *On Christian Doctrine* (which presents a strongly elaborated theory of language and interpretation), joining the problem of general hermeneutics to the particular work of theological hermeneutics. God is not the same as the signs that point to God (whether in creation or human representation). The world that appears to the human mind is shaped by the limitation and distortion (being a creature and being sinful) of being human. Human language says both more and less — and may say it differently — than a speaker may intend; the speaker may not even know what his or her own intentions really are. The same is true of writing, but with the added problems of difference and distance in time, culture, and language. And even if one somehow pierces the veils of appearances of signs and things to glimpse the glory of God, our mortal frame recoils from it, and there is nothing to do but start again. Through the centuries theology has approached the problem by such varied means as doctrines of inspiration, creedal formulations, normative tradition, scholasticism, the teaching office of the church, infallibility, and so on — all of which can be understood as attempts to guarantee some safe passage of truth from God to humankind.

The Kantian "Copernican revolution" in the eighteenth century brought the productive and synthetic power of human imagination to the center of the question of epistemology (how we know). It insisted that our knowledge of the world is knowledge not of things in themselves—as in mimesis, or reproduction — but of things as they appear to us through the structures of our imagination.[32] The dynamics of modern critical consciousness, which may be seen to flow, in part, from this "revolution," are "characterized by the fact that it feels as untrue any immediate relationship to actuality. . . . With critique consciousness takes final leave of the condition in which it can simply accept things as they actually present themselves."[33] That is, our relationship to the world is always mediated, whether by structures of the human mind or the historically conditioned imagination that construes what we perceive according to its own expectations. Neither appearances nor texts are transparent windows. They are *interpretations* that must be themselves interpreted by interpreters formed and limited by their own subjectivity. Critical consciousness applies both to the status of the appearances, texts, and interpretations, and to *self-critical* awareness of the effect of the interpreter on what is interpreted. The development of hermeneutics since that time can be described as interpreters' attempts to take seriously the problem of historical understanding mediated through texts while they remain accountable to the demands of critical consciousness.

This returns us to the core challenge that has marked the hermeneutical discussion for well over a hundred years. We could describe it as a question of the relationship between (so-called) objective and (so-called) subjective approaches to interpretation, or what the debate has termed *explanation* and *understanding*. How can we read in ways that take the text seriously — its referents and the actual interpreter? For help with this, we turn to the interpretation theory of Paul Ricoeur.[34]

---

32. Richard Kearny, *The Wake of Imagination* (London: Routledge, 1988), pp. 156-171.

33. Robert Scharlemann, as quoted in Klemm, *The Hermeneutical Theory of Paul Ricoeur*, p. 19.

34. The following presentation of the hermeneutical challenge is an appropriation of Paul Ricoeur's theory of interpretation, particularly as it is found in Ricoeur, *Interpretation Theory: Discourse and Surplus of Meaning* (Fort Worth, TX: The Texas Christian University Press, 1976). For an excellent analysis, see also Klemm, *The Hermeneutical Theory of Paul Ricoeur*.

Behind the Text

The term "behind the text" designates those locales that precede the setting down of language as writing: God, world, perception, mind of the author, speaker's meaning, hearer's meaning. Each transition, as we have said, entails loss, addition, and change. Having already considered the problem of world and perception, let us look more closely at the transition from speech to writing.

In speech we have a situation of mutual presence and dialogue — and some common context; someone says something to someone about something. The words have a *sense* (that is, they say something) and they have a *referent* (that is, they are about something). In Ricoeur's usage, the sense is found in the semantic structure of the language, and the referents are found in the world about which one speaks. In the event of dialogue, we can question one another: we can ask, "Do you mean this or that?" and we can gesture, point, refer, and clarify. The multiple possibilities, the multiple meanings (polysemeity) of words and grammar, and the world reference can all be narrowed down through this process, and the speakers can come to a closer approximation of what each is saying and what or whom they are saying it about (the ostensible referents). The *event* of speech, however, is fleeting. It comes to an end, and if it is to be preserved, it is preserved not as *event*, but as *meaning*.

The preservation of speech in writing is both gain and loss: in writing the expression is inscribed, but the situation of dialogue is lost. One can read the words years later, but one cannot ask their speaker what the words mean — or what their meaning is about. There is what Ricoeur calls an "alienation" from the event and the context of speech. Undecidability opens up through the loss of context, the loss of dialogue, the multiple possible meanings of words, and their combination. Thus transforming speech into writing entails a *distanciation*[35] and a *decontextualization:* there are a distancing from the event of speech and a loss (decontextualization) of the situation of speech. Yet this loss also brings with it a gain. The loss of the context and determinative referents of the language means a gain of *possible* referents. That is, writing from one time, place, and situation can have possible meanings for another time, place, and situation.

35. This term of Ricoeur is sometimes rendered into English with the spelling "distantiation."

That meaning, however, is not necessarily the same as the original author intended or the original audience understood, nor does it necessarily equal the world or reality beyond the author.

While this uncertainty applies to texts in general, it does so with special significance for the texts of the Bible. Their complex histories of oral tradition, authorship, composition, transmission, and variation do not allow us to claim clear and unequivocal access to the understanding of prior readers, writers, speakers, or realities that lie behind them. Interestingly enough, the effects of distanciation and decontextualization can be found even in a person's own work. A preacher who retrieves old sermon notes or a manuscript will often read his or her own words with a combination of puzzlement and surprise. Words that were spoken on a certain day and for certain reasons (many of which remained unstated) and to certain people may appear strange at a remove of years. In puzzlement one asks, "Why did I say it that way? What was I trying to communicate? What tone did I take? Why was this word so important to me then?" And one may find, with surprise, that the words on the page, prepared for an entirely different reason and season, speak to a situation at hand that was never imagined. The writer's own words come as if from someone else entirely. Even if one recalls perfectly (were such a thing possible) the original reasons for the writing, the distance discloses more than the speaker/writer knew.

Within the Text

When we open the Bible to, let's say, the Gospel of Mark, we are confronted by what Ricoeur calls a *work*.[36] A work is fixed, closed, and finite. It consists of language that has been composed and ordered into a structure. It operates according to certain conventions of genre and is configured by a particular style. The book of Mark is a narrative, for example, and while it contains non-narrative materials, they are included in such a way as to respond to and further the narrative. By contrast, the Gospel of Thomas, though structured (and containing narratives), consists of sayings with

---

36. "The Hermeneutical Function of Distanciation," in *Paul Ricoeur: Hermeneutics and the Human Sciences,* ed. and trans. John B. Thompson (Cambridge, UK: Cambridge University Press, 1981), p. 134.

virtually no overarching narration. Stylistically, to take another example, we could contrast the terseness and action in Mark with John's tendency toward long interpretive speeches. Beyond genre and style, a work has "a teleological system of whole and parts, composed in a hierarchy of ordered relationships."[37] This means that there is a pattern or design to the language, its selection of vocabulary, its syntax, its sequencing, and its correlation of plot, setting, and character. It uses these parts in the service of some overarching goal; indeed, their arrangement is purposeful. These are all to be found inscribed within the text itself, not discovered behind the text.

The distanciation and decontextualization created by the process of writing, as we said, mean the loss of ostensive reference and the opening up of possible reference. If the reference is no longer the understanding of an original audience, author, or world, what can it be? Ricoeur's answer is the "world of the text": "The text speaks of a possible world and of a possible way of orienting oneself within it. The dimensions of this world are opened up by and disclosed by the text."[38] Because of the loss of the first-order reference, the world of the text is a kind of poetic or fictional world. This does not mean that that world isn't true, only that it is a construct, a model proposed to the imagination. The "world" of the Gospel of Mark is different from that of the Gospel of John. Each is a kind of simulacrum (working model or virtual reality) in which narration, action, and meaning are possible. The texts present respective worlds and possibilities for being in those worlds.

To return to the earlier distinction between sense and reference, Ricoeur proposes that "the structure of the work is in fact its sense, and the world of a work is its reference. Hermeneutics then is simply the theory that regulates the transition from structure of the work to world of the work."[39] The immanent structure or design of the text serves this text-world. Interpretation seeks, first of all, to discover and analyze the parts and whole that constitute the sense and reference of the text. The sense is to be found within the text, the reference is found in the world projected *before the text,* rather than one to be retrieved *behind the text.* We shall turn to this question of methodology shortly, under the themes of explanation and understanding; but this category of the "world of the text" is "the cen-

---

37. Poland, *Literary Criticism and Biblical Hermeneutics,* p. 172.
38. Ricoeur, *Interpretation Theory,* p. 88.
39. As quoted in Klemm, *The Hermeneutical Theory of Paul Ricoeur,* p. 85.

tral category to Ricoeur's hermeneutical program because in the end the text-world is what is to be understood and interpreted."[40]

Up to this point we have focused our attention on what a text is and what it might offer. We turn our attention now to the question of the process of interpretation itself.

Before the Text

The actual interpreter enters the process of interpretation from within a particular self-understanding. The interpreter inhabits a "world." There is a world configured in our imaginations, and however it may relate to the environment and other worlds around us, it is within the life-world (Husserl) constructed in our minds that we perceive, act, feel, think, value, believe, and tell our stories.[41] It is also from within this frame of reference that we interpret. This world and how we see our place in it is our *self-understanding.*

Self-understanding is powerfully shaped by the particularity and contingency of our social location, historical situation, and personal experience. Such factors as gender, race, class, ethnicity, nationality, cultural and religious heritage, sexual orientation, political context, family context, personal history, personality, body, education, and more — all contribute to the shaping of one's self-understanding. We are aware of some of this self-understanding and can articulate it. We can recount histories, affirm values, confess beliefs, name fears and hopes, and so on. But much of our self-understanding is hidden from us. It operates behind the lens, so to speak. We do not perceive the understandings themselves any more than we perceive the rods and cones at the back of our eyes that transform light into electrical impulses to send to our brains. Through these self-understandings we both perceive the world around us and perceive it as something with particular meaning. As in our previous discussion of the relationship between the world and our minds, there is no "immaculate perception."

On the one hand, our self-understanding provides a bridge that links us to others. There are things we can perceive precisely because of the

40. Klemm, *The Hermeneutical Theory of Paul Ricoeur,* p. 85.
41. Poland, *Literary Criticism and Biblical Hermeneutics,* p. 174.

imaginative world we inhabit. A person who has suffered the loss of a child may hear the story of Jairus's daughter differently from one who has not. A soldier whose life was saved by a comrade may hear Jesus' saying about laying down one's life for a friend in a special way. A person who has known poverty and hunger may experience meaning in "blessed are the poor" that is hidden from those who have always been well fed.

On the other hand, our self-understandings also serve as barriers. Our understandings of the world are partial and incomplete. We can presuppose (and a presupposition is more hidden than what we consciously think) that our perception is simply the way things are, and thus we can miss, discount, exclude, or erase what doesn't fit. My own self-understanding, especially the more I am persuaded by it, prevents me from recognizing what the self-understanding of others grasps that I do not.

Interpretation inevitably begins, then, with an interpreter who is already in the middle of a prior world of self-understanding that offers both help and hindrance to interpreting a text. What happens when that self-understanding is brought uncritically to interpretation? The text becomes a mirror, simply reflecting back what the interpreter already knows and believes. The *otherness* of the text, the difference, what the text says that does not fit the interpreter's world — or may even overturn it — is simply overwritten (whether consciously or not). The work of interpretation becomes the work of confirmation.

Thus this question arises: Can we get any distance, is there any way we can "bracket" our self-understanding? Even recognizing that the effort will fall short and be incomplete, is it possible to approach a text in such a way that we can find something different from what we see in the mirror? This is the role of so-called critical methods. In Ricoeur's thought, their function is to be explanatory, objectifying, formal, analytical. Their purpose is to help interpretation focus on the structures of the text, the world of the text, and the possibilities for being that the text-world proposes. In the movement from speech to writing, *distanciation* takes place: the language acquires a "semantic autonomy" from the speaker; its meaning is to be sought in the sense and reference of the text itself, not in an author or world behind the text. Similarly, the explanatory, analytical move is also a kind of distanciation. It seeks temporarily — but only temporarily — to focus the interpreter explicitly on the structure and world of the text rather than on the world of the interpreter.

If the interpreter remains within the realm of explanation, however, a new problem arises. Having bracketed one's self-understanding and explored the world of the text and its possibilities for being, what happens next? If the bracket remains in place, then what the text-world and its possibilities for being propose is never put to the world of the interpreter. The interpreter may have a brilliant analysis of the Gospel of Mark that is never brought to bear on the interpreter's own situation and self-understanding.

There is tension, as we have seen elsewhere, between what the hermeneutical tradition has called "explanation" and "understanding." Explanation, with its emphasis on distance, objectivity, and methodology, has been contrasted to understanding, with its emphasis on relationship, subjectivity, and response. In some positions they have been judged to be antithetical — two opposing approaches between which one must choose. Ricoeur, however, sees explanation and understanding in a more dialectical or complementary relationship, each requiring the other. We could describe the interpretive process as a movement that begins with self-understanding, proceeds through explanation, and then moves to *appropriation.* This third step removes the bracket and brings the question of the text-world and its possibilities for being to bear on the situation and self-understanding of the interpreter. Ricoeur describes that movement in this way: "Understanding precedes, accompanies, closes, and thus *envelops* explanation. In return, explanation *develops* understanding analytically."[42]

The process of appropriation means moving from explanation and understanding of the text to understanding yourself *in front of the text.* The text-world and its possibilities for being are brought into confrontation with your own life-world and its ways of being. The world of the Gospel of Mark confronts the world of your community, and the complex process of metaphorical and analogical reasoning reads back and forth between the two. You may accept or reject the claims of Mark's Gospel as you have grasped them. You may modify them in light of other texts. But either way, you will, by your response to them, demonstrate your self-understanding. Ricoeur puts it this way:

> Ultimately, what I appropriate is a proposed world. The latter is not *behind* the text, as a hidden intention would be, but *in front of* it, as

42. "Explanation and Understanding," in *The Philosophy of Paul Ricoeur: An Anthology of His Work,* Charles E. Reagan and David Stewart, eds. (Boston: Beacon Press, 1978), p. 165.

that which the work unfolds, discovers, reveals. Henceforth, to understand is *to understand oneself in front of the text.* It is not a question of imposing upon the text our finite capacity of understanding, but of exposing ourselves to the text and receiving from it an enlarged self, which would be the proposed existence corresponding in the most suitable way to the world proposed.[43]

Recontextualization

The movement from speech to writing, as we noted, also results in a decontextualization, a loss of the eventfulness of speech with the loss of its context and first-order reference. Critical work seeks to establish a text-world and the possibilities for being that it proposes to the imagination. Thus, in order for an appropriation of that world in relationship to the life-world of the interpreter to exist, there must be a *recontextualization.* If we are to understand ourselves in front of the text, it requires bringing those possibilities for being into our own context.

To take a simple example, Jesus pronounced a very clear teaching about giving to those who beg: "Give to everyone who begs from you, and do not refuse anyone who wants to borrow from you" (Matt. 5:42). Walk down an ordinary city street and you are likely to be asked for spare change. You are also likely to see a sign in a window urging you, with very credible reasons, not to give to "panhandlers" but to give instead to the local food pantry. How will you decide what to do? What will count as evidence? How do you conceive the relationship between the words of Jesus in the Sermon on the Mount and the task of discipleship on that particular street? It is one thing to understand the meaning of Jesus' instruction in the world of Matthew's Gospel; it is another thing to decide what that has to do with the request for spare change on this street of your city. When Jesus says, "Follow me," that is not something that is literally possible for a reader to do. The reader who wishes to respond has no choice but to think metaphorically and analogically. The reader must discover what action in his or her own context is a response that corresponds to leaving one's fishing nets or tax table and accompanying Jesus. That is, there must be a process of recontextualization.

43. Ricoeur, "The Hermeneutical Function of Distanciation," p. 143.

It is tempting to think of appropriation as a matter of application (as in an explanation-application movement in a sermon). But this supposes that understanding has already happened — prior to the recontextualization. Ricoeur's approach presses us to recognize that understanding comes only in the movement that brings the world possibilities of the text into the new context of one's own situation. Understanding is actualized in response. Whatever our opinions or analyses may be, our understanding is enacted in what we do. Wherever else we may learn this, we learn it from Scripture itself.

What should we call this response? Ricoeur uses a term that has deep resonance in the Christian tradition: testimony. Testimony here refers to the words and acts — the life — that outwardly attest "to an intention, an inspiration, an idea at the heart of experience and history which nonetheless transcend experience and history."[44] That is to say, one testifies from a concrete place, yet one attests a truth or meaning that is greater than experience and history can demonstrate. Testimony moves from the realm of things seen to the realm of things said and done publicly. The witness is the μάρτυς, the "martyr," whose public profession links the person of the witness to the cause on behalf of which one speaks. The witness testifies in a context of dispute or conflict in which all "technical" means of demonstration are inconclusive; and the work of persuasion must be accomplished by the demonstration of *ethos* and *pathos* (character and willingness to risk and suffer) of one whose life is staked upon the truth of what is said. The witness is one "who is identified with the just cause which the crowd and the great hate and who, for this just cause, risks his [or her] life."[45] The witness suffers (bears) the response to his or her testimony, and this is testimony as well.

Testimony, then, is an explicit and outward attestation of one's understanding of self and world in front of the text. In the hermeneutical spiral, this in turn becomes part of the new beginning place of interpretation. Having read, interpreted, understood, testified, and suffered, one now returns to interpretation knowing in one's own body the meaning of the text. Without recontextualization, testimony remains in the realm of arcane, mythical, or fantastic text-worlds, a kind of historical simulation or

---

44. Paul Ricoeur, "The Hermeneutics of Testimony," in *Essays on Biblical Interpretation*, Lewis S. Mudge, ed. (Philadelphia: Fortress Press, 1980), p. 119.
45. Ricoeur, "The Hermeneutics of Testimony," p. 129.

costume dress-up game. Without testimony, recontextualization remains in the realm of the theoretical, speculative, or imaginary. It is just one more possibility that one does not have to choose.

Frequently Asked Questions

As an interpretive method, incarnational translation raises a number of questions. The following is a sampling of questions that we have considered over the years in conversations between ourselves and with students. Are there risks of misrepresenting Scripture in this kind of translation? What are the limits? What criteria of integrity and faithfulness to Scripture provide checks on our inclinations to make the Bible say whatever we want in our contemporizing translations? Is incarnational translation a modern form of allegorizing? What implications does incarnational translation have for the authority of Scripture? Does contemporizing functional equivalence threaten to become a substitute for the original historical voice of Scripture? Is incarnational translation really *translation,* or is it illustration masquerading as translation and usurping the place of Scripture? Are incarnational translations attempts to improve on Scripture? Does every passage of Scripture need an incarnational translation?

We have made observations relevant to some of these questions in preceding chapters. The preceding discussion of text and meaning also provides a framework for treating them. For some readers, perhaps, most of these questions have been answered by way of the display of incarnational translation in action and the methodological observations we have made thus far. For others, the intensity of the hermeneutical questions may not have subsided but only increased — perhaps to a point of urgency. Whatever the case, questions about the nature and integrity of incarnational translation deserve a thoughtful response.

Are there risks of misrepresenting Scripture in incarnational translation?
Any time we speak about the meaning of Scripture, we run the risk of misrepresenting Scripture. So the real question is whether incarnational translation is riskier than other forms of interpretation. The answer is no. This method does not cause greater risks for misrepresentation of the text. After all, it is not the method but the preacher who decides what the incarnational translation will look like. The method does not cause or encourage

misrepresentation of the text. Used conscientiously, it promotes faithfulness and responsibility in interpretation because it exposes our interpretive judgments in ways that make it difficult to ignore or elide hermeneutical problems. Incarnational translation requires that we either embrace the pattern of the text as a whole in a concrete way of reimagining it for our time and place or else justify the changes we make to that pattern.

What criteria or controls govern incarnational translation?

If preachers determine what their incarnational translations will look like, are their translations subject only to the free sovereignty of their imaginations? Or are there controls and criteria to guide their imaginations? A first response to this question is to consider what the Ricoeurian model we have just described has to say about it. This model is not itself a "method" of interpretation; rather, it is a description of the hermeneutical process. That description serves two purposes. First, it helps us understand what we are doing when we interpret and how and why interpretation works to shape and enrich our lives. Second, by exposing the nature of the hermeneutical process, Ricoeur's description serves to make us more responsible for our interpretations. It reveals our own constructive role in the process, which requires that we take responsibility for our interpretations. The methodological value of the Ricoeurian model (or "theory") of interpretation is that it shows the importance of taking questions of criteria and controls seriously throughout the hermeneutical circle; in critical approaches to the self-understanding that makes possible any relationship to the text; in explanation in which we seek to bracket our self-understanding through the use of critical tools of textual interpretation; and in understanding as appropriation, where the brackets on self-understanding are lifted and the question of where to stand in the world before the text is re-engaged. At each point there are competing possibilities for meaning and hard decisions about which to choose. Too much interpretation poses as what the Bible itself says or obviously means apart from the judgment of the interpreter and the decision of the interpreter among competing possibilities for meaning. Taking responsibility for our interpretations begins with honesty about the criteria by which we choose between competing interpretations — whether in the mode of explanation or understanding. That honesty leads us to examine our chosen criteria in conversation with others, including others who are different from ourselves and who interpret differently.

We do not presume to dictate the criteria that should govern incarnational translation, much less to imply that such criteria ought to be conceived as formulas rather than as principled ways of considering and weighing possibilities. We can only offer a broad framework reflecting some important principles for developing and judging incarnational translations.

1. The Historical-Critical Method as a Guide

We assume that historical-critical exegesis has a legitimate role to play in the process of incarnational translation. The biblical writings are ancient texts that originate in times and places very different from our own. As we understand the task of incarnational translation, our attention to the meaning of Scripture in its original contexts is important. When we read the Bible in a modern-language translation, such as English, we are dependent on the work of historical scholarship: textual criticism along with Greek and Hebrew lexicography. This indebtedness to historical study inherent in the use of a modern translation is a model of the relationship between the ancient text and preaching. We cannot get from *then* to *now* apart from historical understanding.

But a caution is in order. Historical methods are not able to resolve every question of historical interpretation. Historical criticism cannot fully cross the gap created by distanciation so as to give "assured" results for reconstruction of the world "behind" the text or the world "in" the text. Often, a biblical passage is susceptible to more than one reasonable historical interpretation (even when many implausible interpretations can also be excluded on historical grounds). In fact, there is good reason to believe that in many cases a given unit of tradition or authorial composition was open to multiple reasonable interpretations by its *original* audience. Therefore, historical criticism by itself cannot settle all questions of what the text originally meant as a basis for determining what it means for us.[46]

The polyvalence of the biblical text is the font of its surplus of mean-

---

46. For an acute and balanced discussion of the conflict between adherents to traditional historical-critical hermeneutics and postmodern hermeneutics, see A. K. M. Adam, "Integral and Differential Hermeneutics," in *The Meanings We Choose: Hermeneutical Ethics, Indeterminacy, and the Conflict of Interpretations*, Charles H. Cosgrove, ed. (London and New York: T. & T. Clark International, 2004), pp. 24-38.

ing through time. Distanciation creates the conditions for this surplus, which serves the church's hunger for interpretation in different ways from time to time and place to place. The loosing of the text from its original time and place limits our ability to recover the possibilities of the text's original meaning, but distanciation also makes the text available for interpretation in other times and places. Historical-critical interpretation sets bounds for interpretation, but the bounds are matters of judgment and allow for competing possibilities for meaning. When we wrestle with possibilities of meaning "in front of" the text, our appropriation involves choosing among these possibilities.

For example, there is no consensus — and no way of knowing with confidence — whether, from the standpoint of historical interpretation (i.e., what Paul likely meant), the "I" of Romans 7 is autobiographical, or, if it is, whether it represents Paul the Pharisee, Paul the follower of Christ, Paul the youth passing through the age of accountability, or some other Paul. Commentators have offered many interpretations of the "I" in Romans 7, some more plausible than others. Hence, when we stand before Romans 7, we meet a collection of reasonable interpretations from which to choose. We have no infallible divining rod for selecting one of these as the most accurate interpretation of Paul's original meaning. But our choosing can be guided by a narrowing of choices based on historical-exegetical plausibility and by theological criteria analogous to what ancient interpreters called the "rule of faith."

2. Moral-Theological Considerations as Criteria for Judging Between Competing Possibilities for Understanding[47]

As interpreters, we are already guided by such hermeneutical criteria or rules. The challenge is to make them explicit so that we can subject them to critique rather than follow them unconsciously. For example, in the interpretation of the story of the "rich young ruler," a Lutheran and a Wesleyan are likely to bring different considerations to bear in choosing to embrace

---

47. On the role of moral-theological criteria in the use of the Bible for theology and ethics, see Charles H. Cosgrove, "Toward a Postmodern *Hermeneutica Sacra*: Guiding Considerations in Choosing between Competing Plausible Interpretations of Scripture," in *The Meanings We Choose*, pp. 39-61; see also Cosgrove, *Appealing to Scripture in Moral Debate: Five Hermeneutical Rules* (Grand Rapids: Eerdmans, 2002), pp. 154-180.

one interpretation among a number of plausible ones. The Lutheran, guided by the law-gospel distinction as a hermeneutical principle, is likely to favor an interpretation that does not violate this principle. Moreover, the principle itself may assist the Lutheran in arriving at a particular interpretation. Hence, a classical Lutheran interpretation of Mark 10:17-22 (par. Matt. 19:16-30; Luke 18:18-30) is that Jesus' command "go and sell all. . ." is a calculated word of law designed to drive the man to despair so that he will see his need for the gospel. But the Wesleyan, for whom James's "faith without works is dead" is defining for the way of salvation, is likely to insist that Jesus' command is not death-dealing law but a life-giving commandment that is positively related to grace as forgiveness and moral empowerment. Historical-critical exegesis may shed light on the text in ways that challenge both the Lutheran and the Wesleyan interpretations; but it cannot resolve the meaning of the text so as to obviate theological guides for preaching or teaching the story.

Ancient interpreters such as Irenaeus and Augustine spoke of a "rule of faith" as a guide in choosing between competing interpretations of Scripture. They understood this rule as a summary of the Bible's primary teachings. Today we may be more aware of the subjectivity involved in ancient formulations of rules of faith. But the important thing to observe is that ancient interpreters were aware that the accepted methods of exegesis in their time could produce multiple conflicting results, just as the accepted methods of interpretation in our time produce competing results. The rule of faith as a *hermeneutical rule* provided a means of adjudication between interpretations.

We operate with our own rules of faith, whether we call them that or not, or whether or not we recognize their influence on our exegetical and homiletical decisions. They enable us to discover things in the text that we would otherwise miss. They provide controls, so far as we accept them, on our interpretations. But they can also lead us to construe the text in historically implausible ways and to miss genuine possibilities for meaning available in the interpretive traditions of other Christians. A healthy interpretive environment requires conversation between our own tradition, the varied results of historical criticism, and the voices of other traditions.

3. Analogical Reasoning as the Way We Imagine Incarnational Possibilities[48]

No one-to-one correspondence exists between life as it could once be lived in accordance with Scripture in its original cultural contexts and life as it might now be lived in accordance with Scripture in contemporary cultural contexts. Any faithful correlation between then and now necessarily takes the form of resemblance, not exact identity. We live by analogy.

Modern-language translations from Greek and Hebrew are necessarily analogical. If we are unaware of this truism, we can easily fail to recognize that, even when we imagine we are living according to the letter of Scripture, we are in fact living at best on the basis of analogy. Even what look like the most obvious possibilities for perfect equivalence turn out to contain inherent differences. For example, when Jesus teaches about divorce in Matthew 5:31-32, we may seek to obey his "rule" for divorce literally. But whatever rule we adopt for ourselves, it will be about a social institution that *we* call "divorce," which is similar to but not identical with the ancient Mediterranean social institution Jesus was talking about in Matthew.[49]

It is more obvious to us that analogy is required to live out the teaching of other biblical texts. How do we avoid being like the Pharisees, who "tithe mint, dill, and cumin" but "have neglected the weightier matters of the law"? How do we find daily manna in the wilderness, as Israel did, or recognize a word of judgment for ourselves in Amos's warning that "the songs of the temple will become wailings in that day"? The analogies to our own lives may seem obvious to us. Certainly our various Christian traditions contain vast supplies of analogical connections, discovered by those who have gone before us, so that we do not have to forge all the links ourselves. Long before we came on the scene, Christians analogized from corrupt temple worship to vain Christian worship, from Israel's liberation from Egypt to the end of African-American slavery, from Jesus' night in

---

48. On the nature of analogical reasoning, see Cosgrove, *Appealing to Scripture in Moral Debate*, pp. 51-89.

49. One question is whether we should even translate the verb *apoluō* in Matt. 5:31-32 and other texts about marital relations with the English word "divorce." At least one scholar thinks this translation is misleading. See Gerald L. Borchert, "1 Corinthians 7:15 and the Church's Historic Misunderstanding of Divorce and Remarriage," *Review and Expositor* 96 (1999): 125-29.

Gethsemane to gethsemanes in our lives, and so on. One interpretive task is to test these traditional analogies.

This brings us to the question of whether there are any controls on analogizing. How do we judge whether an analogy is apt or farfetched, genuine or superficial? A first response is that the controls are not hard-and-fast rules but a wisdom or capacity for judgment in us. As individual interpreters and as communities of interpretation, we judge whether a proposed analogical connection between Scripture and some practice or self-understanding in our own world is justified or rightly conceived. We make the analogies and we have the power to break them. When a contemporary preacher or theologian suggests that the gentiles in Acts 15, who are shown to be acceptable to God (despite their nonconformity to the Mosaic Law) because God has given them the Spirit, are like gay and lesbian persons today who have received God's Spirit, we — either as individuals or communities of interpretation — may say, "Yes, that analogical connection is persuasive," or "No, it fails to convince."

And this is true of any of our other efforts to shine the biblical text on an event, idea, experience, or claim in our time, for instance, that the tower of Babel is like the attempt by Dale Kohler in John Updike's novel *Roger's Version* to prove the existence of God with the help of a computer; that the destruction of the World Trade towers in New York is like the destruction of Sodom and Gemorrah; that failing to go to the aid of a man lying in an alley in St. Louis is like the priest passing by the man in the ditch in the Good Samaritan story; that the help Jesus gives to the hemorrhaging woman who has suffered at the hands of many doctors is like the help faith healers today offer to cancer patients and disabled people who have not found cures from modern medicine; that victims of AIDS in our time are like lepers in Jesus' time; that corporate America today is like the wealthy priestly-aristoctratic establishment in Jesus' day; that requiring literal belief in biblical miracles is like requiring works of the law as a condition of true faith; that immersion in a water-filled tub at the front of a sanctuary is like immersion in the Jordan river or in a lake in ancient Palestine; that the state of Israel's military action in the Six Days War is like the battle led by Gideon and his troops against the Midianites; that the bombing of Cambodia during the Vietnam War is like Egyptian oppression of the Israelites in the story of the Exodus; that the claim that we meet God in our neighbor is like the claim that the Word became flesh and dwelt among us; that psalmody in the monastery is like the prayer without ceasing that Paul advocated.

The preceding is a hodgepodge of examples of many different types and orders of analogy. We may scratch our heads about some (what do these two things have to do with each other?), charge others with the error of "comparing apples and oranges," or enthusiastically affirm others. How do we know when an analogical connection is justified?

The figure of speech about comparing apples with apples and not with oranges provides a clue. There are many different kinds of apples, but they share a family resemblance; likewise, when we judge an analogical connection, we are looking for a family resemblance. The crucial question is whether sufficient relevant similarities exist between two things to justify a comparison in which we say the one is like the other. The quality and weight of similarities must overcome our perception of the differences. This has to do with similarities between the elements of each and similarities of relationships between elements, the kinship of patterns or inner logic between two things.

The points of similarity must be substantial and relevant. Some differences or similarities may be trivial, superficial, and unimportant. So how do we distinguish between the relevant and the irrelevant? There is no "rule" for this. Life experience and practice in assimilating and distinguishing create in us a capacity for analogical reasoning, a capacity that is social — formed in community. We learn in community how to discover and evaluate analogical relationships. A pedestrian example may illustrate this. Steve Garvey's employer establishes a "casual Friday" on which employees are permitted to wear jeans and shorts. On a very hot day in the middle of July, when the air-conditioning is broken at work, Steve cannot find any of his shorts (they're all in the wash), so he wears a longish bathing suit instead. His supervisor threatens to write him up, charging that a bathing suit is not a pair of shorts. How will he and his supervisor (and perhaps others brought into the dispute) settle this question? They may begin by debating the technical meaning of shorts, which won't get them very far — because there is no technical meaning. Very quickly, they will begin the process of analogical reasoning via a comparison of similarities and differences. Is the bathing suit, the particular one Steve is wearing, sufficiently like the shorts that he and other people have been wearing without incident over the summer? You can imagine the ensuing conversation and the range of considerations the participants will bring to it.

Everyday life teaches us how to reason analogically about matters of modest and momentous import. Life draws us into innumerable debates (with ourselves and with others) in which analogical reasoning is the primary mode of judgment. Sometimes we are able to work to consensus; sometimes we end up disagreeing. Unless we are of such a dogmatic psychological makeup that we can never see anyone else's point of view or recognize the weaknesses in our own arguments, we know that the everyday process of analogical reasoning is not arbitrary in its assignment of significance or subject to unlimited fancy. At the same time, it involves judgment and is thus subjective and perspectival. Sometimes we reach analogical conclusions about which we have great confidence; other times we draw analogies only tentatively.

We deal with the question of apples or oranges in biblical hermeneutics in basically the same way as we do in everyday life. We rely on our socially shaped capacity for seeing similarities and differences and judging their saliency. That capacity for analogical reasoning is further refined for the particular subject matters of theology and draws on a fund of examples (or "precedents") in the traditions of which we are a part. Some analogies seem obvious to us because they have been handed down from the tradition. The logic of these obvious analogies, the ones we take for granted, models analogical reasoning to new questions. All the sermonic analogies we have heard over our lives contribute to our own capacity for analogical reasoning. We cannot escape analogizing unless we are to treat the Bible as a dead, obsolete letter. We cannot practice analogical reasoning without the help of the traditions of analogizing in our culture and in our churches. We cannot discover the weaknesses or faults in our received analogies or patterns of analogical reasoning unless we engage in conversation with persons and communities that see things differently than we do.

Is incarnational translation really translation, or is it illustration masquerading as translation and usurping the authority of Scripture?

This question is closely connected with some others posed at the beginning of this chapter. Does contemporizing functional equivalence threaten to become a substitute for the original historical voice of Scripture? Does every passage of Scripture need an incarnational translation?

We have noted that translation from the ancient biblical languages into any modern language involves analogical reasoning. Whether we call what we are doing in incarnational translation by the name "translation" or not, it is a translation model that guides our contemporizing restatement of Scripture. But there are important differences between historical translation that seeks not to contemporize but to convey the original sense of the text and incarnational translation in which contemporizing is the primary purpose. Perhaps that is an argument for restricting the term "translation" to only the historical kind. Nevertheless, whatever we call it, what we are proposing draws inspiration from a translation model. Whether we use the label or not, "translation" is a guiding concept for how to do what we have described in this book.

Having said that, however, we must also say that incarnational translation is not translation in the ordinary sense of the word. It is a kind of illustration, illustration that imitates, by means of contemporizing analogy, the form and content of the text. In this imitation it resembles translation. But we have observed again and again the difficulty of doing justice to the whole of a biblical passage — much less a whole biblical book — in the contemporizing recontextualization process. The cultural differences between then and now make thoroughgoing incarnational translation almost always impossible. Our translations are always incomplete, partial representations.

The purpose of incarnational translation is not to replace Scripture but to encounter it in a fresh way. There has always been a tendency in the church to pay lip service to the primacy of Scripture over commentary and yet, in practice, to elevate commentary over recital, suggesting that the Bible is in such great need of our commentary that we must spend more time commenting than reciting. We can justify this by saying that the Bible is full of riches that must be extracted and displayed, that it contains puzzles that must be explained, that it stands at a distance from us that we must overcome. All of this extraction, display, explanation, and application takes many words. So let's admit that we do substitute our own words, as commentary, for the words of Scripture. We say "this" (the text) means "that" (our interpretation). The implication is that the hearers cannot understand "this" without help, cannot live by it unless we translate it into "that" — "that" being our commentary. Incarnational translation is no different. If commentary is a kind of substitute for Scripture, so is incarnational translation. But "substitute" is a misleading term in both cases, because we are not talking about displacement or usurpation. The commentary points back to Scripture, and so does incarnational translation: it offers a restatement of the text to help the reader encounter the text afresh.

One more pertinent consideration about whether incarnational translation competes with the biblical text is the way any sermonic illustration functions for hearers. It is often an illustration in a sermon that people remember best or leave worship with as a relevant word for their lives. If that is true, then the illustrations that have been carefully crafted by asking, at every point, about their analogical connection with the pattern of the Scripture text as a whole in the unity of its form and content are likely to do a better job of communicating Scripture's message than illustrations chosen because they exemplify a selected part of the text without regard for how other elements in the text and its illustration cohere.

Certainly, there are occasions when incarnational translation is not necessary or appropriate. We will probably not offer a contemporary version of Psalm 23 at the bedside of a dying parishioner. And some passages of Scripture communicate well enough in preaching without contemporizing translation. Moreover, variety in preaching has its virtues. Any technique in preaching can get tiresome. Preaching that always includes a dynamic translation can wear out a good thing through overuse. On the other hand, the variety of biblical genres and ways of mixing genres ensures at least a great formal variety of incarnational translation.

Is incarnational translation an attempt to "improve on" Scripture?

This question arises for two reasons. One is rather trivial. When, through the power of contemporizing and recontextualizing, an incarnational translation helps us understand the text in a more immediate way as a word for our lives, one might say that it is a kind of "improvement" on the original. But the term is misleading. We could equally say that anything we propose — in commentary or in other forms of illustration — is an attempt to improve on the text's ability to speak to us on its own. What is improved here is not the text but the communicative process from the text to us.

But there is another, weightier sense to the question about incarnational translation's aims to improve the text. It has to do with ways in which theological judgments guide certain decisions in contemporizing translation. For example, when we decide that a story of holy war in Judges cannot be taken over by the church in a literal sense as a praxis for us but must be appropriated at another level of generality (its larger principles) or by analogy (e.g., taking "war" in the sense of missional struggle), one might call these decisions "efforts at improvement" when they show up in incarnational translation. But again, that criticism would be misplaced. Preaching has always entailed decisions about how to appropriate it. Those decisions are necessarily guided by perceptions of situation (one's own and that of one's hearers), pastoral and missional purpose, and theological convictions, including perceptions of how the Bible as a canonical whole shapes our understanding of its parts. For example, when the early Christian theologians determined that they should allegorize the Levitical laws concerning things such as diet as a precondition for appropriating those laws for the life of the church, they were making hermeneutical judgments about how the church is supposed to hear those laws. They did not understand themselves as "improving on" Scripture, and they adduced Scripture in support of these transformative interpretations. The same is true in incarnational translation. As translation for Christian appropriation, it is necessarily guided by theological considerations, including perceptions of how the separate parts of the Bible should be heard by the church in the context of Scripture as a whole.

Is incarnational translation a form of allegorizing?

The discussion of the preceding paragraph leads directly to a final question: Is incarnational translation a kind of allegorizing? We see some resemblances between allegorical exegesis and most, if not all, forms of contemporary exegesis in the service of Christian life. One of the judgments of at least some traditions of postmodern hermeneutics is that modernist theological hermeneutics, which involves the rejection of allegorical interpretation, has been insufficiently self-aware. In fact, the use of historical methods in the service of faith and practice has necessarily entailed *theological* forms of interpretation that resemble allegorical exegesis.[50] Moreover, post-Enlightenment preachers, most of whom have sworn off allegorizing, have nevertheless practiced their own forms of it.

Consider how most preachers today appropriate the story of the Battle of Jericho in Joshua 6. They typically associate the "walls of Jericho" with things in our world or in our own lives. They invite us to bring down these walls by God's power rather than imagining that we can rely on our own

---

50. On similarities between modern interpretation and ancient allegorical interpretation of the Bible, see James Barr, "The Literal, the Allegorical, and Modern Biblical Scholarship," *Journal for the Study of the Old Testament* 44 (1989): 3-17. Barr also points out differences between ancient and modern allegorizing.

strength. Often preachers follow the cue in Hebrews that Joshua brought down the walls by faith. They may emphasize that God, in Christ, has torn down the walls of sin and death in our lives and ushered us into the Promised Land of the new creation. They may associate the siege of the walls with the struggle against injustice in our society or with personal spiritual battles. For example:

> The walls of Jericho collapse at the sound of the trumpets. Through prayer and faith in God's liberating power, the walls of hatred collapse, the walls of prejudice come down, the walls of injustice crumble, the walls of despair give way. . . .

It is not hard to imagine a sermon in which this kind of allegorizing appears. How is it different from the following allegorical interpretation by Origen, the third-century church father?

> The walls of Jericho collapse at the sound of the trumpets. Jericho is the picture of this age, whose mighty ramparts we see destroyed by the prayers of priests. These mighty ramparts were idol worship. . . . But Our Lord Jesus Christ, whose coming the son of Nun prefigured, sends his apostles as priests, and they bear resounding trumpets, namely, the Gospel . . . and all the engines of idolatry and the dogmas of the philosophers are laid waste from top to bottom. . . .[51]

We may not agree with all the connections Origen makes, but he is doing the same kind of thing that preachers have always done: he draws analogies between the text and the lives of his hearers according to his theological understanding of his hearers and the world in which they live.

The check on ancient and medieval allegorizing was what people — the interpretive communities in which this kind of interpretation was carried out — found plausible. Likewise, we operate by plausibility structures that tell us whether to accept or reject a given analogical claim about, say, the form that the walls of Jericho might take in our time or who the Samaritan in Jesus' parable might be for us. What once looked like a legitimate association to Origen or St. Bernard of Clairvaux may strike us as ar-

---

51. Origen, *In Jos.*, hom. 7 as quoted in Henri de Lubac, *Medieval Exegesis: The Four Senses of Scripture*, vol. 1, trans. Mark Sebanc (Grand Rapids: Eerdmans, 1998; Edinburgh: T. & T. Clark, 1998), p. 152.

bitrary. Likewise, if they were still around to contemplate the analogical connections we make, they might find arbitrariness in our interpretations.

Our disagreements with premodern approaches and results in interpretation owe to differences of culture and theology. Ancient and medieval allegorists worked with traditional spiritual tropes on the assumption that a person, place, or thing carries the same meaning wherever it is found in Scripture. They interpreted the Old Testament in terms of the New on the assumption that the Old Testament prophesies Jesus Christ and his work in both explicit and hidden ways. They thought of resemblance as a matter of appearance: the outward form or surface of things. They conceived of the human subject, the Bible, and nature as mirroring each other in form, and they treated the resemblance of form (appearance) as proof of inner unity, sameness, connection. Ancient and medieval allegorists often ignored the genre of the texts they interpreted. Notoriously, in assigning spiritual meanings to persons, places, and things in biblical stories, they did not require that the interpretive result was also a narrative. Therefore, the explicit narrative character of stories (as well as the implicit narrative elements of other genres) was often violated in their allegorical exegesis. Elements in stories were equated with things that, when combined, did not add up to another story.

Ancient and medieval interpreters also operated with a different sense of history and homiletical context than we do, which caused them to cast their allegories in general, universal terms. The allegorical interpretations they offer in their sermons often strike us as overly general and abstract, lacking concreteness in life for a particular time and place. Our historical sense makes us attend to the particular and unrepeatable. Therefore, our analogical illustrations tend not to be about, say, the universal human soul but about Emily or Steve or the First Baptist Church of Memphis or the people of New York on 9/11. That is, we think it is crucial to particularize and contextualize the general. Finally, ancient and medieval allegorists tended to treat all the meanings they found in Scripture as divinely intended meanings *in* the text. We tend to think that our *exegesis uncovers* what is in the text, but we regard our analogical illustrations as our own creations. We want these analogies to be faithful to the text, but we do not claim that they are divinely intended meanings hidden in Scripture. Herein lies a fundamental difference between modern and premodern interpretation: modern interpretation assumes that there is a gulf between then and now. Even when we acknowledge that all exegesis is shaped by our own assumptions and our cultural horizons, most of us still make a distinction between what the text meant and what it means, between the possibilities for meaning Scripture carried in its original settings and the appropriations of the text that we make in our settings. It is only where this distinction is rejected (as in some forms of fundamentalism) or has completely collapsed (as in some postmodern hermeneutics) that a fully allegorical hermeneutic is conceivable.

The differences we have outlined justify a distinction between allegorical exegesis and analogical illustration. As a sophisticated form of analogical illustration, incarnational translation has some features in common with allegorical interpretation, but the two are not identical.

Selected Bibliography

Biblical Genres

Bible dictionaries and introductions to commentaries are valuable resources for information about biblical genres. In addition to these, the following books offer helpful guidance.

General

Alter, Robert. *The World of Biblical Literature.* New York: Basic Books, 1992.

Goldingay, John. *Models for Interpretation of Scripture.* Grand Rapids: Eerdmans, 1995.

Long, Thomas G. *Preaching and the Literary Forms of the Bible.* Philadelphia: Fortress Press, 1989.

Terrien, Samuel. *The Elusive Presence: Toward a New Biblical Theology.* San Francisco: Harper & Row, 1978.

Poetry

Gerstenberger, Erhard S. *Psalms: Part 1 with an Introduction to Hebrew Poetry.* Grand Rapids: Eerdmans, 1998.

Gunkel, Hermann. *Introduction to Psalms: The Genres of the Religious Lyric of Israel.* Completed by Joachim Bergrich. Translated by James D. Nogalski. Macon, GA: Mercer University Press, 1998.

Kugel, James L. *The Idea of Biblical Poetry: Parallelism and Its History.* Baltimore and London: Johns Hopkins University Press, 1998.

Watson, Wilfred G. E. *Classical Hebrew Poetry: A Guide to Its Techniques.* Sheffield, UK: JSOT Press, 1984.

Narrative

Alter, Robert. *The Art of Biblical Narrative.* New York: Basic Books, 1981.

Berlin, Adele. *Poetics and Interpretation of Biblical Narrative.* Sheffield, UK: Almond, 1983.

Gunn, David N., and Danna N. Fewell. *Narrative in the Hebrew Bible.* Oxford: Oxford University Press, 1993.

Herzog, William R. *Parables as Subversive Speech: Jesus as Pedagogue of the Oppressed.* Louisville: Westminster/John Knox Press, 1994.

Hultgren, Arland J. *The Parables of Jesus: A Commentary.* Grand Rapids: Eerdmans, 2000.

Rhoads, David, and Donald Michie. *Mark as Story: An Introduction to the Narrative of a Gospel.* Philadelphia: Fortress Press, 1982.

Scott, Bernard Brandon. *Hear Then the Parable: A Commentary on the Parables of Jesus.* Minneapolis: Fortress Press, 1989.

Sternberg, Meir. *The Poetics of Biblical Narrative: Ideological Literature and the Drama of Reading.* Bloomington, IN: Indiana University Press, 1985.

Tolbert, Mary Ann. *Sowing the Gospel: Mark's World in Literary-Historical Perspective.* Minneapolis: Fortress Press, 1989.

Law

Brueggemann, Walter, and Patrick D. Miller. *The Covenanted Self: Explorations in Law and Covenant.* Minneapolis: Fortress Press, 1999.

Jackson, Bernard S. *Studies in the Semiotics of Biblical Law.* Sheffield: Sheffield Academic Press, 2000.

Patrick, Dale. *Old Testament Law.* Atlanta: John Knox Press, 1985.

Sonsino, Rifat. *Motive Clauses in Biblical Law: Biblical Forms and Near Eastern Parallels.* SBLDS 45. Chico, CA: Scholars Press, 1980.

Stamm, J. J., and M. E. Andrew. *The Ten Commandments in Recent Research.* London: SCM Press, 1967.

Wisdom Literature

Crenshaw, James L. *Old Testament Wisdom: An Introduction.* Atlanta: John Knox Press, 1981.

Murphy, Roland E. *The Tree of Life: An Exploration of Biblical Wisdom Literature*. Grand Rapids: Eerdmans, 1996; 2002.

O'Connor, Kathleen M. *The Wisdom Literature*. Wilmington, DE: Michael Glazier, 1988.

Hermeneutics

The fields of biblical studies and homiletics have been influenced enormously by postmodern hermeneutics in all its variety. This has included questions of the ethics of interpretation, the possibility of knowing the past, semantic polyvalence and indeterminacy, the ideological freight of texts, intertextuality, and rhetorical dimensions of texts — to name some of the notable fields of inquiry. The selection below gives some of this range, with a special emphasis on the broad-ranging work of Paul Ricoeur, which we find especially helpful and integrative for the theological disciplines.

Bleicher, Josef. *Contemporary Hermeneutics: Hermeneutics as Method, Philosophy, and Critique*. London: Routledge & Kegan Paul, 1980.

Bozarth-Campbell, Alla. *The Word's Body: An Incarnational Aesthetic of Interpretation*. Tuscaloosa: University of Alabama Press, 1979.

Cosgrove, Charles H. *Appealing to Scripture in Moral Debate: Five Hermeneutical Rules*. Grand Rapids: Eerdmans, 2002.

Cosgrove, Charles H., ed. *The Meanings We Choose: Hermeneutical Ethics, Indeterminacy, and the Conflict of Interpretations*. London and New York: T. & T. Clark International, 2004.

Edgerton, W. Dow. *The Passion of Interpretation*. Louisville: Westminster/John Knox Press, 1992.

————. *Speak to Me That I May Speak: A Spirituality of Preaching*. Cleveland: Pilgrim Press, 2006.

Klemm, David E. *The Hermeneutical Theory of Paul Ricoeur: A Constructive Analysis*. New Brunswick, NJ: Associated University Presses, 1983.

Mueller-Vollmer, Kurt, ed. *The Hermeneutics Reader*. New York: Continuum, 1988.

Palmer, Richard. *Hermeneutics: Interpretation Theory in Schleiermacher, Dilthey, Heidegger, and Gadamer*. Evanston, IL: Northwestern University Press, 1969.

Poland, Lynn. *Literary Criticism and Biblical Hermeneutics: A Critique of Formalist Approaches*. Chico, CA: Scholars Press, 1985.

Ricoeur, Paul. *Essays on Biblical Interpretation*. Edited by Lewis S. Mudge. Philadelphia: Fortress Press, 1980.

————. *Figuring the Sacred: Religion, Narrative, and Imagination*. Minneapolis: Fortress Press, 1995.

————. *Interpretation Theory: Discourse and Surplus of Meaning*. Fort Worth, TX: The Texas Christian University Press, 1976.

————. *Paul Ricoeur: Hermeneutics and the Human Sciences*. Edited and translated by John B. Thompson. Cambridge, UK: Cambridge University Press, 1981.

————. *The Philosophy of Paul Ricoeur: An Anthology of His Work*. Edited by Charles E. Reagan and David Stewart. Boston: Beacon Press, 1978.

Segovia, Fernando F., and Mary Ann Tolbert, eds. *Reading from This Place: Social Location and Biblical Interpretation in the United States*. 2 volumes. Minneapolis: Fortress Press, 1995.

Silverman, Hugh J., ed. *Gadamer and Hermeneutics*. New York and London: Routledge, 1991.

Homiletics

In Chapter 1 we have described certain trends in homiletics over the past twenty years or so. The following selection represents some of the signal works that have shaped the new homiletics.

Childers, Jana. *Performing the Word: Preaching as Theater*. Nashville: Abingdon Press, 1998.

Craddock, Fred B. *As One without Authority*. 3rd edition. Nashville: Abingdon Press, 1979.

Eslinger, Richard L. *Narrative and Imagination: Preaching the Worlds That Shape Us*. Minneapolis: Fortress Press, 1995.

————. *A New Hearing: Living Options in Homiletic Methods*. Nashville: Abingdon Press, 1987.

————. *The Web of Preaching: New Options in Homiletical Method*. Nashville: Abingdon Press, 2002.

Long, Thomas G. *Preaching and the Literary Forms of the Bible*. Philadelphia: Fortress Press, 1989.

Lowry, Eugene L. *The Sermon: Dancing on the Edge of Mystery*. Nashville: Abingdon Press, 1997.

McClure, John S. *Other-wise Preaching: A Postmodern Ethic for Homiletics*. St. Louis: Chalice Press, 2001.

Mitchell, Henry H. *Celebration and Experience in Preaching.* Nashville: Abingdon Press, 1990.

Rice, Charles. *The Embodied Word: Preaching as Art and Liturgy.* Minneapolis: Fortress Press, 1991.

Thomas, Frank A. *They Like to Never Quit Praisin' God: The Role of Celebration in Preaching.* Cleveland: United Church Press, 1997.

Wardlaw, Don M., ed. *Preaching Biblically: Creating Sermons in the Shape of Scripture.* Philadelphia: Westminster, 1983.

Translation Theory

The last twenty years have seen an explosion in practical and theoretical studies of translation. The work of Eugene Nida has been especially formative. The science of translation has also become highly interdisciplinary, as the following sampling of the vast literature reflects. In thinking through the relationship between the translation theory and incarnational translation, we have found the following books helpful.

de Waard, Jan, and Eugene A. Nida. *From One Language to Another: Functional Equivalence in Bible Translating.* Nashville: Thomas Nelson, 1986.

Hodgson, Robert, and Paul A. Soukup, eds. *From One Medium to Another: Communicating the Bible through Multimedia.* Kansas City, MO: Sheed and Ward, 1997.

————. *Fidelity and Translation: Communicating the Bible in New Media.* Kansas City, MO: Sheed and Ward; New York: American Bible Society, 1999.

Nord, Christine. *Translating as a Purposeful Activity: Functionalist Approaches Explained.* Manchester, UK: St. Jerome, 1997.

Pym, Anthony. *Translation and Text Transfer. An Essay on the Principles of Intercultural Communication.* Frankfurt: Peter Lang, 1992.

Scorgie, Glen G., et al., eds. *The Challenge of Bible Translation: Communicating God's Word to the World.* Grand Rapids: Zondervan, 2003.

Scripture Index

Genesis

1	117-26
1:1	124
1:1-2	123
1:1–2:4	117
2:2-3	153
29	46

Exodus

15	64, 90
20:1-17	157-58
20:3	157
20:8-11	153
20:22	153

Leviticus

19:18	158
21:16-24	93
24:5-9	141

Deuteronomy

5:15	153
6:7-9	153
7:7-9	153
8:1-2	153
23:1	93
32	90

Judges

6–8	125-26
6:6-10	125
7	117, 125
7:9-15	129-30, 137
7:12	125
7:19-15	129, 130-31
8:1-29	129
8:27	125

1 Samuel

15:1-3	45-47
21	140-41

Job

24:1-8	174-76
25	176
28:1-28	166
33:26-28	71
34–38	179
38–41	177-78
38	176, 180
38:4-11	176
38:8-11	177
38:12	177
38:12-13	177
38:16	178
38:28-29	177
38:31-32	179

38:32	177
38:33	178
38:34	177
38:37	177

Psalms

8	75-76
18	71
22	67-68
23	76-78
30	71
32	71
33:1-3	90
34	71
40:1-12	71
41	71
42	68-70
66	71-74
73:5	65
75:10	65
92	71
102:3	65, 66
116	71
118	71
136	120
138	71
146–50	64
149:3	90
150:4	90

Scripture Index